ROUTLEDGE LIBRARY EDITIONS:
EPISTEMOLOGY

Volume 1

PLATO'S THEAETETUS

PLATO'S THEAETETUS

JOHN M. COOPER

Routledge
Taylor & Francis Group
LONDON AND NEW YORK

First published in 1990

This edition first published in 2015
by Routledge
2 Park Square, Milton Park, Abingdon, Oxon OX14 4RN

and by Routledge
711 Third Avenue, New York, NY 10017

Routledge is an imprint of the Taylor & Francis Group, an informa business

British Library Cataloguing in Publication Data
A catalogue record for this book is available from the British Library

ISBN: 978-1-138-80196-7 (Set)
ISBN: 978-1-315-69475-7 (Set) (ebk)
ISBN: 978-1-138-90516-0 (Volume 1) (hbk)
ISBN: 978-1-138-90869-7 (Volume 1) (pbk)
ISBN: 978-1-315-69474-0 (Volume 1) (ebk)

Publisher's Note
The publisher has gone to great lengths to ensure the quality of this reprint but points out that some imperfections in the original copies may be apparent.

Disclaimer
The publisher has made every effort to trace copyright holders and would welcome correspondence from those they have been unable to trace.

Plato's *Theaetetus*

John M. Cooper

GARLAND PUBLISHING
NEW YORK & LONDON
1990

Library of Congress Cataloging-in-Publication Data

Cooper, John M. (John Madison), 1939–
Plato's Theaetetus / John M. Cooper.
p. cm. — (Harvard dissertations in philosophy)
Thesis (Ph.D.)—Harvard University, 1967.
Includes bibliographical references.
ISBN 0-8240-3200-4
1. Plato. Theaetetus. 2. Knowledge, Theory of. I. Title. II. Series.
B386.C66 1990
121—dc20 89-49392

All volumes printed on acid-free, 250-year-life paper
Manufactured in the United States of America

Design by Julie Threlkeld

Preface

In 1965 when I began work on the *Theaetetus* for my dissertation not much was in print that discussed in a philosophically responsible and illuminating way either the progress of the dialogue as a whole or any of its more or less separate sections. My aim was to do whatever with my neophyte's abilities and experience I could to bring our philosophical understanding of the dialogue up to the standards of clarity and penetration that my teacher G.E.L. Owen had established in his publications and (even more) in his lectures and seminars at Oxford on the pre-Socratics, Plato, and Aristotle.

Through the work of a number of excellent philosophers and scholars since the late 1960's, the best of it inspired directly or indirectly by Owen's example, if not also his teaching, our understanding of the *Theaetetus* has dramatically and, I hope, permanently improved. Anyone writing a dissertation on the *Theaetetus* in 1989 would have vastly improved resources to use in grappling with the interpretation of the dialogue, and the product would necessarily read very differently from my own 1967 effort. Obviously I cannot in the space available do justice to the philosophical and scholarly literature on the *Theaetetus* published over the past twenty-odd years in English and other European languages. I must, however, mention two papers that have significantly altered my own thinking. These are: "Observations on Perception in Plato's Later Dialogues" by Michael Frede (first published in his *Essays on Ancient Philosophy* (Minneapolis, 1987) but presented already at a Princeton Ancient Philosophy conference in 1973), and "Plato on the Grammar of Perceiving" by Myles Burnyeat (*Classical Quarterly*, N.S. 26 [1967]). Both authors address issues raised in a paper of mine, a reworking of material found in chapter IV of my dissertation, published in *Phronesis* XV (1970): "Plato on Sense-Perception and Knowledge: *Theaetetus* 184–187." This was my only publication deriving from the dissertation.

—J.M.C.

Princeton, New Jersey

September 1989

TABLE OF CONTENTS

CHAPTER PAGE

INTRODUCTION

The *Theaetetus* is almost alone among Plato's dialogues in being fairly precisely datable. In the "preface" which precedes the dialogue proper Theaetetus is said to have just been brought back from battle near Corinth, wounded and suffering from dysentery; it seems clear that he is about to die. Euclides, who reports these facts to Terpsion, is reminded of a conversation Socrates once had with Theaetetus when he was quite a young man, not long before Socrates' death. On this occasion Socrates was much impressed with Theaetetus' mental powers, and predicted for him the illustrious future he in fact turned out to have. It is this conversation which the main dialogue records. The tributes to Theaetetus' prowess in the preface and in the dialogue proper, where one of his main mathematical achievements is described and celebrated (147d-148b), strongly suggest that Plato composed the dialogue as a memorial to him. If so, the date of composition must fall not long after the battle in which Theaetetus was fatally wounded. Now there were only two battles of Corinth during Plato's lifetime, one in 394 and one in 369,[1] and the earlier date, though it has had some supporters, notable among them Lewis Campbell,[2] is hardly acceptable if the dialogue was composed shortly after Theaetetus' death, and has not generally been adopted by scholars. The *Theaetetus*, then, seems fairly firmly assignable to the early 360's.

This date makes the *Theaetetus* pretty certainly written after the *Republic*, which is at the latest a composition of the 370's.[3] And as the *Theaetetus* is the first of the series of dialogues--*Theaetetus*, *Sophist*, *Statesman*, and *Philebus*--which Campbell liked to call "dialectical" because of their more alert critical stance and their heightened interest in examining the first principles not only of Socratic but also of pre-Socratic thought,[4] this date fixes also a *terminus post quem* for the whole series of dialectical and critical dialogues. If we are justified in thinking that the *Parmenides* as well, even if it antedates the *Theaetetus*,[5] has close temporal affinities to the dialectical group, then from about 370 onwards, or a little earlier, and certainly after the completion of the *Republic*, a considerable portion of Plato's philosophical work was devoted to the close and often abstruse and difficult reasoning which characterizes these five dialogues. In fact, Plato's whole literary output during the last twenty-odd years of his life probably includes, besides these works, only the *Laws* and, if now-traditional interpretations of the evidence concerning Plato's "later style" are accepted, the *Timaeus* and *Critias*. Thus Plato's last two decades were occupied partly with the political and legal researches of the *Laws*, and, so far as his more purely philosophical activity is concerned, were either limited to the composition of the series of critical dialogues (if those are right who place the *Timaeus* and *Critias* before the *Parmenides*)[6] or at any rate primarily devoted to them. The growing interest of scholars and philosophers in the *Parmenides* and *Theaetetus* and their successors is thus hardly surprising.

The interpretation of the dialectical dialogues, and perhaps particularly of the *Theaetetus*, has inevitably been the center of considerable controversy. Interpretations of these dialogues have in general fallen into two rough categories. On the one hand, there are scholars who, though differing widely from one another in other respects, agree in finding the arguments and conclusions of the dialectical dialogues at variance in important respects with the central metaphysical and epistemological doctrines of the *Republic* and other middle period writings. When such interpreters speak of the critical character of these works they at least partly mean that they contain critical reëvaluations of the doctrines of middle period Platonism. On the other side stand those who think that, in the main, the philosophical conclusions of the Republic and allied dialogues are to be regarded as constituting the permanent core of Plato's philosophy which, once he adopted it, he firmly retained throughout the remainder of his philosophical career. These interpreters allow the *Parmenides* and *Theaetetus* and their successors to contain elaborations and defenses, and in some cases developments, but never revisions or rejections of the earlier doctrines. With such writers the thesis that the aim of the *Theaetetus* is to support by an indirect argument the *Republic's* central contentions about knowledge has been very popular, and this view is in fact the main thesis of F. M. Cornford's analysis of the dialogue in his well-known book, *Plato's Theory of Knowledge*.

I will be arguing below for interpretations of several particular passages of the *Theaetetus* which will make their arguments and conclusions incompatible with doctrines maintained in the *Republic* and other middle period dialogues. I therefore accept the view that the

Theaetetus, at least, engages in reëvaluation and criticism of some of the doctrines of middle period Platonism, and is not restricted in its aims to the reaffirmation of the *Republic*'s theories about knowledge. It must be admitted, however, that scholars falling into the general category of those who find in the dialectical dialogues no important revisions or criticisms of middle period doctrines, have up until now generally carried the day. Their influence on the prevailing understanding of Plato's writings has been preponderant, and this is particularly true of the United States. For many people in this country it is simply axiomatic that canonical Platonism is to be found in the *Republic*, and that the dialogues which follow maintain, or at least do not destructively criticize or contradict, the main doctrines expounded there. And to allege inconsistencies between what is said in later dialogues and the doctrines of canonical Platonism is often taken as virtual proof of faulty scholarship or a diseased critical sense. Now I think it is not an exaggeration to say that this widespread attitude is to a great extent traceable, so far at least as Platonic studies in America are concerned, to the influence, direct or indirect, of one man, Paul Shorey.

Shorey's war against the whole idea of revisions or developments in Plato's views is well-known; he rejected not only the thesis that the dialectical dialogues criticize and reject some theories of middle period Platonism but also any attempt to find in the dialogues *any* significant development or alteration of view on any topic whatever, whether before or after the *Republic*. It was Shorey's opinion that the dialogues could be assumed to have been written in whatever order you please without requiring any change in the interpretation of Plato's philosophical views.[7] Now it is obvious that in denying development of every sort Shorey puts himself into opposition to widely differing types of interpretation representing quite different interests in and approaches to Plato's writings. Thus one main object of his attack was the so-called genetic school of interpretation which flourished in the latter half of the last century, particularly in Germany. The concern of these interpreters to find in the dialogues a beginning point and a definite development of the theory of Forms, the Platonic theory of the soul, etc., led them to emphasize the _manner_ in which a view is stated or referred to, and to argue from the absence of a certain doctrine in, say, the _Phaedo_ to its not yet having been formulated then; and in general every possible nuance of exposition was found by someone to be fraught with meaning. Thus some writers,[8] in searching for the place where the Forms are first introduced, hit upon the passage at the end of the _Cratylus_ (439c) where Socrates, by a conceit, is presented as having dreamed a theory of Forms; to them the talk of a dream in connection with the Forms marked this reference to the doctrine as tentative and therefore earlier than places like the _Phaedo_ where the doctrine is openly displayed. Shorey's exasperation with the methods and results of such enquiries is easily understandable, and in the main his complaints against the distortions which they produced are well-founded.

But though it was perhaps dissatisfaction with this style of criticism which led him to formulate his thesis of the "unity of Plato's thought," Shorey also rejected and attacked, wholesale, methods of interpretation which represent quite different approaches to Plato's writings. For example, the attempt of Henry Jackson[9] to interpret important and difficult arguments of the *Philebus* and other late dialogues as introducing a new, quasi-Hegelian conception of Forms, was regarded by Shorey as just as unbalanced and just as much a tissue of distortions as the genetic interpreters' views. But Jackson's effort to interpret Plato's *arguments* and self-conscious statements of Plato's philosophical *conclusions* is quite a different matter from the reliance on such tenuous external indications as the manner of expression or the completeness of exposition of some reference to a Platonic doctrine. To refute an interpretation of an argument completely, one must provide a better interpretation of what the argument says. If Jackson's interpretation of a certain argument construes Plato as having revised certain of his earlier views, and someone thinks this an unlikely thing for Plato to have done, then what he must do is try to understand the argument as closely and carefully as possible and show that the alleged conflict is not in fact to be found in it. But in the case of Jackson's views, and in general where the interpretation of arguments in the later dialogues is concerned, Shorey fails, and indeed refuses, to meet his opponents on their own ground. Thus he simply denies that the passage of the *Philebus* (23c ff.) on which Jackson bases his views contains any argument at all bearing on general metaphysical questions,[10] and he therefore refuses to commit himself to any detailed analysis of the passage. Similar tricks are played with the *Sophist*'s examination of ὄν and μὴ ὄν, where Shorey takes Plato not to be discussing the philosophical question what οὐσία *is* (a question raised in the *Republic*), but rather working out the solution to a question of "practical logic," namely how we can without contradicting ourselves *speak* about οὐσία.[11] Shorey has to bring in this dubious distinction in order to prevent the otherwise natural inference from what according to Plato cannot be thought without inconsistency, to what in his view cannot be the case. These ruses must not, however, be tolerated, and the right to treat philosophy as philosophy and arguments as arguments must be absolutely insisted upon. So far as the dialectical dialogues are concerned, the important question is whether the arguments found in them can be interpreted, in detail, so as to accord with the thesis of the "unity of Plato's thought," and I think it must be admitted that Shorey's discussion of them is too superficial to come close to justifying the widespread conviction that canonical Platonism is in no way threatened by arguments and conclusions of the *Theaetetus* and its successors.

There are of course other sources of the present general allegiance to the view that the dialectical dialogues produce nothing fundamentally at variance with the doctrines of the middle period works. Among other things, the fact that such important scholars as Cornford and H. F. Cherniss have vigorously taken this line has no doubt had its influence. In the course of my analysis I will have occasion to consider in close detail the interpretations these writers have adopted of crucial passages of the *Theaetetus*; and in general the result of such examinations is not favorable to currently accepted views. My commentary on the *Theaetetus* can, in fact, be regarded as in part a detailed attempt to subject the thesis of the "unity of Plato's thought" to the one test that matters--its ability to produce a sustained and detailed interpretation of the arguments Plato actually employs in a single dialogue. If a careful interpretation of the *Theaetetus*, as a whole and argument by argument, cannot be made in conformity with that thesis, then, whatever turns out to be the case for the other dialectical dialogues, it can no longer be maintained that canonical Platonism was always accepted by Plato.

There is one further matter which should be mentioned here, even if only briefly. This is the question of the dating of the *Timaeus* (and its companion-piece, the *Critias*). As is well known, the *Timaeus'* cosmology is rather emphatically grounded on the canonical theory of Forms, and maintains a number of metaphysical and epistemological theses associated with it. Since the evidence drawn from considerations of style is usually taken to point to a date for the *Timaeus* at least as late as any of the dialectical dialogues, the *Timaeus* seems a powerful witness to the correctness of the prevailing view of the relation of the dialectical dialogues to canonical Platonism. If the *Timaeus* knows nothing of supposed revisions in central doctrines, so the argument runs, it must be wrong to find dialogues written around the same time or earlier arguing in favor of such changes. Now even if the *Timaeus* were known to be later than the whole series of critical works, it would obviously still be necessary to study the arguments of the *Theaetetus* and its successors to see whether or not they were compatible with the *Republic*'s and *Timaeus'* views. It must be insisted on that in all such matters the interpretation of particular arguments must have priority over any considerations of probability drawn from such externals as relative dating. It may be improbable and unfortunate that the *Theaetetus* and *Sophist* should argue against views accepted both in the *Republic* and the *Timaeus*, but it is not impossible, and the only way to find out whether they do is to study them carefully.

But in fact the evidence adduced to support the *Timaeus'* claim to belong to the last twenty-odd years of Plato's life can be, and has been, strongly questioned.[12] This is a very large and complicated topic, and I shall mention here only one aspect of one issue, though a very important one. The most imposing ground[13] for assuming a late date for the *Timaeus* is that it, in common with just five other dialogues (*Critias*, *Sophist*, *Statesman*, *Philebus*, and *Laws*), shows such a marked tendency to avoid illegitimate hiatus that, as Cherniss and others have emphasized, the decision to write in this way must have been quite deliberate. Taylor justly remarks[14] that in these dialogues Plato attempts to "adapt the style invented for the topical pamphlet by Isocrates to the purposes of sustained philosophical and scientific exposition . . . [with] . . . the general effect . . . that we no longer have the approximation to the tone of well-bred conversation [characteristic of the *Republic*, but instead] . . . are getting something much more like a formal treatise or essay."

Now it is usually assumed, and is roundly asserted by Cherniss,[15] that the decision to avoid hiatus was made once and for all for literary activity of all types, so that any work which avoids hiatus is later than any which does not. And this at once ranks the *Timaeus* as later than the *Theaetetus* and *Parmenides*. But I see absolutely no reason to accept this unargued assumption. If the effect of the avoidance of hiatus is, as Taylor says, to write in the style of a treatise or essay, why should we not think that the decision to avoid hiatus in works where the essay style was thought appropriate preceded the decision to avoid it generally? Why should not the tone of well-bred conversation have been desired in some works (say the *Theaetetus*) even after essay style had been adopted for other purposes and in other works (say the *Timaeus*)? Since Owen had already clearly enunciated this alternative,[16] it is distressing to find that Cherniss has misunderstood the suggestion.[17] Cherniss thinks it follows from Owen's emphasis on the fact that the *Timaeus* is, after all, an essay, to which Plato might have thought an Isocratean essay style appropriate even while not avoiding hiatus in conversational dialogues, that Plato would at any time in his life have avoided hiatus in writing it. And he then goes on to point out that the *Symposium* and *Menexenus*, which though not essays are at least like the *Timaeus* in being *tours de force* of style, do not exhibit this feature. This is of course an *ignoratio elenchi*: the suggestion is that at *some* time Plato decided to adopt an Isocratean essay style for treatises, not that he *always* had two styles, one for essays (and other stylistic *tours de force*) and one for dialogue. And Cherniss has not, in fact, rebutted this suggestion in any way. It seems evident to me that, in the present state of our research into questions of Plato's style, Owen's interpretation of the avoidance of hiatus in the *Timaeus* has at least as much plausibility as the orthodox view. I do not, therefore, see any force at all in the claim that an interpretation which attributes to the *Theaetetus* views which are inconsistent with those of the *Republic* flies in the face of very well established facts about the order of Plato's dialogues.

In sum, there is, so far as I can see, no justified general presumption in favor of the prevalent thesis that the dialectical dialogues, including the *Theaetetus*, must be interpreted as maintaining the doctrines of canonical Platonism. There is no even *prima facie* reason not to turn to the examination of the *Theaetetus* with a willingness to construe its arguments in whatever way seems most natural, given their context within the dialogue itself, to an alert and sober philosophical reader. It is this effort that I undertake in the commentary which follows.

CHAPTER I

THE AMALGAMATION OF THE THEORIES OF THEAETETUS, PROTAGORAS, AND HERACLEITUS (151-161)

A. The Elements of Protagoreanism and Heracleiteanism (151-155)

The main dialogue of the *Theaetetus*, a conversation between Socrates, the geometer Theodorus, and his pupil Theaetetus, begins with a brief introductory discussion (143d 1-151d 6) in which Socrates engages Theaetetus (146c) as his respondent in an investigation of the question, What is knowledge? At first Theaetetus replies by citing various sciences, arts, and crafts as "knowledges" (ἐπιστῆμαι), much as under similar circumstances Meno thinks to say what virtue is by explaining what the virtue of a man, a woman, and so on, consist in (*Meno* 71e ff.). Socrates explains that he wants to know what knowledge itself is and not how many varieties of it there may be, and after a digression showing Theaetetus' geometrical prowess and explaining Socrates' avocation as intellectual midwife, the discussion turns in earnest to the attempt to define knowledge.

Once Theaetetus understands that in asking ἐπιστήμη ὅτι ποτὲ τυγχάνει ὄν Socrates wishes to be given a general characterization of all things that are called ἐπιστῆμαι, he is pretty easily persuaded to put aside his initial diffidence (148e) and propose a definition of knowledge. The definition, that knowledge is nothing else than perception, is no sooner announced than Socrates embarks on a lengthy development of the grounds which might lead one to accept this doctrine. He first associates Theaetetus' thesis with the Protagorean doctrine that man is the measure of all things and then contrives to make Protagoras' theory itself a kind of epistemological offshoot of a Heracleitean theory of reality. The views of Theaetetus, Protagoras, and Heracleitus are said, as Socrates concludes his development and exposition of them, to "come to the same thing" (160d), and Theaetetus is represented as holding that if Heracleitus' and Protagoras' views are correct then perception turns out to be knowledge (160e 1-2).[1] In the subsequent criticism of the amalgamated doctrine these different elements are, in the main, separately investigated and tested. First Protagoreanism (160c-179c) and then Heracleiteanism (181b-183c) are examined and found to be false doctrines and therefore not safe bases on which to defend Theaetetus' definition of knowledge as perception. It is only at this point in the argument (184b-186e) that Socrates and Theaetetus confront directly the proposed definition, without reference either to Protagorean or to Heracleitean doctrines; and, in fact, it does not take Socrates very long to show that perception, correctly conceived, is not only not identical with knowledge but never amounts to knowledge at all.

The first large section of the dialogue (151d-161b), then, has the purpose of constructing a two-sided philosophical underpinning for Theaetetus' definition of knowledge as perception. Plato's interests in the dialogue are, nonetheless, as much engaged by Protagoreanism and Heracleiteanism on their own account as they are by these doctrines as supports for the sense-perception theory of knowledge. This is why his subsequent criticism considers each strand in the philosophical expansion of Theaetetus' theory in isolation from the other, as well as in virtual independence of its role in the expansion and defense of Theaetetus' definition.

There is little difficulty in understanding how the thesis comes to be associated with Progagoras' doctrine that man is the measure of all things. Protagoras, as Plato represents him,[2] holds what may be called a relativist position about truth and existence: he believes that it is incorrect ever to say that something is *true*, or *is the case*, or that anything *exists* or *is* such-and-such, without saying to whom or for whom these things are so. Later on (166-168) in response to criticism Protagoras' theory will be explained more at large, but here (152) only the fundamental doctrine is stated. And although Protagoras evidently means to assert his thesis quite unrestrictedly and for judgments of all types, it is here illustrated only by reference to judgments about the qualities a thing is *perceived* to have. The correct thing to say about a wind is that it is not in itself (ἐφ' ἑαυτοῦ 152b 5) either cold or not cold: it *is* cold *to* a person who feels it so and not cold *to* one who feels it not so. What any one feels or sees or otherwise perceives to be the case *is* the case for him (c 2-3). Thus Protagoras' theory implies that every perception is true (to him who has it) and that perception is always of something that exists or is the case (for him who has it) (c 5-6).

In this way Protagoras' doctrine maintains the existence of the qualities and objects which any one perceives. It is not however entirely clear how he means to argue for this: he seems to be saying (152a 6-8) that truth and existence, taken without explicit reference to the person to whom something is true or for whom it exists, are empty concepts--that there isn't any truth or existence, but only truth-for-x and existence-for-x. If, however, his intention is to do away with the concepts of truth and existence and introduce instead his relative truth and relative existence, it is not easy to see how he can argue that perception is a case of knowledge. For "The wind is cold to me" will then not differ materially from "The wind appears cold to me." Thus, in the first place the effect will be to reduce all thinking to the reporting of appearances; and, in the second place, in these reports there will be nothing true but, at best, true-for-the-reporter. But knowledge (as Protagoras is represented as arguing, 152c 5-6) implies truth and the existence of its object, not mere truth-for-x and existence-for-x (which comes to no more than appearance). It seems then that if he wishes to introduce these new concepts he ought to conclude that there is nothing that exists and no knowledge, only appearances and reports of appearances, rather than that perceiving is getting at what exists, and, therefore, amounts to knowleage. It seems possible, then, that what he really wishes to argue for is not the abandonment of the concepts of existence and truth, with their freedom from "for-x" suffixes, but rather an adjustment in the criteria for their application: a thing is hot not if it so appears to the normal observer (or whatever) but if it so appears to any one (and the paradox that then the same thing will have contradictory predicates can be softened somewhat by pointing out that if a thing is both hot and cold it is so for different observers).

But however exactly Protagoras wishes to explain and support his thesis (the alternatives will become important later on in connection with Plato's refutation of his doctrine), here at the beginning the position is so briefly stated that all one has a right to conclude is that Protagoras is appealing to the facts about perceptual relativity to support some doctrine to the effect that what <u>one</u> person experiences cannot be allowed to discredit the judgments any one else makes on the basis of <u>his</u> experience. The conclusion that perception is knowledge is then brought in on the ground that no perceptual judgment can be refuted. (Since there are other types of judgments besides perceptual ones, and Protagoras' theory has the same implications for all judgments, it does not imply that <u>every</u> case of knowledge is a case of perception and therefore does not support Theaetetus' <u>identification</u> of perception and knowledge. But a discreet silence is maintained here, and indeed throughout the whole discussion, about this discrepancy between Protagoras and Theaetetus.)

Having established this degree of harmony between the views of Theaetetus and Protagoras, Plato goes right on (152d ff.), without pause, to connect Protagoras with Heracleitus' doctrine of universal flux. This he does by suggesting, facetiously, that the doctrine about truth and existence just outlined was a mere popular version of the doctrine which Protagoras really meant to uphold and which he taught his pupils in private. His private doctrine, we are given to understand, coincided with that of Heracleitus. In attributing this view to Protagoras as his secret teaching Plato is no doubt giving a hint, if hint is needed, that it is he and not Protagoras who first discovered the affinity between the two doctrines.[3]

It is not easy to see at first how the two views can come to the same, or how Protagoreanism can be construed as a consequence of Heracleiteanism. Heracleitus' doctrine is a doctrine about change, which is to say about the constant succession of qualities and other properties, whereas Protagoras is evidently interested in the simultaneous predication of different and apparently conflicting qualities. They do, indeed, share one feature, namely the denial that anything is in itself (152b 5-6, d 2-3, 7-8) any given thing or of any particular quality: but the Heracleiteans point to the fact that qualities come and go, arising under certain circumstances and passing away or failing to arise under others, whereas Protagoras' appeal would seem to be to the fact that at one and the same time different perceivers see a thing as (e.g.) blue and green. And to say that something is not in itself green because it looks blue to some people at the same time as it looks green to others, is at least apparently quite a separate point from the Heracleitean view that you should not say a thing is in itself green because before you know it it will have become blue. The one seems to envisage lack of duration as the cause why nothing is anything or of any quality, whereas the other is preoccupied with indeterminacy and ambiguity at any single moment. There is, then, an initial doubt how Plato thinks Protagoreanism reduces to Heracleiteanism.

Now Plato does provide an argument of sorts which is intended to show how Protagoras' point is basically just the Heracleitean flux story applied to perception: I take it that the discussion (154b-155e) of the puzzles about size and number is supposed to provide the rationale for the reduction of Protagoreanism to Heracleiteanism, and that the theory of perception then outlined (156a-157c) is intended to carry through the assimilation. But even before those arguments are produced the two theories are already quite abruptly associated. For in the initial statement of Heracleiteanism (152d 2-e 1) itself it is apparently the Protagorean type of relativity that is introduced as posing the problem to which the Heracleitean doctrine of flux is the answer. The passage reads:

> Nothing is, taken by itself, one thing, nor could you rightly call it just _this_ thing or a thing of just _this_ sort, but if you say it is large it will appear small as well, and if heavy it will appear light, and similarly for all predicates, since nothing is one thing or just _this_ thing or of just _this_ sort. All the things which we say, speaking not correctly, _are_, become as a result of motion and change and mingling with one another: for nothing ever is, but always becomes.

Now the first sentence of this statement relies in its examples exclusively upon the kind of indeterminacy which is associated with the behavior of predicates which have been conveniently dubbed "incomplete."[4] None of these--ugly and beautiful, equal and unequal are other examples dwelt upon in Plato's middle period dialogues--can be simply predicated of any subject, at least not of anything in the ordinary world, but on each occasion the predicate must be "completed" by means of a reference to a person to whom the things are equal, or to things in comparison with which a thing is beautiful, and so forth. Nothing is _just_ beautiful, but, as Plato says in the _Hippias Major_ (289a-b), not even Helen is beautiful whatever she is compared with (for example the gods): one ought to call a woman beautiful with the qualification "for a human being." And one seems to be invited to think of Protagoras' interest in perceptual predicates as involving the view that they are all of them incomplete in just the same way--one can never say a thing is just green without adding (either explicitly or implicitly) to what observer it is so. The apparent effect of Protagoras' denial that the wind is ever ἐφ' ἑαυτοῦ cold, but always only cold to the man who shivers (and not to him who does not shiver), is to require a completion whenever any of these predicates is applied to anything.

In the middle period dialogues, as here, it is argued that, because a thing that is heavy in one respect or in reference to one standard of measurement will equally turn out light in another respect or reference, it must be wrong to say of any such thing that it *is* heavy: only something which has the quality of heaviness however it measured and in whatever respect can be truly said to *be* heavy. When this topic is discussed in the *Republic* (479a-d) things other than Forms, which alone bear the predicates in question without requiring qualification, are said to waver between being and not-being, since one cannot be satisfied to think either that they are (e.g.) heavy or that they are not, nor that they are both, nor yet that they are neither. And neither in this passage nor, I think, anywhere[5] in the *Republic* is there any suggestion that when a predicate is used in an incomplete application one ought to say that the thing *becomes* (e.g.) heavy in comparison with so-and-so, rather than that it is or appears heavy in one reference and not in another.

In the *Theaetetus*, however, the reference to the behavior of incomplete predicates is followed up immediately with a statement that we should never say that anything is (e g.) heavy but rather that in its intermingling with other things it becomes so. We need to know how the theory of becoming introduced here is to be applied to the incomplete predicates, among them the perceptual ones. It is in the analysis of the puzzles about size and number that, as I have already said, Plato indicates how the theory of becoming is supposed to account for the behavior of incomplete predicates. But before considering that passage we must have a more definite notion about what the theory of becoming maintains.

The thesis that nothing is anything, but merely becomes this or that, is variously given in the *Theaetetus* as holding that (156a 5) everything is change and there is nothing besides change, and as proposing (157b 1) to remove "is" everywhere in favor of "becomes." The intention of the theory, given these two claims, is to assert (181d 8-e 7) that everything is constantly changing in every respect.

To find out more precisely what the theory of flux involves it is necessary to recall the *Timaeus*.[6] The *Timaeus* begins its cosmology (27d 6 f.) with a division between τὸ ὂν ἀεί, γένεσιν δὲ οὐκ ἔχον and τὸ γιγνόμενον μὲν ἀεί, ὂν δὲ οὐδέποτε, and this second realm is patently one in which the thesis of the *Theaetetus*, ἔστι μὲν γὰρ οὐδέποτ' οὐδέν, ἀεὶ δὲ γίγνεται, applies with full rigor. Now when the *Timaeus* says that all αἰσθητά, which make up the realm of γιγνόμενα, become but never are, it has in mind a contrast between things that undergo change and things (the Forms) that never change in any respect and cannot indeed ever have significantly tensed propositions asserted about them (37e-38a). Perceptible things are *created* (28b), have a career in time, and pass away. Existence or being so-and-so belongs only to things which are eternal and have whatever properties they have always and without change (28a 2, 38a 2-6). Other things both come into being and come to be hot or a house, passing out of being later on and losing whatever properties they may chance to have. These facts are taken to show that being and existence do not belong to transient things, and this makes it clear that being and existence are thought to imply a duration and stability to which no γιγνόμενον can lay claim. Thus the fact that the physical elements give place to one another in an unending cycle, none of them retaining its own character, shows (49b-d) that it cannot be right to say that anything in the world *is fire*: the most one should say is that some part of the world[7] *becomes fiery* (51b 4-6). The contrast between γένεσις and οὐσία is here a contrast between change and permanence.

Now the *Timaeus* maintains not merely that physical, perceptible objects undergo change, but also that, as γιγνόμενα ἀεί, they are *always* changing and never at rest. The contrast of γένεσις and οὐσία is therefore a contrast between what is *always* the same and what *never* remains the same even for the shortest period of time. This doctrine of γένεσις is transferred into Whiteheadian terminology by Taylor, who writes that[8] "'passage' is a fundamental character" of the sensible universe and that[9] the physical world consists of events in which "objects" are ingredient. Everything in the physical world loses its characters as soon as it gets them and never has for any stretch of time any character whatever; during any period, however short, it takes on a succession of different characters. When therefore Timaeus denies οὐσία to αἰσθητά he means to deny them not only the absolute permanence of the Forms but also the lesser stability that would be implied by the continued possession of some property for any period of time.

This is so far intelligible enough: γένεσις means change, and constant γένεσις altogether without οὐσία means constant change without stable possession of any property. And this way of understanding the theory fits nicely with what the Theaetetus says in defense of the Heracleitean theory introduced there. Thus Socrates points out that warmth, which creates and preserves life, is itself the product of rubbing, which involves motion and change (153a); likewise, it is activity which preserves a good condition of mind and body (153b), so that motion and change for physical things means existence and lack of it means their destruction. Hence Socrates paraphrases the flux thesis by saying (156a) that the world is just change and besides change there is nothing.

On the other hand, Socrates also says that the intention and effect of the Heracleitean theory is to remove altogether the verb εἶναι from use in connection with physical objects (157a-b). This of course means that physical objects must not be implied to have settled possession of any character for any period of time, as the emphasis in the context on the denial of rest and stability (157b 5, 7) shows. But it appears that the theory as I have so far been construing it does not in fact ban <u>every</u> use of εἶναι, as the theory literally interpreted wishes to do. For if the theory holds that, for example, a chair is always changing its color--there is a succession of shades of green followed without interval by a succession of shades of blue, none of which remains in the chair for two moments together--it must allow a minimum use of εἶναι to express the possession of each of the characters for the moment at which it is present. If at moment <u>t</u> the chair becomes green, then at that moment it <u>is</u> green--not in any sense which implies the continued existence of that color but in the minimal sense that it is green that then comes to <u>be</u>.[10] It is obvious to us, because of the structure of the English word "becomes," that this minimal "is" cannot be avoided; the implication would not be so obvious to a Greek, whose word for "become" (γίγνεσθαι) bears no evident relation to the verb "to be" (εἶναι). For this reason Plato's Heracleiteans can express the successive momentary possession of characters by use only of "becomes" locutions, without bringing in any overt use of εἶναι, however minimal: they can say "It becomes green, then blue, then purple," and abstain from saying, what evidently amounts to the same, "Now it is green, now blue, now purple." There will in any case be no harm in such use of what one may call momentary-εἶναι, since it is evidently only duration-εἶναι that the Heracleiteans wish to remove altogether. Only duration-εἶναι involves rest and abstention from change, which it is the Heracleiteans' primary aim to do away with.

Now I think it is important to notice the distinction between momentary-εἶναι and duration-εἶναι and to observe that the Heracleitean theory is a theory of constant succession and therefore denies only the application of duration-εἶναι to physical things, being content to use momentary-εἶναι even though without avowing the fact. For sometimes commentators, perhaps half-aware of the anomaly of a theory which holds that τὸ εἶναι πανταχόθεν ἐξαιρετέον (157b 1) nevertheless allowing a use of εἶναι, speak as if they thought the theory of flux involved the substitution of γίγνεσθαι for εἶναι in all contexts, including those where only momentary-εἶναι occurs and not duration-εἶναι. Thus when Taylor speaks, as he often does, of the physical universe as always "in the making" and essentially incomplete,[11] he sometimes seems to have in mind not the fact that neither it nor any part of it ever acquires any characteristic for good or for any length of time, but that it never even momentarily quite exemplifies any quality. Thus he sometimes interprets Timaeus' class of γιγνόμενα ἀεί as things which are always becoming something but never finally are that something (Commentary, p. 128); and this is in turn to be explained (p. 348; cf p. 63) by reference to the remark in the Phaedo (75a 2) that physical equals "desire" to be such as the Form of the equal but, falling short of this, they merely "tend to be something to which they never do more than approximate" (p. 348). Now in the Phaedo the failure is not due to the fact that a physical equal doesn't remain equal to anything for any period of time but changes to become unequal before you know it; rather[12] it is that a physical equal is simultaneously unequal, e. g., equal to one thing and not equal to another.[13] The thesis is, then, that no physical equal is really equal because it is never at any given moment unambiguously equal. The suggestion in Taylor's references to it and his way of connecting it to the theory of γένεσις is that the relation between a physical equal and the Equal itself is *at any given moment* one of incomplete γένεσις or incomplete exemplification--the physical thing is becoming equal but destined never to complete the process; it will never *be* equal even for a moment. But *this* sense of becoming is quite a different one from that which we have seen to be introduced and supported in both *Timaeus* and *Theaetetus* by references to change and motion. For, to alter the example, if something is a γιγνόμενον in the sense that it undergoes an uninterrupted succession of colors, no one of which it possesses during any period of time, we shall not want to say that no process it undergoes is ever completed. To be sure, we will not say that any property becomes its lasting possession, but the process of becoming red, e. g., will terminate in the momentary-εἶναι of red (even though there will be a new process immediately underway); and there is no indication in the *Timaeus'* account of γένεσις or the *Theaetetus'* introduction of ὄντα μὲν οὐδέποτε, ἀεὶ δὲ γιγνόμενα that the momentary possession of redness or equality or whatever is to be disallowed on the ground that at any given moment nothing exhibits these qualities but at best *tends to exemplify* or *is in process of becoming* an instance of them. The γένεσις theory, to be intelligible at all, must be distinguished from the point, whatever exactly it is, that is being argued when the *Phaedo* says that physical equals ὀρέγεται . . . εἶναι οἷον τὸ ἴσον (75a 2). If when something is, as we should say, equal to something else it is really only striving after equality and in that sense merely becoming equal but never quite finishing the process, this is quite a different use of "becomes" from that which the Timaeus invokes to explain how the elements (earth, fire, etc.) succeed one another without cessation. The Timaeus' point would be ruined if one refused to say when part of the Receptacle becomes fiery that it is at that moment fiery, and recommended instead saying that even then it is only in process of becoming fiery.[14] For then we would have no succession of properties but a succession of incomplete momentary processes, which if intelligible at all introduces two levels of processes where the theory of constant change evidently only wants one.

It is, then, important to distinguish momentary from duration εἶναι and to see that it is only the latter whose use the theory of flux is refusing to grant. In Theaetetus 152d-e, consequently, Plato is suggesting that Protagoras' views about truth and existence amount to the Heracleitean theory that everything in the world is constantly taking on and losing characteristics, and that there is nothing that has any character for any duration. And this account is to apply to all characters (152d 5-6, σύμπαντά τε οὕτως), colors, weight, and size as well as properties like fieriness and being a man. The incomplete predicates "large," "small," "heavy," and "light," mentioned at 152d 4-5, are to be conceived as coming to be true of an object at a certain moment, and never remaining true of it, just as "fiery" in the

Timaeus comes to be true but does not remain true of a part of the Receptacle in the unceasing cycle of the elements. As we shall see in a moment, according to Heracleitean doctrines a thing becomes small when brought into comparison with one object or group of objects, and becomes large when compared with others. And if the same thing may be both large and small at once (in different connections) this will be explained by saying that a thing may come into comparison at once with two sets of objects, and so become at once large in one comparison and small in the other. In this way, as we shall see more fully just below, the Heracleitean flux story, as implying constant succession of characters, also does duty for the kind of simultaneous indefiniteness which is characteristic of the incomplete predicates attended to in the Republic.

The way in which a Heracleitean account can be made to yield basically the same result as Protagoras' theory about perceptual qualities, but with an improvement, is illustrated at 153d 8-155e 2. Socrates begins by suggesting on behalf of the Heracleiteans (153d 8-e 2) that colors (which do duty pretty much throughout for perceptual properties in general) must not be thought of as possessions of bodies; rather they arise under certain circumstances when bodies come into contact. No body ever is red (if that implies fixed position and rest, e 1-2) but at most becomes red on some occasion under certain circumstances. This first rough statement of the Heracleitean theory of sense perception is expanded below (156a-157c), but before that Socrates pauses to consider two puzzles concerning size and number which are supposed to illustrate the necessity of adopting the Heracleitean theory that things only become large or white or warm (under certain circumstances) and never are any of these things.

The puzzles themselves and the lesson to be drawn from them are extremely difficult to construe. They are introduced as an example of the contradictions which arise if we say that the things we perceive <u>are</u> white or hot or large, etc. The facts of perception seem to show that no person perceives the same thing in connection with an object as any other person (still more as any dog); a single given man doesn't even have the same experiences on two different occasions, due to the fact that he is never in a constant state (154a). And from this it is supposed to follow (154b 1-6) that one ought not to say that either perceived object or percipient organ is white, warm, etc. Now Protagoras has already been represented (152b) as holding that one should never say that a wind is <u>in itself</u> cold, but he has allowed the use of "is," so long as one adds to or for whom the wind is cold. But Protagoras did not, in allowing the use of "is," take account of the fact, urged by the Heracleiteans, that everything is constantly changing. It seems therefore that the argument at 154b should not be merely a repetition of Protagoras' point about the temperature of the wind, and it seems possible that a correction or clarification in Protagoras' thesis is being urged. For if his view is to be compatible with the Heracleiteans', his use of "is cold to me" must mean no more than "becomes cold to me," and hence must not be construed as involving a use of duration-"is." That is to say, when in accordance with Protagoras' views someone says the wind is cold to him he must not be understood as implying that it has been so for him for some time or that it will go on having that property for him for any period. Because Protagoras was not concerned with change but with simultaneous observer-relativity he has left it an open question whether in saying the chair is green to me I imply the continued possession of this color (for me) by the chair. But in order to reduce Protagoreanism to Heracleiteanism this implication must be denied. Hence in 154b and the discussion which follows Protagoras' "is green to me" is being replaced by the Heracleitean "becomes green in connection with me."

But if this is what Socrates intends to be arguing at 154a-b and reinforcing by the example which follows, it must be admitted that the point is obscurely brought out. He says: "Therefore if the thing we measure ourselves against or touch were large or white or warm [when we so perceive it], it could not ever have become different by encountering something different [i. e., by being perceived by someone else], at any rate if it does not itself change." (154b 1-3). This evidently assumes that the thesis to be overturned holds both that objects have continuing properties and that one can attribute these to them without having to mention any person for whom the property exists. And whereas Protagoras' original position might be construed as including the first point it seems that the second is explicitly denied by him. On the other hand, as we shall see in a moment, in the example which follows Socrates refuses to draw a distinction between a thing's being larger than something else and its being larger simpliciter (i. e., than it was); and this suggests that Socrates is for some reason assuming that if someone says something is warm _to him_ or larger _than something else_, and means to attribute continuing properties to the thing, he must accept the consequence that the thing is warm or larger (_sans phrase_). Implausible though this assumption is, if Socrates is accepting it then he may think that by showing difficulties in the continued possession of properties _sans phrase_ he can show the necessity of not allowing any lasting properties of any sort for any time.

In any case the argument presented in connection with the puzzles about size and number does rely upon this assumption, in order, apparently, to draw the conclusion that one should never speak of characters as possessed by anything for any duration but only for an indivisible moment during a period of uninterrupted change.

The example Socrates introduces in order to illustrate this point concerns, in the first instance, six dice. If we compare six dice with another group of four, we shall have to say that the six are more than the four; and likewise in comparing them with twelve dice we have no alternative but to say they are less. (Later on [155b 6 ff.] a parallel case concerning not number but size is introduced: Socrates is at one time larger than Theaetetus, but later, due to Theaetetus' growing, he is smaller.) We must then, it seems, say of the dice that they are more and, again, that they are less, and similarly of Socrates that he is larger and, later, that he is smaller.

But if we do say these things we appear to come into conflict with certain other true statements which we cannot help affirming.

These are:

(1) Nothing can become greater or less in size or number so long as it remains the same size as it was (lit., "so long as it is equal to itself") (155a 3-5).

(2) What has not been added to or taken away from neither grows nor shrinks, but is always equal to itself (a 7-9).

(3) What was not (i. e., what was not in existence or was not the case) at an earlier time cannot be at a later unless there intervenes some process of change (b 1-2).

The conflict arises because we wish to say at different times that the dice are more and that they are less and this commits us, by (3), to saying that some process of change must intervene between the time when they are more and the time when they are less. But we do not think the dice have been added to or subtracted from, so that, by (2), they do not (at any rate) undergo the changes called growth or shrinking; there are always just the same number of them. But in that case, by (1), they cannot be at one time more and at another less, because the only process of change that could bring this about is increase or diminution of their number (which we have ruled out). Hence if we say that the dice are greater when compared with the smaller quantity we cannot also say that they remain the same in number as they were; and conversely if we say they remain the same they cannot be first less and then more than anything: the three enumerated propositions "fight amongst themselves" when we say the things we have decided we must say about the dice (155b 4-6).[15]

Now it is evident that the air of paradox here is generated by first permitting the inference from judgments of the type of "These dice are more than those dice" to "These dice are more (simpliciter)," and then covertly interpreting the latter to mean "These dice are more than they were." Thus the word "more" is being treated as if it had a relative and a non-relative use: relative when a reference to some second thing is intended, and non-relative when no external reference is intended but, at most, a reference to the former state of the one thing being talked about. The paradox thus arises because we are permitted to go from the one to the other of these uses without noticing that they are different. Obviously no even apparent contradiction would arise if at every point in the argument the two uses were carefully kept apart by adding the qualifying clauses wherever necessary. Thus there is nothing remotely contradictory about saying that Socrates comes to be smaller than Theaetetus even though he remains his same size, because becoming smaller than Theaetetus is quite a different thing from becoming smaller simpliciter. And this shows that propositions (1) and (3) above are acceptable only if qualified so as to distinguish these two things.

But, though Plato does not explicitly say what moral he wishes to elicit from these puzzles, he cannot be recommending that we distinguish relative from non-relative uses of such words as "more." The puzzles themselves are to be resolved by following Heracleitean principles as introduced earlier and applied in the sequel to the case of perceptual properties (cf. 155d 5 ff.); hence the doctrine of constant change should provide the solution of the conflict which Plato here creates. If this is so then the source of the contradiction as Plato construes it must be located in the attempt to describe the dice as continuing to be the same number and Socrates as continuing to maintain his same size. If nothing remains the same and nothing has the stable possession of any feature, then it must be wrong to speak of Socrates' size and the number of the dice as ever constant. Number and size are things which they are constantly acquiring and losing, as they come into contact with other things; that being so, if Socrates' becoming smaller than Theaetetus involves a change in Socrates as well as in Theaetetus (as Socrates implies that it does), this cannot cause difficulty, since propositions (1) and (2), which speak of Socrates' size as a continuing possession, have no application to anything in a world of constant flux. If a change in the things against which you measure something implies a change in the thing measured, as Socrates has evidently been assuming, this consequence can be accepted with equanimity by a Heracleitean, since he thinks everything is always changing in every respect. Socrates at time *t* is brought into connection with Theaetetus, and in this κρᾶσις πρὸς ἄλληλα (152d 7) Socrates becomes smaller. Taken together with other objects at other times other predicates come to be true, momentarily, of him; but as every predicate is true only for a moment and (at least in the cases we have been considering) only comes to apply within a certain configuration of objects at that time, the contradiction alleged by Socrates cannot arise.

The upshot is that in alleging a difficulty which unwary non-

Heracleiteans fall into when they try to talk about dice or Socrates under certain circumstances, Plato has not given any good argument for preferring Heracleiteanism to ordinary ways of speaking. If "larger" is treated as a real comparative, requiring completion on every occasion of use, no contradiction arises, and a non-Heracleitean can go on speaking of things as existing and being so-and-so for a period of time, as well as becoming so-and-so.[16] The examples considered do not really require, if treated in a non-Heracleitean way, a change where there is no change. Socrates, however, thinks that they do imply this impossibility, and evidently draws the conslusion that the Heracleitean view that there is always change everywhere offers the only way out.

But the interesting point in the passage is that by considering what Socrates evidently recommends on behalf of the Heracleiteans it is possible to see how Protagoreanism is being reduced to Heracleiteanism. If the moral extracted above is applied to the case of perceptual qualities, as 154b implies it is meant to be, then the following account emerges. One must abandon every effort to speak of any characteristics as belonging to anything for any period of time. When one says, "The wind is cold for me," this must be understood as the report of a momentary event, and a completely accurate way of speaking would be to say "The wind becomes cold for me now." Perceptual predicates, like "larger" and "more" as illustrated in the puzzles, come to apply to a thing only within a configuration of objects. When something becomes green it does so in connection with some particular percipient at some definite moment of time, just as it is by taking Socrates together with Theaetetus at a certain time that one can say that he becomes smaller. When taken together with something else at another time or even at the same time Socrates may well become larger: his possession of the predicate "larger" is always limited to a certain context of other objects. Likewise colors always qualify a thing in a context involving a perceiver (as well, no doubt, as other surrounding circumstances), and if a thing becomes green in one context it may very well in another context later on or at the same time become blue.

This consideration suggests an answer to the question which arose at the very beginning (p. 17 above), about how Plato thinks Protagoras' point about the relativity of perceptual (and other) qualities to the observer can be an offshoot of a theory of constant change. For some qualities, among them the perceptual ones, arise only within a certain context or configuration of objects, and if an alteration of contexts can bring with it an alteration of a thing's qualities, then when a thing is at once part of several configurations it will have at one and the same time all the different qualities which it would acquire in succession if it entered the different contexts one after another. Perceptual relativity thus comes down to change of perceptual context, with its consequent change of perceptual quality. A thing can simultaneously become blue and green, because it belongs to two different perceptual contexts. In this way the private doctrine attributed to Protagoras substitutes for his loose "is to me" the completely accurate "becomes in connection with me." Protagoras' "what appears to each is for him" is acceptable as an informal and popular way of putting the real truth, which is that what appears to each in perception becomes in connection with him and some object. And since these becomings are always connected with some particular subject it is necessary, in order to identify and characterize a color-process, to refer to the person for whom the process happens (154a 2, μεταξύ τι ἑκάστῳ ἴδιον γεγονός). This fact at once justifies Protagoras' insistence that every perceptual predicate should be qualified by a reference to some person, and explains how Heracleiteanism can seem to support the view that perception is knowledge. For according to this theory every judgment about color, for example, will be a report of the color-process which comes into being in connection with the person making the judgment, and matters have been so arranged that he must apparently be right in his report. Therefore, even though one cannot say about his own or any one else's perceptions that they report what _exists_ or _is_ the case for him, it appears to be enough to say that they report infallibly what comes to be, or comes to be the case, for him. Even in this latter circumstance perception seems to amount to knowledge.

This opening exposition of Heracleitean doctrines, then, shows how an uncritical Protagorean theory about perceptual judgments is to be refashioned into a combined Heracleitean-Protagorean account. It is argued that certain predicates--"larger," "more"--cannot without generating difficulties be applied so long as a theory of constant change is not adopted. The same argument is invoked to show that difficulties arise when one tries to apply perceptual predicates. The Heracleitean way of handling such predicates is recommended as the remedy for the embarrassments referred to, and a brief indication (153d 8-154a 2) is given of how this method will treat perceptual judgments. The detailed Heracleitean theory of perception is expounded in the section immediately following.

B. The Heracleitean Theory of Perception (156a-157b)

The puzzles about size and number and Socrates' apparent inference from them have suggested how the Protagorean theory of the relativity of perceptual qualities is to be reduced to a Heracleitean account of reality. The proper objects of perception--colors, temperatures, tastes, sounds, etc.--are going to be regarded as arising momentarily in a world of total flux as a result of the mutual influence of perceptual organs and external objects. The emphasis on the context in which they arise will ensure their relativity to observers, and by treating them as momentary becomings the account will make them amenable to a general Heracleitean metaphysics. In the immediately succeeding passage (156a 2 ff.) a theory of perception is presented which claims to be a Heracleitean account and which in its broad outlines clearly follows the pattern just adumbrated. On the basis of this theory of perception it is then argued (157e-160c) that each man's perceptions are necessarily true and, therefore, each man has a right to claim knowledge about what he perceives. The ultimate effect, then, of the Heracleitean theory of perception is to vindicate Protagoras' claim that what appears to each man is the case for him, and therefore to support Theaetetus' definition of knowledge as perception.

The theory of perception itself begins by citing its allegiance to the Heracleitean principle that τὸ πᾶν κίνησις ἦν καὶ ἄλλο παρὰ τοῦτο οὐδέν (156a 5), and concludes with the announcement that as expounded just before it has kept to the stricture that τὸ εἶναι πανταχόθεν ἐξαιρετέον (157b 1) and that one must never bring anything to rest (b 7-8). But if these strictures express the ideals directing the construction of the theory, it cannot be denied that the exposition itself fails to put them into practice. The theory is at least careless in its manner of speaking about the elements of the perceptual situation which it introduces; and ultimately, as I shall show below, the account it gives is really incompatible with Heracleiteanism.

The exposition begins by distinguishing two kinds of change, those with an "active capacity" and those with a "passive capacity." This distinction is alleged to be the basis of the difference between things capable of being perceived (agents) and organs or persons capable of perceiving (patients); but how we are to understand these differences as differences in type of <u>motion</u> is neither indicated nor, probably, worth inquiring into. In any event it is the other broad division of kinds of motion, the distinction with respect to speed of change (156c 6 ff.), which is most important. The active and passive motions just mentioned are said to generate, by coming together and interfering with one another, two other motions, corresponding to a perceived quality and the perceiving of it. This latter pair of motions is contrasted with the former as being very rapid, in comparison with the slow rate of change characterizing the other pair. A "slow motion" is further explained by the remark that it "has its motion in the same place and with reference to the things that come within its vicinity" (156c 9-f); the more rapid motions are explicitly said to be changes of place, and their greater rapidity is supposed to be due to the fact that locomotion is their mode of change (d 2-3). This suggests, though it does not quite say, that the slow motions are changes in quality while the rapid are changes in place; and, *per contra*, as the things that undergo qualitative change are said to have location, the αἰσθητά and αἰσθήσεις, which are changing place, are apparently at rest with respect to change of quality.

If this is correct, then the theory being suggested here amounts to the following. A stick or a stone is to be regarded as constantly losing and gaining qualities. Each quality it gains comes into being together with an awareness of it on the part of somebody, and though each quality moves in place constantly so long as it exists, it is nevertheless quite firmly some one quality--say whiteness--and not any other during the time it is moving in place. Therefore it *is* definitely whiteness that comes to be and *exists* during the time it is perceived; and equally, the stick really *is* white at that time, at least for the percipient in question. The qualities which as it were succeed one another in the stick do *exist* and *are* whatever they are during the time they are perceived. Such a theory of perception would result in the stick's becoming white to me for a certain time in such a sense that during that time it *is* white to me; in short, the sense of becoming such a theory would employ would be one which was not incompatible with existence, but strictly implied it. The process in question would terminate in fixed and lasting states, and for the description of these states not γίγνεσθαι but εἶναι would be the correct locution.

But, as I have already remarked, although the actual account of perception thus leaves open, and perhaps even envisages the possibility of requiring, some uses of duration- εἶναι after all, the Heracleiteans expressly claim (157a 7 ff.) for this theory that in it εἶναι is πανταχόθεν ἐξαιρετέον. Perhaps, therefore, the theory of perception expounded in 156-157 should not be interpreted as attributing only one kind of change to each of the elements it introduces in its analysis of the perceptual situation. Possibly it is only looseness of expression which makes the theory appear to condone some uses of duration- εἶναι, and in interpreting it we should make explicit all that is involved in the banishment of εἶναι. According to such a more extreme theory the αἰσθητά which are generated by the interference of perceived object with sense organ would not <u>be</u> whiteness or redness, but would become momentarily one or another of these things without remaining for any period of time. On this theory a stick or a stone will be thought of as endlessly changing its place as well as all its qualities; and it will never actually gain and have any quality whatever. Sense-qualities and awarenesses of them will come paired together, but neither a sense-quality nor an awareness is fixed in any way, either in place or in any other respect: redness comes to be in the space between the percipient and the object, but immediately not only changes in place but also becomes some other color. Reports of perception are thus of something absolutely momentary.

Now either of these theories of perception would serve some of the purposes for which a theory of perception is introduced at this point in the argument. Whether perceptual qualities exist when they are perceived or merely come to be at that time, each αἰσθητόν has correlated with it an αἴσθησις of the appropriate sort. Quality and perception are, as the theory says (156b 1), "twin" offspring of organ and perceived object. The theory of perception, then, whichever of the two versions just outlined is intended, has the important consequence that there is never a sense-quality which belongs to no one; to pick out a sense-quality one must always refer, even if only implicitly, to the experience of someone for whom it exists (or becomes). Therefore the theory supports Protagoras' views about the relativity of perceptual qualities (as it claims to do) by requiring every predication of a sense-quality to carry a reference to the subject for whom it exists or becomes. It also seems suited, in either of the two versions, to make a start, at least, toward justifying Protagoras' claim that perception always yields truth. For just as nothing either is or becomes red all by itself, so no one either is or becomes percipient-of-red by himself: there cannot be an αἴσθησις that lacks an αἰσθητόν. And each percipient's title to freedom of error in his perceptual judgments is protected at least from attack by anyone else on the basis of his own experiences: there is no conflict between what any two persons perceive, because the qualities in question are separately generated and separately experienced.

On the other hand the two theories <u>are</u> different, and if we are to have a truly Heracleitean account of perception at this stage of the argument we had better have the second and not the first of the two theories outlined above. Only the second, furthermore, provides a replacement and clarification of the Protagorean "is for X" locution--and as I have interpreted the moral of the puzzles about size and number, which introduce the account of perception, it is just such a replacement that is here to be spelled out. It has to be admitted, however, that in the theory of perception itself Plato makes no serious attempt to formulate the thorough-going Heracleitean theory that this would require. If nevertheless we are to prefer the full Heracleitean account, we must attempt to find some explanation for Plato's not having <u>stated</u> such a theory.

In part, this failure can be explained by the consideration that in order to rectify it he would have had to distinguish between locomotion and alteration, as I have done in formulating the second version of the theory above, and attribute both sorts of change to the "slow" motions as well as to the "fast." But to do this would tip his hand prematurely: precisely the fact that according to the γένεσις -doctrine of the Heracleiteans everything must have every sort of change is made the basis for his own refutation of this view of γένεσις later on (181-183). Here, he purposely slurs over the distinction between kinds of motion in order, as Campbell puts it,[17] "that it may come in as a fresh point at a later stage." Hence, it might be said, we have sufficient ground for discounting the fact that in the exposition of the theory of perception αἰσθητά are only given φορά, and we should mentally alter it to make them constantly change all their qualities as well. Indeed, it might be added, that it does wish to get rid of lasting qualities is shown by the fact that even in the exposition itself the theory adheres strictly to forms of γίγνεσθαι in detailing what happens in perception, as if this were required by the fact that αἰσθητά and αἰσθήσεις are φοραί.

This line of reasoning does not however really make the theory as actually expounded any the more easily understandable as a serious Heracleitean theory. For it attempts to show how a theory which distinguishes slow from fast motions can be brought into line with Heracleitean presuppositions, and to explain why it was not explicitly brought into line in the first place. But it is easy to see that if even rudimentary attention is paid to Heracleitean principles the distinction between slow and fast motions cannot be introduced at all. The slow motions, or physical objects, are apparently supposed to be incessant qualitative changes. A stick or a stone--a slow motion--becomes a succession of, for example, colors without interruption. As I said above, the theory ought not to give these motions stability of place, as it does; but even if this is allowed to pass the theory obviously still contravenes Heracleitean principles. For if the colors and other qualities that a stick comes to have are to be understood in accordance with a theory even of constant flux of qualities they obviously ought not to be given any duration at all. Thus in the perceptual situation, as the theory says, the stick or the stone becomes not whiteness but white

(156e 5): but if so then the whiteness it comes to have had better not last for any time. If the stick becomes white and stays white for any period of time then during that time it will <u>be</u> white and rest will have been introduced into the world. Why then does the question ever arise what kind of motion the αἰσθητά have? Having no duration they ought not to have any motion of <u>any</u> sort. As soon, therefore, as the theory distinguishes slow from fast motions, regardless of what sorts of motion the latter have and whether the former have every type of motion or only some, it has ceased to be a serious Heracleitean theory. Αἰσθητά patently must be momentary becomings, and as soon as the theory treats them as motions, which must have duration, it not only brings αἰσθητά to a standstill, but also gives sticks and stones lasting properties. Rescue operations may or may not succeed in introducing motions of all sorts into every element of the theory, as Heracleitean metaphysics require, but they cannot explain away the fact that in even embarking on a theory of the type found at 156-157 Plato cannot have paid any serious attention to the Heracleiteanism he claims to be following.

If the theory of perception is only superficially a Heracleitean theory, how are we to explain its appearance here in the <u>Theaetetus</u>? I think the answer must be that Plato is already preparing for the refutation of the flux theory which he will produce below (181-183): since the argument he will press against Heracleiteanism is more effectively deployable against a theory which has naively and half-consciously been thinking of αἰσθητά as having duration (though it is valid against any theory which denies duration to everything), he here sets the Heracleiteans up with a theory that is ripe for refutation. Plato wants to argue in his refutation that the doctrine of general flux is not only false but even unable to support the thesis that what any one judges in perception is true. The latter point goes home more impressively against a theory which has been thinking of the qualities reported in perception as having a duration. For it can then be pointed out that if what one perceives has a duration it must have a succession of qualities, so that one cannot say that what one perceives is (e. g.) red rather than any other color: during the time when one perceives it it must become in succession all the other colors, so that it admits no color-name in preference to any other. The result is that no report of perception one might make at any time is any truer than any other one might have made then, and perceptual judgments lose all claim to truth. It seems that his desire to show not merely that no judgment has any claim to truth in a world of flux but, especially, that no perceptual judgment can be true, has led Plato to give his Heracleiteans a theory of perception which really does not fit their principles at all.

Now if this way of looking at the theory of perception is correct, the Heracleitean theory and the reduction of Protagoreanism to Heracleiteanism had better not be too firmly wedded to the details of the account of perception given in 156-157. And in fact the defense of perception as knowledge which is made in 157e-160c, though at various places in it details of the perception theory are recalled (e. g., 159d, e), does not rely heavily on the fact that αἰσθητά have duration. The essential point is that perceived qualities are things which objects come to have at a certain moment in connection with certain other objects as they are at that moment; and one need not think of them as having any duration in order to follow the subsequent argumentation.

C. Heracleiteanism and the Truth of Perception (157e-160d)

One can think of the basic principles of Heracleiteanism, as applied to perception in 153d-157d, as effectively removing one potential source of objection to the view that all perceptions are true. Because a perceptual quality always arises within a certain configuration of object and percipient, no color or taste or smell can be attributed to an object without reference to the percipient in connection with whom it arises. No object has, as it is put below (160b 1-3, 10-c2), any quality for and by itself. Hence the truth of one's perceptions cannot be impugned by the claim that they fail to correspond to the quality the object _itself_ actually has: it, by itself, has no qualities at all.

But there are other threats to the truth of each man's perceptions. The failure of one's perceptions to correspond with those which other people experience, or which a person in normal circumstances or healthy condition would experience, might also be appealed to as grounds for rejecting them as false. Thus if a certain wine tastes bitter to me in ill-health but sweet to me and others under normal conditions, one might well argue that though I am certainly correct in saying that bitterness is what I now experience my perception is nevertheless false because the wine is not bitter but sweet to the normal palate.

This objection does not depend upon saying that the wine has the quality of sweetness altogether in independence of perceivers--this has already been ruled out--but only that we should refuse to say that what seems to anyone _is_ so unless he is in normal circumstances, healthy condition, etc. The normal person's experiences are the criterion of what is the case, and not those of any indiscriminate person in just any circumstances. Sometimes a person's experiences are similar to those which other people do, or would, experience in connection with a certain object, and sometimes they vary from this norm. And when they vary they must be pronounced false, however much they may be what really _appears_ to be the case to the person in question.

This objection is raised by Plato at 157e-158a and in order to answer it on behalf of his Protagorean Heracleiteans he develops from the elements of Heracleitean metaphysics a more stringent relativism than has yet appeared. The effect of his reply is to argue that on Heracleitean assumptions there can be no place for the concept of a normal observer. Such a conception requires, at a minimum, that we should be able to say that one person's experience is _similar_ to another's, so that the experiences of certain persons can be grouped together and pronounced "normal" by contrast to the deviant experiences of the abnormal. But given a Heracleitean theory of reality, Plato will argue, this condition fails of fulfillment. The upshot is that each man is entirely cut off from every other man and from himself at every other moment, and his experiences have no possible connection with what anyone else experiences or what he himself experiences at any other moment. Each man's perceptions will turn out to be free from criticism of any and every sort because they have been made in the strongest possible sense private to himself at the time he has them.

The nub of this further development consists in the two assertions (1) that no αἴσθησις or αἰσθητόν is ever like any other and (2) that each person (and, of course, though this is not emphasized in the text [but cf. 160c 4-5], each object) is really an infinity[18] of successive persons, no one of which is ever like another. These two theses are enunciated at the very outset of the account of perception on Heracleitean assumptions (154a 6-8), but the matter is not pressed there. It is only after the exposition of the theory of perception, and in answer to the imagined objection explained just above, that this stronger sort of relativity and subjectivism comes forcibly to the forefront. Plato considers two types of case, the discrepancies between waking and dreaming experience and those between a healthy and a diseased person's perceptual judgments. As for waking and dreaming experience (158b 5-d 7), he contents himself with the remark that when one is in either of the two states he places the very strongest credence in the things that then seem to him to be true, so that, since the same amount of time is spent dreaming as waking, there is no ground on which to appeal to what seems true to you in the one condition as refuting what seems true to you in the other.

In considering the contrast between health and sickness (158e 5-160c 10), however, Plato attempts to carry the consequences of Heracleiteanism further. The argument proceeds by means of the following three assertions:

(1) A "person" is really a succession of different persons, inasmuch as he is constantly changing. (159c 8-9)

(2) But what appears and is to one person appears and is different to a different person. (159c 8-9)

(3) Therefore not only is it the case (as was argued in the previous analysis of perception) that what I at any time perceive really is (becomes) so for me then, but also nothing that appears to me at any time is like what appears to any one else or to me at another time. (159e 7-160a 2)

The implied conclusion is:

(4) There can be no ground whatsoever for calling some experiences true and others false. The illusions of dreaming and madness and the "abnormal" impressions due to illness are "real to us at the time when we experience them; which is all the reality anything is permitted to claim."[19] Each perceptual experience is totally unlike and unconnected with any other perceptual experience. There is no ground for appeal to anything beyond the momentary experience itself as a criterion of truth, since all one finds elsewhere is an infinite variation of different persons' quite different and mutually dissimilar and unconnected perceptions. Each person is totally confined within a momentary private world and can do nothing but report his momentary experience. In fact (160b 5-c 10), person, external object, perceived quality and act of perceiving are bound together in such a way that they all come to be for one another and for nothing else.

What reasons are there for accepting (1) and (2)? Neither of them seems, at first sight, true at all: even if a person is constantly changing it does not follow that he is constantly changing his identity. One might, however, allow this to pass in view of the Heracleitean denial of duration in every regard. The difficulties with (2) are more intractable; even if different people may have different experiences in connection with the same object, that is no reason to think that no two people can ever have the same perceptions. (Granted, one might think that two people could not have the same experiences, as [it might be said] one cannot have anyone else's smile or identically the same [abstract particular] sallowness. But Plato is clearly saying that difference of person makes experience qualitatively, and not merely [if there could be such a thing] numerically, different: cf. 159e 7 οὕτως, e 8 ἀλλοῖον, 160a 2 τοιοῦτον).[20]

The reasons Socrates actually proposes to Theaetetus for accepting these propositions seem inadequate on one of two grounds. Either the logic by which they are established involves a fallacious principle of reasoning[21] or there is an equivocation on a key term appearing in premiss and conclusion. Socrates begins by laying it down that something altogether (ὅλως, 158e 10) different from something else cannot have any capacity in common with that other thing; and, he adds,, anything that is entirely different must be unlike (ἀνόμοιον, 159a 3) the thing it is different from. But then he enunciates the dubious proposition that "if anything happens to be like or unlike something (itself or another), we shall say that in being made like, it becomes the same, and in being made unlike, different." (159a 6-8). Now this might be construed as an instance of the fallacy of affirming the consequent: if anything is different, it is unlike, here is something unlike, *ergo* it is different. And there are indications that this is just how Socrates intends to be reasoning. For in what follows he establishes that Socrates-ill is unlike Socrates-well, draws the inference that therefore the two Socrateses are different from one another (159b 10), and considers himself thereby licensed to apply the initial premiss (that two different things do not share any capacity) in order to conclude that the respective Socrateses do not have the capacity to be similarly affected. If this is his argument, then we have quite certainly been given no reason (not even one which assumes the truth of Heracleiteanism) for thinking either that Socrates-well and Socrates-ill are two different persons, or for accepting that neither they nor any other pair of different persons can have the same experiences.

The alternative to so construing the argument is to take 159a 6-8 not as committing the fallacy of affirming the consequent but rather as enunciating an independent axiom about things that are like or unlike one another. This axiom, expressed in the *Parmenides* (139e-140a), holds that to say that something is like something else is to say that they are the same in some respect (που, *Parm*. 139e 8) (and similarly for unlikeness). But even if this is what Socrates means to be saying at 159a 6-8 we are still not brought any closer to a valid reason, even assuming the truth of Heracleiteanism, for accepting (1) and (2) above. For when Socrates goes on to argue that because Socrates-ill and Socrates-well are unlike they must be different, he is entitled only to conclude that they are different *in some respect*. But, as he has made quite explicit just before, it is only when two things are ὅλως different that we have the right to conclude that they do not share any capacity (and so do not have the capacity to be similarly affected in sense perception). Nothing has been said to show that two things in *some* respect different cannot have *any* capacity in common. Only by an equivocation on the word "different" could Socrates pretend that this has been shown. In the conclusion, "difference" means "difference in some respect," while in the premiss it means "difference in every respect." There are indications in the text that this is how Socrates reaches the conclusion that each temporal stage of a "person" is a different person and has entirely different experiences from those of any other person. For in establishing that Socrates-ill is unlike Socrates-well Plato has Theaetetus, to Socrates' evident delight (159b 8), slip in references to τὸν ἀσθενοῦντα Σωκράτη, ὅλον τοῦτο (159b 6), suggesting that because Socrates at any given moment is ὅλον ("as a whole," "taken all together") unlike himself at any other moment taken as a whole, he is *ὅλως* ἕτερος (cf. 158e 10) and ὅλως ἀνόμοιος (entirely different and unlike). But he isn't, and this attempt to cover up the transition from difference in some respect to difference in every respect is not very convincing.

It therefore appears that the reasons Socrates gives in support of his two theses (1) and (2) above are, however one interprets the train of reasoning, inadequate to permit them to serve as premisses to his desired conclusions (3) and (4). Though it may be true that each man is constantly changing, it has not been shown that he is at any two moments entirely unlike; and this is what is required in order to allow the inferences in (3) and (4). It has not been shown that different temporal person-stages must have qualitatively different perceptions.

Faced with this situation it is not easy to decide what to say It seems certain on careful examination of 158e-159c that one or the other of the two fallacious arguments outlined above is indeed the sole support given anywhere in the text for the very important thesis that no one's experiences are ever like anyone else's. Is there any reason to think, independently of the argument in the text, that on Heracleitean principles the thesis must be true? It has been argued[22] that Heracleiteanism implies no such thing, that it only holds that no quality survives for any period of time, and does not deny that the same quality might recur after an interval or come into being in two places at once. And it must be admitted that this is a very plausible account of the true implications of the theory. The possibility therefore suggests itself that Plato has, in his desire to make Heracleiteanism imply Protagoreanism and support the thesis that sense perception is always true, simply forced the consequence on the theory. Wishing to show that if Heracleiteanism is true what anyone perceives to be the case is so, and seeing that to this end he must disallow appeals to the normal observer as the standard of what is so, he has just *made* the flux theory imply the total difference of each person's experience from every other's. And it might be said that the confusion over which of two fallacious arguments he uses to plaster over the gap in his reasoning is deliberate, or half-deliberate, auxiliary obfuscation.

Now ordinarily such an hypothesis would be acceptable only in the last resort. Before embracing it one should exercise all his ingenuity in order to find more than a palpable fallacy in such a crucial argument, or, failing that, one would at least attempt to devise some reasons for accepting the conclusion argued for. But in the present instance I not only doubt that exercises of ingenuity would be of any avail, but even think the hypothesis can be made plausible on its own account.

What reasons are there for thinking that the arguments deducing from Heracleiteanism the truth of perception must be able to be represented as plausible or correct? Presumably something like the following: Plato has undertaken to examine the claim of perception to be knowledge and has introduced Protagorean and Heracleitean doctrines because they support this claim. If a Heracleitean could not plausibly appeal to his basic principles in support of the truth of every perception, then an essential link in Plato's argument fails. At the conclusion of the passage we have just been considering Socrates says that the three views, those of Theaetetus, Protagoras, and Heracleitus, all come to the same; all amount to the claim that perception is knowledge (160d 5-e 2). But if the view expressed above is correct, then they do not come to the same thing, nor did Plato really think they did: he just fraudulently pasted them together as best he could without caring whether they really did harmonize. And surely this wrecks the whole line of argument which Plato has evidently been mounting from 152 onwards.

But what exactly is this line of argument? If one read no further than 160d-e it would be easy to have the impression that what Plato wished to do was to show how all these doctrines amounted to the same thing, so as to refute all three at once--for example, by showing that perception is <u>not</u> knowledge he would refute Protagoreanism and Heracleiteanism, which imply that it is. In fact, however, he does nothing of the sort. Immediately after having reduced Theaetetus' and Protagoras' doctrines to Heracleitus' he sets about pulling them apart again. He first considers Protagoras' doctrine that man is the measure of all things (161c-179a), no longer taking it as merely a theory about the truth of perception, but treating it in its full extension as covering all judgments. And though in the course of the refutation Protagoras is represented as the author of Theaetetus' claim that perception and knowledge are simply identical, and is even made to defend it (163a ff., 166a-c), and though he is permitted to make appeal to Heracleitean principles when they help in turning an objection (166b, cf. also 168b 4-5), the main lines of the discussion and the eventual refutation are clearly directed against Protagoras' views without any real concern about their connection with those of Theaetetus and Heracleitus. Likewise in the refutation of Heracleiteanism which follows (181c-183b), even though the pretense is kept up that Protagoras' views are being tested (cf. 183c 7), it is obvious that the flux doctrine is being directly assaulted on its own account. It is true that the flux doctrine is formally rejected only because it does not help Theaetetus in his claim that perception is knowledge (183e 6-11, 183c 1-4), but this failure is, and is presented as, only the special case of a perfectly general inadequacy in the flux theory itself. And, finally, the refutation of Theaetetus' original definition (184b-186e), when it is at long last attempted, treats the claim of perception to be knowledge altogether independently of any supporting hypothesis. It therefore appears that, whatever the line of argument apparently being prepared in 152-160, Plato's subsequent argument nowhere depends upon the plausibility or correctness of his amalgamation of the three doctrines he considers. It suggests itself that the amalgamation is not much more than a means of getting into a single dialogue three doctrines which he wished to consider and refute. If so, then the quality of the arguments produced in the amalgamation does not matter to his real aims, and one is free to think that he did not care whether or not they were either quite plausible or finally convincing.[23]

In any case there seem to be only two alternatives: either Plato did mean the argument of 157-160 seriously (and then one can only plead, with Campbell,[24] "the imperfect state of logic" in Plato's time), or else he only pretends to think that its conclusion follows from Heracleitean principles and that the argument given is valid. We seem forced to choose between these two interpretations. It should be emphasized, however, that whichever of these alternatives is opted for, the inadequacy of the argument does not affect anything said later on, since from 160e onwards the three theories are kept well apart from one another and examined on their own accounts.

My own inclination is to take the latter alternative, and not be concerned at the inadequacy of the argumentation in 158-159. It seems desirable not to attribute to Plato a bad argument, except when he is speaking half in jest, and the fact that one need not do so here in order to preserve intact the cogency of the refutations which follow, where the really serious argument occurs, weighs heavily with me. The other alternative is to give him a bad argument, seriously meant, on which nothing of importance hangs. It seems to me preferable to avoid doing this, but I do not see how to show this interpretation to be wrong.

The conclusion Plato aims at in the passage is in any case worth emphasizing. It is alleged that in a world of total flux, in which nothing has any duration, no momentary person in any way resembles any other, and in particular no person has a capacity for sensory affection similar to anyone else's. Hence no perceived quality produced in connection with one person-stage has any resemblance to that produced in connection with any other person-stage; and similarly for objects and their capacity to sensibly affect a percipient. Each person is thus confined within the moment when he exists and restricted to the registering of the sense-quality that comes to be then. Because of the total difference of each person and quality from every other, there is no ground for alleging that what comes to be in perception for any one is in any way false or misrepresents anything. No perception can be impugned either by reference to what any object is really in itself like, or by appeal to what normal persons experience in connection with it.

In formulating these conclusions (159e 7-160c 10) Plato abruptly reintroduces the uses of εἶναι which it has been the purpose of the reduction of Protagoreanism to Heracleiteanism to remove. Thus

160b 8-10: "so that whether one says a thing is or that it becomes, it must be said to be or become for someone or someone's or with reference to something." The fact that here at the end of the amalgamation of the two theories Plato is still allowing Protagoras to say that what one perceives not merely becomes but even is for someone, is further evidence that he has not seriously wished to replace the Protagorean doctrine about εἶναι with the Heracleitean theory of constant flux. We end, where we started (cf. 152c 5-6), with Protagoras asserting that "Therefore for me my perception is true--for it is always of what exists for me (ἡ ἐμὴ οὐσία) (160c 7-8)." On this ground, here (d 1-3) as earlier, rests the claim that perceiving is knowing.

CHAPTER II

THE REFUTATION OF PROTAGORAS

A. Introduction

In the exposition of the theory of perception and the discussions associated with it Protagoras' doctrine about truth has been grounded in the flux theory so far as its implications for Theaetetus' views on knowledge are concerned. His theory that what seems to be the case (τὸ φαινόμενον) to each person is the case for him has been taken (152c 1-3) to imply that what appears to each person in perception is true for him who perceives it, on the ground that in the case of perceptual properties seeming to be, e.g., red amounts to being perceived as red (152b 11). The flux theory was then brought in and developed as a means of defending his view in its application to perception and perceptual judgments. But of course Protagoras meant to be upholding a universal thesis about truth and wished to assert that whatever a person might make (sincerely) an assertion about he necessarily said something true about it--as true, that is, as anything anyone could ever assert. When, therefore, Socrates begins his criticism of the theories he has just managed to amalgamate in his account of perception, he undertakes to test and refute Protagoras' thesis understood in its largest sense. The effect of refuting it as a general doctrine about truth, and not merely one concerning the truth of reports of perception, will be to take one prop out from under Theaetetus' sense-perception theory of knowledge. For if Protagoras' doctrine about truth is false, in general, then the question whether it is true within the limited field of perception will have to be examined on its own merits; one must not derive any assurance that perception will turn out to be true from a preconceived faith in Protagoreanism.[1] The criticism of Protagoras, then, aims to eliminate his views as an independent source of support for Theaetetus' definition of knowledge.

Protagoras' theory consists of two parts. The first, with which the explicit refutations of the *Theaetetus* are concerned, is a doctrine about the truth of the opinions of individual men--opinions about the qualities they perceive things to have or otherwise judge to be present in them. The second part of the theory concerns the judgments in matters of morality and social convention and policy which whole cities make: these too, it turns out (cf. 167c 4-5, 172a), are all true, because true for any city so long as it continues to accept them. This part of the theory does not figure prominently in the discussions of the *Theaetetus*, which is concerned throughout with individual men and their knowledge or lack of it: but even political Protagoreanism is rejected (though not formally refuted), as I shall show, in an admitted digression (172c-177c) interrupting the refutation of Protagoras' views about individual men's judgments.

There is a certain difficulty, though Plato does not mention it, in understanding how Protagoras conceived these two parts of his philosophy to be related. He appears to have thought of the political component as an independent theory asserting the view, common among the sophists, that there is no truth in moral, political, and social matters beyond what is accepted and acted upon in different nations (cities): so that for any given man the truth in these matters is whatever the people around him unquestioningly accept and act upon. But it is hard to see how this can be prevented from coming into conflict with the fundamental doctrine about the truth of each man's opinions. For it certainly happens that sometimes some one in a social group rejects one or another of the opinions or practices which members of the group ordinarily accept naturally and unquestioningly. And then in order not to overrule his "man the measure" slogan, Protagoras will have to affirm the truth of the dissident's opinion. In doing so, however, he makes the general or canonical opinion on the matter of morality or social policy in question not true for the <u>city</u> where it is canonical, if that means true for all its citizens, but rather true for just those citizens who accept and follow the general opinion. And in that case the alleged independence of political Protagoreanism is an illusion: it really says no more than that each man's individual view on moral and social questions is correct. The fact that there is normally substantial agreement in any group on some such questions may permit use of the expression "true for this group," but this usage can always be cashed by saying for precisely whom the thing in question is true.

What Protagoras would reply to this is matter for conjecture. The general intention of his doctrines, however, both in their political and their specifically epistemological bearing, is clear. The thrust of his argument is to deny that there is any truth or existence or reality except what appears to a person to be true or existent or real: he attempts, as we have seen (152a-c), to make every assertion true by denying everything that might be taken as a criterion by which one person might test and pass judgment upon anyone else's statements. Ultimately the only criterion for the truth of an assertion is that it is made.[2]

Now, as I remarked above (pp. 14-15 of Chapter I), there are two possible ways in which Protagoras might intend these theses. He might mean to ban truth and existence as implying an objectivity which he refuses to tolerate, introducing in their stead new concepts "truth-for-x" and "existence-for-x." In that case assertions of the form "It is true that p" and "Such-and-such exists" would be ill-formed, requiring completion by the addition of a reference to some person or persons by whom (as we non-Protagoreans should say) these things are thought to be true or to whom they appear to exist. This is, in fact, the way in which his doctrine is usually interpreted: I have mentioned above some difficulties which arise if this is Protagoras' teaching, but it must be admitted that Plato nowhere quite firmly explains what he held, and that his habit of always adding "to me" or its equivalents to occurrences of the key terms "exists" and "true"[3] strongly suggests that as Plato understood it the Protagorean doctrine required the addition. Certainly by the time when Socrates begins his examination of Protagoras' views in 161c the presumption is on the side of this interpretation. One should, however, in reading the arguments which follow retain in mind the possibility that the title of Protagoras' book, Truth, means that in it he expounded a theory of truth, and did not merely abandon truth for something else. This theory would hold that the only criterion of something's being true is its being (sincerely) believed by someone to be true, or, in the case of perceptual judgments, whatever appears in perception to be the case to any one _is_ the case.

The doctrine then is that whatever any one thinks to be the case is the case, or, alternatively, is the case for him. It is against this general doctrine that Socrates argues beginning at 161b. Ultimately his refutation consists of two attempts (169d-171d, 177c-179b) to draw out the consequences of Protagoras' program sufficiently to reduce it to absurdity; but before doing this he makes several briefer criticisms (161c-165e), one of which contains the germ of his later refutation while the others are rather carping and inconclusive. One main purpose of these arguments seems to be to permit Protagoras to expand his theories in various directions so as to give Socrates entrée for his _reductio_ arguments. In his own defense Protagoras is made (166a-168c) to sketch a reply to the objections just brought against him, and at the same time to supplement his theory as it has appeared up until then by explicitly adopting what I have called political Protagoreanism and adding an account of wisdom which does not require abandonment of his principle that no one's opinions are false.

In order to give a complete summary of the contents of 161-179, mention must be made also of the digression, 172-177, in which political Protagoreanism is railed against, though not refuted.

B. The Preliminary Arguments (161c-165e)

Socrates begins by taking the bull directly by the horns. Protagoras has wished to rid us of every possible means of criticizing or refuting one another's judgments. The only sort of truth he trusts is the kind which every opinion must possess: for him, all one needs to do, and all one can do, in order to find out whether an opinion is true is to discover what the opinion is. Finding out the content of a thought is finding out something true. To know what one thinks about the world is to know what the world is like, insofar as the world has any character at all. Socrates pounces directly upon this and points out that it has the consequence (161d 3-e 3) that no man is better informed than any other, nor is there any possibility of discriminating between men with respect to wisdom and stupidity. This denial that any man is wiser than any other, in the sense of knowing more, is the kernel from which Plato will later develop his refutation of Protagoras. Here in its first appearance it is very closely connected with two different but related points, whose inclusion permits Protagoras to postpone his demise by answering the objections contained in them, as if they were the whole substance of the criticism Socrates has raised. Socrates acquiesces in this move, content to have started a hare which he can hunt down later, after Protagoras in his Defense (166d 1-167d 4) has promulgated an official teaching about wisdom.

The two points just mentioned as related to the denial that men differ in wisdom are these: (a) If what seems or appears to be the case to each man _is_ the case for him, presumably also every animal which has the power of perception must be granted at least this much share in truth, that what it perceives to be so _is_ so for it. And in that case, one wonders at Protagoras' preferring to begin his book by saying "_Man_ is the measure of all things." Why not "pig" or "baboon"? No doubt _more_ things seem or appear to men than do to pigs, since men can think whereas pigs cannot; but at any rate there is nothing that appears to a pig that is _false_, and to this extent a pig has as much right to be pronounced the measure of all things as any man does. No man is the measure of anything except for himself, and any pig is to precisely the same extent and in precisely the same way a measure--namely, a measure for itself. So the difference in _number_ of things that can seem to men and pigs is no ground for thinking men measures in preference to pigs.[4] So Protagoras' views have the bizarre result that Protagoras himself, and any other luminary, is no wiser than a pig!

(b) On the other hand, of course, any man is as wise as any god; being the only measure there can be for him, he knows everything there is to know for him, and nothing a god could know would give him the advantage. Here too there is absolute parity.

There is obviously justice as well as humor in these objections. But Protagoras is permitted to fend them off (162d 5-163a 1). He observes that in his writings he has explicitly refrained from expressing either belief or disbelief in gods, so that whether they are measures of anything is for him an open question. Hence, he implies, no comparison between men and gods is warranted on his views. As for pigs, Socrates has unfairly and frivolously played to the crowd by pretending to deduce the spectacular consequence that pigs are as wise as men: but he has given no valid proof either that this does follow or that it implies a fault in the theory if it does. (Presumably Protagoras has partly in mind that Socrates has assumed that the only, or the correct, account of wisdom will make a creature wiser than another just in case it believes fewer falsehoods: but, as Protagoras will try to argue below, the correct account of wisdom makes some men wiser than others without making any excel in the truth of their beliefs.)

Socrates, chastened by Protagoras' appeal to fairness and seriousness, takes a new tack, shifting his attention from Protagoras' general doctrine to the theory that perception is knowledge, which the general doctrine is intended to support (163a).[5] Against this theory he raises two objections, one of which Theaetetus himself immediately parries, while the other is declared merely contentious, as involving the theory in a merely verbal inconsistency, and left to Protagoras to rebut in his Defense. A third objection, together with a group of smaller cavils, is added in illustration of what a really contentious person could do in attacking the sense-perception theory of knowledge (165b-e); this one seems not to be taken seriously and does, indeed, rest on an obvious misunderstanding of the thesis being examined.

What is the purpose of this set of small criticisms? As previously noted, they are all directed against the equation of sense-perception with knowledge, and though Protagoras is represented as holding this theory (by implication), it is and remains Theaetetus' peculiar contribution. Cornford therefore thought that these criticisms are directed against a simple identification of perception and knowledge, and are designed to force Theaetetus to amend and extend his theory in a couple of ways in order to make it more satisfactory without at the same time giving up the spirit of the original definition:[6] the objections are therefore in his view instructional in intent. On the other hand Cornford also thought the third objection a *reductio ad absurdum* valid against Theaetetus' position, though not against Protagoras, presumably since Protagoras did not restrict knowledge to sense-perception.[7] And it is not clear what Cornford thinks Theaetetus should do to evade what he regards as this argument's consequence; though he appears to think that all three objections are only valid against Theaetetus' definition construed more narrowly than he intended it.

I am therefore not convinced that these arguments are posed here in order to show Theaetetus what a painfully literal interpretation of his thesis will commit him to and thereby point the way to a more adequate version of his basic doctrine. It is certainly not true that all three have this effect, and it may be doubted that the passage as a whole was intended to have it. For one thing neither in the refutation of Theaetetus' theory (184-186) nor before that (except here) is any attention paid to the fact that according to him not only is all perception knowledge but also all knowledge is perception: the refutation is able to show that no perception is knowledge, so it does not need to press Theaetetus on the other half of the thesis. Emphasizing this side of the definition would therefore tend to confuse the issue, particularly since later no difficulty is pressed upon it on this ground and no difficulty raised in these arguments is permanently remedied in what follows. For another thing, as I shall show, only the second objection can be interpreted as forcing an extension of the definition to include a kind of knowledge that is usually, at least, not thought of as perception. Thirdly, there seems to be no explanation why Plato should have begun the examination of Protagoras' dictum and then dropped Protagoras altogether for a few pages *merely* in order to apprise Theaetetus of some dangers lying in wait for his thesis if unamended or taken quite strictly.

It seems to me that the chief purposes of these three arguments are two: to provide amusement and to prepare in a smooth and natural way for the Defense which follows, where, as I have said, the grounds are finally laid for Protagoras' ultimate defeat. The second argument does indeed force an extension of the simple theory adopted by Theaetetus, and there is no reason not to recognize this as one aim of that argument; but, at the same time, there is no reason for forcing all three arguments into the same mold. The passage as a whole can have the purposes I have suggested, while the second has the additional aim of showing Theaetetus one of the errors of his ways.

That the third argument is a joke has already been remarked by Runciman;[8] and though the kind of dialectical display Socrates engages in in this and the other arguments may not seem funny to us there is ample proof that the ancients delighted in it.[9] These few pages of word-play provide just the right amount of needling to provoke Protagoras into a full-scale defense of his doctrines, and it is in this that I believe they find their dramatic justification and the key to their interpretation.

The arguments run, in outline, as follows:

(1) (163b 1-c 3) One may see letters of the alphabet (or hear words of another language spoken), yet for all that not know the letters or words in question: hence we can see something and yet not know it. To this Theaetetus himself gives essentially the correct reply: that which the man sees he knows, but you must just be careful how you describe this. What you might see as the letter Ψ he sees as colors and shapes of certain sorts in a certain arrangement, and the theory only implies that he's right about these things.[10] In effect, Theaetetus is pointing out the intentionality of perception, and he is right to say that appeal to it enables him to preserve his definition against Socrates' thrust.

(2) (163c 4-164b 12) Anyone who has learned (or seen) something and retains his memory of it knows that thing, when and so long as he does remember it. But a person who has looked at a thing and then closed his eyes must, by Theaetetus' definition, not know the thing at the time when, his eyes being closed, he is not perceiving it. Yet surely he may retain a memory of the object, and from our initial admission it follows that in that case he knows it. We have thus the formal contradiction that the same man knows and does not know the same thing at the same time. Therefore, if our initial agreement about remembering is to be retained--and it seems entirely unobjectionable--we shall have to abandon Theaetetus' definition.

Socrates at first (164c 1-2) feigns to think that this argument has by itself refuted the definition and starts as if to find a new one to try out. But at this point he stops short, accusing himself of paying more attention to words than to the truth; and as an illustration of how far one can go in producing frightening consequences by seeking a merely verbal self-contradiction he offers the third argument.

(3) (165b 2-d 1) The same contradiction--that the same man knows and does not know the same thing at the same time--can be even more neatly produced from Theaetetus' definition than the preceding argument has managed to do. For it is possible to look at a thing with one eye open and the other closed, and then the contradiction follows directly from the definition without auxiliary premiss: for if perceiving is knowing, and a man in the situation described both sees (with his open eye) and does not see (with his closed eye) the same thing, then he both knows and does not know it.

The error in this argument is easy to see. In defining knowledge as perception one means (since there are more than one sense, and more than one sense organ) to hold that to know something is to perceive it by some sense or other, some organ or other, etc. To show that someone both perceives and does not perceive (knows and does not know) something, and force a <u>true</u> contradiction, one must show that someone both has perception, in this sense, and its contradictory. Now the contradictory of "perceives by some sense, some organs, etc." is "perceives by <u>no</u> sense, <u>no</u> organ, etc." Socrates does not however adduce a case where a man both has and has not perception understood in this way. The negative predicate he applies to the man in the described circumstances is "does not perceive with his right eye" and this is not the same as "does not perceive by _any_ sense, by _any_ organ, etc." Hence there is no contradiction in saying that someone both sees (= perceives by some organ of sight or other) and does not see (= does not perceive with some _particular_ organ of sight) the same thing; and therefore Theaetetus has no need to accept the consequence that some one knows and doesn't know the same thing.[11] (Of course he can even grant Socrates the inference from "sees and does not see" to "knows and does not know"; then it will be necessary to accept the legitimacy of such odd locutions as "knows by some means of acquaintance" and "does not know by means of his right eye." But by accepting this he will be able to dispel the air of contradiction. And there is no reason why a determined theorist should refuse to swallow this, along with "know sharply," "know dimly," "from a distance," etc., which Socrates himself mentions [165d 2-6]. Odd they may be, but if the theory requires them diffidence on their account can hardly be permitted to wreck an otherwise attractive definition.)

The argument involving memory admits of essentially the same reply. For if Protagoras is willing, as it appears he is,[12] to treat remembering as a kind of perceiving--a kind of quasi-sensory awareness of some contemporary object--then what the argument shows is that one can at the same time be perceiving something by one sense or mode of perception and not by another. And this is no more objectionable than seeing and not seeing turned out to be; remarks can be made about perceiving (by memory) and not perceiving (by sight) parallel to those made about seeing (with one eye) and not seeing (with the other).

C. Protagoras' Defense (166a-168c)

These final two arguments are briefly replied to by Protagoras himself at the beginning of the Defense of his views which Socrates himself is forced, on account of Protagoras' absence, to provide. The reply is very briefly stated, altogether without elaboration (166a 2-c 2). But Socrates seems to contemplate three answers on Protagoras' behalf, each involving a different method of dispelling the menace in granting that the same man both knows and does not know the same thing. These methods are (1) to deny that the thing known is really one and the same thing as the thing not known; (2) to question directly the idea that knowing and not knowing are somehow incompatible; (3) to deny that it is the same person who knows and does not know the thing. The first reply involves admitting, as I have admitted above, memory as a kind of perception. But it turns upon treating the object perceived in memory as the contemporaneous memory-image, and not the object once perceived by sight (say). When a person knows and doesn't know a thing because he remembers but does not see it, the thing which he does not see (the house he saw a moment ago, say) is a different thing from the thing which he remembers (the memory-house). The second reply may be making the point mentioned above, that just to the extent that there is no contradiction in seeing (with one eye) and not seeing (with the other) there is no contradiction in knowing (with one organ or by one mode of awareness) and not knowing (by another): if one understands what is being said and why, there is no incompatibility between the two states.[13]

The third reply is difficult to construe: its appeal to the constant succession of "persons" in any single man evidently only shows that the "same" person can know and not know a thing when the times of knowing are different; but both of the arguments being replied to allege that a person at the same time knows and doesn't know a thing. The infinite succession of person-stages seems at first sight not capable of reducing the paradox contained in the suggestion that a man at the same time remembers (and so knows) and does not see (and so does not know) a certain house. But perhaps the intention is to suggest that because the man who sees the house and the man who later remembers it are different persons it is wrong to treat memory as a source of knowledge of the same thing as one can know by sense-perception. The man who perceives a thing and the man who remembers it are not the same man, and one cannot hold that the very thing which one man saw the other remembers seeing. Since each person is entirely momentary there is no alternative to taking the object of his memory as something contemporaneous and not past. If this is what Protagoras has in mind, then the third reply reinforces the first.

In any event Protagoras considers the arguments so far advanced against Theaetetus' definition to be insincere and urges Socrates to direct his attention to the actual theories that have been invoked and not to the words in which they are expressed: once he examines fully and fairly the theses that everything is in motion and that what appears to each man is so for him, he can proceed to investigate whether the identity of knowledge and perception can be maintained on grounds drawn from these theories (168b 2-c 2). Verbal paradoxes or anomolous modes of expression resulting from the definition cannot be allowed to stand in the way of the conclusion, if it is in fact defensible in the way suggested.

As for his own peculiar contribution, Protagoras seizes the opportunity to expand his theories by adding an account of wisdom (in answer to the stimulus of Socrates' original objection) and explicitly including sovereign states as among those who are measures of their own truth. As for wisdom, Protagoras' insistence that no one's beliefs are false does not prevent him, as Socrates implied it did, from making a distinction between wise men and others. The wise man is simply (166d 6-8) the man who can change another's perceptions and opinions, when they both seem and are bad or harmful to him who has them: neither before nor after the change does the man hold <u>false</u> beliefs; neither the man who is ill nor the man who is well has any beliefs or experiences that are false, though the one's are better than the other's (167a 1-3, d 1-3). Wise men excel only in their ability to replace a bad set of perceptions or beliefs, or a bad condition of body or soul, with a better. Thus doctors apply herbs to bring about health, and in doing so they cause the patient's perceptions to change, so that wine which appeared and was bitter to him becomes sweet for him: but they do not remove false beliefs for true ones. Likewise wisdom in public affairs does not consist in the ability to substitute true laws and regulations for false ones--whatever laws and regulations are accepted as right by a city are right so long as they are accepted. The wise man of public affairs has rather the ability to change for the better the opinions which a state holds in matters of right and wrong.

Now it is obvious that by admitting that one man can be wiser than another, even in the attenuated sense which he is willing to grant, Protagoras has practically resigned from the argument. For though he does claim (167d 1-4) to be consistently defending his thesis that no one holds any false beliefs, even while granting differences in wisdom, he really cannot do both things at once. For if a doctor is a wise man who can change peoples' perceptions for the better, he must hold certain opinions about what perceptions will result from the application of certain herbs, etc., and he must be right in thinking that certain procedures will produce a better state of the patient's body. What then must one say about a non-doctor, an unwise man who holds opinions on just the same matters as those with which the doctor's wisdom is concerned? Surely Protagoras must say that the unwise man holds false opinions, and in that event, as I say, Protagoras has in effect resigned his case. It appears on examination of the text that he has been able to overlook the fact that his doctrine about wisdom does contradict his thesis about truth only because he nowhere clearly faces the question whether his wise men hold any beliefs that are truer than those held by other people: when he reasserts his view that every one's beliefs are true (167d 1-4, cf. 166e 4-167a 4, b 1-4), he chiefly has in mind the healthy as opposed to the sick man or the city with good, as against the city with bad, regulations governing right conduct. By reaffirming that both well and ill men are right about what they experience, he thinks he retains his view that no one believes anything false; but, obviously, all he needs to do is compare his wise with an unwise man in order to see that he has in fact given it up.

Socrates himself will press just this objection upon Protagoras, and on the basis of it will pronounce (179a 10-b 5, c 1-2) his doctrine that every man is indiscriminately a measure of all things a certainly mistaken thesis. Why then does Protagoras here so rashly commit himself to a doctrine of wisdom fundamentally at variance with his basic contentions? One reason is the threat of an inconsistency in his personal behavior: as Socrates pointed out in his initial objection (161d 7-e 3), if Protagoras really believes that no one's opinions on any matter are false, then how does he explain his setting up as a teacher and a wise man whose instruction is worth large sums of money?[14] Earlier Protagoras left the query unanswered, but clearly enough not only his devotion to personal instruction but also his having written a book imply that he has something of which to apprise other people. There is, then, it would seem, something he knows that they do not know, and any of them who thinks he does know it is wrong. And in answer, as we have seen, he clutches at the straw of saying that he and any other wise person differ from ordinary people only in the ability to bring about in others better experiences and opinions than they earlier possessed.

D. The Refutation and Digression (169d-179c)

It may seem, in view of the considerations just advanced, that Socrates in the Defense has merely set up a straw man in order to have the pleasure of knocking him down. Perhaps the line taken by Protagoras in the Defense as a means of retaining some sort of difference in wisdom among men is not his most effective reply, or the one which he would himself have made.[15] As if in anticipation of this objection, Socrates opens his refutation of the Protagorean dictum by proposing to prove (169d 10-170a 1), by considering just the dictum itself and its consequences, that (171d 5-7) even Protagoras must admit that some men are wiser than others and that (171b 11-c 3) this difference involves a difference in knowledge and truth as well. Socrates' first argument against Protagoras therefore seeks to establish that there must be some false beliefs, even granted Protagoras' dictum; in his second argument (177c 6-179b 9) he will specify the class of judgments wherein falsity resides, and these will turn out to include opinions in the matters to which Protagoras' Defense appealed in its account of wisdom.

The total effect of the two arguments will therefore be to vindicate Socrates' attribution to Protagoras of the doctrine of wisdom explained above--with the important addition that this doctrine commits Protagoras to the view that some men excel others with respect to attainment of truth. It cannot be maintained that every judgment is true.

Socrates' first argument has, at least since Grote's spirited attack[16] upon Plato's account and refutation of Protagoras' dictum, been generally thought to be fallacious. What Socrates wishes to show is that if Protagoras accepts his dictum and applies it consistently he will have to admit the truth of those beliefs of others which contradict his own. Inasmuch as every ordinary person thinks that not every man is the measure of the truth, Protagoras must hold that his dictum is false, if he is to hold it to be true. For this reason the dictum is alleged to be self-refuting, and Protagoras, as much as any one else, is made to grant the falsity of some people's beliefs. Now Grote's opinion that this argument is fallacious is founded upon the presumption that Protagoras meant his man-the-measure dictum to require the addition after every use of the words "true," "exists," etc., of an index expression specifying some person for whom whatever it is is true or exists, etc. And it is true that if Protagoras has wished, as I put it above (Chapter I, pp. 14-15), to replace the concept of truth by a concept truth-for-x, Socrates' argument does fail. For Socrates' argument requires to have the following form:

Suppose (1): Man is the measure of all things, i. e., every opinion any man holds is true.

But (2) some men think it is not true that man is the measure of all things.

Ergo (3) it is not true that man is the measure of all things, i. e., not every opinion is true.

But if one follows Protagoras' stipulation about index expressions, this argument must be recast in the following non-obnoxious form.

Suppose (1a): Man is the measure of all things, i.e., every opinion any man holds is true-for-him.

But (2a) some men think it is not true-for-them that man is the measure of all things.

Ergo (3a) it is not true-for-them that man is the measure of all things, i.e., some opinions are false-for-them.

And there is evidently no inconsistency in Protagoras' accepting his dictum while maintaining its falsehood-for-others. So long as *he* does not hold it to be both true and false *for himself* he is in no logical bind whatsoever.

Of course even if this reply were entirely adequate one important result would still have been achieved: it would have been shown that if there is no truth but only truth-for-me, as Protagoras thinks, then his own doctrine has no special claim to validity. It is just a belief like any other and cannot claim any truth beyond that which accrues to it from being believed. It is not *true*, but merely true-for-Protagoras. Consequently the impression that he has revealed to us the *nature* of truth and reality is necessarily illusory. As a philosophical insight, therefore, the doctrine that each man is the measure of all things for himself fails to be the compelling and revolutionary thesis it seemed to be: whatever attitude any one takes towards it will be the correct attitude for him to take and all discussion of it turns out to be otiose.

This is no mean consequence to have derived. But the fact will still remain that Socrates' argument is fallacious, since it misrepresents the thesis he pretends to be attacking. The possibility remains, however, that it is not Socrates but modern commentators who misrepresent the thesis. For if Protagoras meant not to replace truth with truth-for-x, but to offer a thesis about what criteria are properly invoked in order to establish that something is true, the line taken above against Socrates' argument fails. For then Protagoras will merely be saying that all one has to do in order to determine whether something is true is to find out whether any one believes it. And if someone, for example, perceives a thing as red it will *be* red and not merely be-to-him red. This being so, Protagoras in accepting his man-the-measure dictum accepts that whatever any one believes is *true*; and if someone thinks the dictum false then Protagoras must accept that it *is* false, since someone so thinks. The consequence (3) does unavoidably follow, and it cannot be converted into (3a).

Which of the two interpretations of Protagoras' doctrine is correct? I have already remarked (above, p. 62 and n. 3) that in stating his thesis Plato regularly does introduce the expression "for him" in the way in which the first interpretation would require. On the other hand Protagoras certainly wants to say (cf. 161d 6-7, 167d 2) that everyone's beliefs are true and none false, in such a way that he can defend the claim that perception is knowledge, and it seems that in order to do this he should be telling us that what any one perceives is true (and not merely true-for-him). Perhaps it is not possible to be entirely sure what he meant; and perhaps his 'Αλήθεια was not more decisive one way or the other than Plato's testimony is. In any event, if Socrates' argument at 169-171 is to be anything but a mere _petitio principi_ then we must preserve at least the ambiguity in Protagoras' views. He must be not unfairly represented as recommending not the abandonment of the concept of truth but an adjustment in the criteria for its application.

By his first argument, then, Socrates has drawn from Protagoras' own words the admission that some men hold false opinions; and the Defense has not been unfair in granting for Protagoras that there are differences of wisdom among men. Socrates' argument has, indeed, shown that the difference in wisdom brings with it differences in attainment to truth which the Defense attempted to deny or conceal. But with the important exception of this one clarification Socrates' aim has been to vindicate his attribution of a doctrine of wisdom to Protagoras, and I think he has achieved his purpose.

What then are the matters upon which men may differ with respect to wisdom and attainment of truth? Socrates will argue in his second refutation (178a 5-179b 5) that wherever predictions or future-tense judgments of any kind are involved not every person is equally a measure of the truth. From this he will infer that doctors, farmers, and others who have a special competence--those whom the Defense characterized as wise--are more likely to be right in their opinions on matters within their own areas of competence than any chance person. He will show, therefore, by an independent argument that the line drawn in the Defense between the area where each man's opinions are true and that in which falsehood occurs, is correctly drawn. But before beginning this line of reasoning he states, by way of anticipation, the conclusion to which he will be tending. The argument just concluded has shown that there is an area where falsehood can occur, and it is natural to suggest (171d 9 ff.) that Protagoras' distinction between judgments about how to change someone's experience for the better points the way to the area of falsehood. According to this distinction, as Socrates now summarizes it, in most matters what seems so to each man is so, but not in such matters as what is healthful or noxious; and likewise for nations, error never occurs in such matters as what is right or disgraceful, or proper in religious observances, but only when it is a question of what is beneficial to the state. Here, then, he says, we may hope to rest our whole discussion, and reject Protagoras' dictum as a general account of truth.

At this point Socrates interrupts himself and begins a long digression (172c-177c) contrasting the philosopher and the man of public affairs. This passage has been the subject of the most extravagant flights of misinterpretation. Cornford discerned in it allusions to the _Republic_ which he roundly pronounced (_PTK_, p. 89) to be "intended to recall the whole argument of" that dialogue, with its "intelligible region of Forms, the true objects of knowledge." Plato's purpose according to Cornford in inserting the passage was to remind us of the correct answer to the _Theaetetus'_ question, What is knowledge?, without actually coming right out and arguing for it: knowledge is acquaintance with Forms.[17] Cornford holds that in the digression Plato is attacking a view which somehow goes beyond Protagoras and which he

vaguely and puzzlingly associates with Thrasymachus; in fact, however, this part of his view is demonstrably a tissue of misreadings of the passage which immediately precedes the digression proper.[18] But even if some ultra-Protagoreanism were the target of the discussion it would be totally impermissible to interpret whatever allusions to the cave allegory there may be in the passage as implying "the whole argument of the Republic" or the doctrine that knowledge in each and every case is acquaintance with Forms.

The true impact of the digression is really easy to see. Socrates has just summarized Protagoras' views, as now emended to allow some judgments of individuals and states to be possibly false. This emendation he will argue for below; what he will not examine then is the other contentions that no one can be in error about his immediate experience and that no state can be in error so far as the rightness of its established customs and practices is concerned. Immediate experience will however be examined in connection with the Heracleitean theory of perception (181-183); this leaves only the Protagorean doctrine about rightness and religious propriety untouched, and, as can easily be seen from careful reading of the text, it is to this and this alone that the digression addresses itself.

Those who have knocked about the law-courts from childhood up and have received their training there, says Socrates, are to be regarded as house-slaves by comparison with the true free-men educated in philosophy. Those who have learned about right and wrong in the law-courts have necessarily directed their attention to the means of successfully avoiding punishment; for them it matters not whether they must cheat or otherwise wrong their fellow-citizens so long as what they do is not judged wrong by the court and punished. The whole body of legal institutions and rules is regarded by them as something to be fended off, manipulated, or argued over in the pursuit of their own gain. The philosopher, by contrast, knows nothing of the particular customs and practices of any city, and does not concern himself with right and wrong as these are conceived in any particular place. In fact, Socrates says, the philosopher's body alone resides in his city while his mind is in the universe at large, spying into the things beneath the earth and doing geometry on the earth's expanses. Such a man asks not particular questions about whether this or that person has wronged the other--the sort of question the law-courts are always concerned with--but is rather interested in what right and wrong themselves are, or what in general human happiness consists in.[19]

The fundamental mistake which the man of affairs makes is in being concerned only with what is regarded as right and wrong in his state and not caring how much wrong he does so long as it is not so pronounced by his state's institutions: in this he shows himself unaware of the real penalties in store for real, and not merely legal, wrong. Happiness consists in being as like god as possible, but god is in no way unrighteous, so that to become like god is to become as righteous as possible. However adept, therefore, the man of practical affairs may be at obtaining his ends by attending to and manipulating the accepted standards of right in his state, he displays the greater folly of losing sight of the more important end of his own ultimate happiness. For the penalty for going really wrong, and not merely wrong in the eyes of the law, is not the physical pain inflicted by the law but the ineluctable condemnation to an after-life of association with evil. Freedom from κακά comes only to those who have led lives as much as possible like god's, and hence only to those who are really just and righteous.

Protagoras, then, is wrong to say that the only criterion of something's rightness or religious propriety is some state's opinions and enactments. There is an independent standard and those who ignore it do so at their own peril. The digression makes this point, naturally enough, by invoking some of the same images as those employed by the Republic for its somewhat similar purposes: the notion of the philosopher as occupied with general questions, the investigation of which takes him up out of the limits of everyday life, and the idea of an after-life whose delights are strictly apportioned according to merit. But the point being made is clearly only one about the objectivity of moral judgments, and even then it is not said or implied that this objectivity is grounded in transcendent Forms or that to know right from wrong is to be acquainted with a Form of rightness.

Thus there is neither any general appeal to Forms as the only objects of knowledge on whatever subject, nor even an appeal to Forms as what makes possible objectively valid moral judgments. The passage merely, in a quite general way, affirms against Protagoras and others who share his political views that there are standards of right and wrong other than those which particular states happen to enshrine in their legal and other institutions. Nothing more than this can be found in the passage; it certainly requires wrenching it badly out of context to find in it any hints about what objects knowledge in general must be directed toward.

After the digression Socrates returns to the discussion just broached before the digression itself began. It seemed likely, Socrates was saying, that Protagoras, having been driven to grant that some beliefs of some people are false, would be willing to accept the distinction between wisdom and ignorance which Socrates had sketched in the Defense, and would grant that with respect to what is better or worse both men and states differ in degree of attainment to truth. Now (178a 5-179b 5) Socrates undertakes to show that in fact there are differences in truth among judgments of this latter sort, which anyone must recognize. For these judgments all have reference to what will turn out to be the case in the future, and not all judgments about the future can be true.

Socrates attempts to prove this by showing that when a layman and a doctor disagree over whether a certain course of action will result in the layman's getting a fever one of them (usually the doctor) is right and the other wrong. Either he does acquire the predicted body-temperature or he does not, and the outcome shows one judgment to have been true and the other false. Protagoras might reply that there is no such thing as the predicted body-temperature just occurring or not, but one must say for <u>whom</u> it exists. Why should not both layman and doctor be right--the fever coming to exist for the one and failing to occur for the other? In that case both predictions could be admitted to be true. The answer to this is that it doesn't matter who is the criterion of the existence or not of the fever when the time comes: so long as what is judged then is judged by reference to <u>some</u> standard the result will depend upon the application of the standard then, and not upon what some one predicts the test will show. Once the prediction is made there is nothing to do but wait and see how the facts turn out; hence when a person judges how he himself will feel, and even though he is the sole judge of how he feels when he's feeling that way, he makes a judgment that cannot be said to be true just because he makes it. If it is true it will be so because of the way he later does in fact feel, and there is no guarantee that this will accord with his prediction. Hence the logic of the situation is not changed by assuming, as Socrates does, that in the dispute between the doctor and the layman the fever either comes or doesn't, without saying for whom it exists or does not exist. This point is made explicit immediately afterwards (178d 4-6), where Socrates clinches his argument by remarking that when it is a question of something's turning out to be in tune a gymnastic trainer will not be better than a musician at judging what will turn out <u>even to the trainer</u> himself to be in tune. Future-tense judgments cannot be declared true on principle, however true on principle all present-tense judgments are, because they necessarily find their validation in some present-tense judgment at a later time and not in anything contemporaneous with themselves or private to the man who makes them at the time when he makes them.

We have, then, found a class of judgments where error may occur, and since included among them are the judgments by reference to which Protagoras was represented as introducing differences among men with respect to wisdom, it has turned out that in recognizing the existence of wisdom Protagoras has in fact refuted his own theory; but we have also seen that he has no alternative but to accept some men as wiser than others in the sense of having the truth in a higher degree, and that wisdom primarily finds its expression in the ability to make true predictions. It has therefore emerged that no man of sense can give credence to Protagoras' theory of truth, as a general proposition; if any part of it--e.g., the truth of all judgments of perception--is to be retained it will have to be argued independently of the thesis that each man is the measure of all things. Socrates therefore concludes the refutation of Protagoras (179c) by remarking that what remains is to see whether each man is always right about τὸ παρὸν ἑαυτῷ πάθος since it is here that perception's claim to be knowledge must either succeed or fail. He therefore turns in the next section to the Heracleitean theory of perception constructed above, and tests whether its foundation-- τὸ πᾶν κίνησις ἦν -- is sound, and whether it can support Theaetetus' definition of knowledge.

CHAPTER III

THE REFUTATION OF HERACLEITUS

A. The Argument Against Flux in the Theaetetus (181-183)

Plato has now shown that insofar as Theaetetus' definition of knowledge as perception coincides with and draws support from the Protagorean doctrine of man the measure, it is not acceptable. As soon as Protagoreanism is extended beyond the judgments which each man makes about the sense-contents actually present to his consciousness at the time of speaking (179c 1-4), and made to apply to judgments about future events, what is advantageous, etc., it is quite certainly a false doctrine. Protagoreanism, as a distinctive theory, must be rejected. If any part of it is to be retained it will be its application to judgments of immediate sense-perception (cf. 171e 1-3). But, now that as a general doctrine Protagoreanism has been refuted, immediate sense perception must be examined on its own ground to see whether it is always true and whether its judgments are always known to be true. If it turns out that they are known, then to this extent Protagoreanism will have been vindicated; but one cannot any longer reason in the other direction and use Protagoreanism to vindicate sense-perception's claim to be knowledge.

For this reason Socrates announces (179d 1-5) that it is now time to approach closer to τὴν φερομένην ταύτην οὐσίαν and examine whether the Heracleitean metaphysics of the κομψότεροι is sound or unsound. The Heracleitean doctrine of reality was ostensibly introduced, as we have seen, as a means of supporting Theaetetus' contention that about what appears to him a man has knowledge: for if everything is in constant flux there are at most momentary appearances, about which no one but the person to whom the appearance appears can logically be in a position to judge. Since, according to this doctrine (152d 8, 157b 1), it is never correct to use the word "is" or "exists" of anything, it is not possible to get to know how anything is in itself (152d 2-3)--about which each man would not be the only judge--and appearances must be the most any one can get to know. It therefore seems to follow from the Heracleitean doctrine that knowledge must be restricted to immediate perception (cf. 151e 1-2).

What Plato does, therefore, beginning at 181b 8, is to inquire whether knowledge can be shown to be identical with perception by appeal to the doctrine that everything is in constant flux. There are two ways in which he might argue that it cannot: he might show that the consequences deduced from the doctrine of flux in support of the equation of sense perception and knowledge are incorrectly deduced; or he might argue that Heracleiteanism is a false doctrine, so that, whatever its consequences, the equation cannot be supported by appeal to them. In fact I believe that Plato shows both of these things: Heracleiteanism is not only false but, even if true, it would not imply that a man _knows_ what appears to him in immediate sense perception. The result of showing this will be to disengage Theaetetus' equation of perception with knowledge from the Heracleitean metaphysics which was brought to its support; at that point, when neither Protagoreanism nor

Heracleiteanism has been found to "ring true" (179d 3-4), Theaetetus has no alternative but to permit a frontal assault on his thesis. This assault is made at 184b-186e, where it is finally proved that in itself perception does not amount to knowledge.

But for the moment we are still concerned with the Heracleiteans and with sense perception as conceived by them. Plato begins his examination by pointing out that Heracleiteanism logically involves not only that everything is in motion but even that everything is in motion in every respect: if all stability of every sort is to be denied to reality then of course everything must be moving with every sort of motion (181e 9 f.). That consistent Heracleiteanism involves the absolute banishment of "is," "exists," "this," "that," and any other word that would introduce stability into the world, has already been shown (157a-b): only verbs of becoming and change, and whatever is consistent with these, are permissible for talking about what is in constant flux. Plato now goes one step further and shows that in order to avoid introducing stability it is necessary to insist upon each thing's becoming and changing constantly with every kind of change and becoming. In accordance with the extreme economy with which the argument of the whole dialogue is constructed, he actually only mentions two sorts of change, local motion and change of quality (181d 5-6). Though Plato elsewhere[1] divides change into these two kinds, his argument does not depend on the exhaustiveness of the division. In order to explain his contention that in a Heracleitean world change of everything in every respect must be the universal rule the division of motion into two kinds is sufficient. For granted that there are just two kinds of motion, a thing must be in motion of both sorts in order for it to be true that it is in motion and not also at rest (181e 5-7). In any case, it is clear that Plato has a firm grasp of the general principle that motion of every sort (however many sorts there may be) is implied by the Heracleitean doctrine: for he explicitly takes his distinction of motion into two kinds to show that in a Heracleitean world everything must be moving with <u>every</u> sort of motion (πᾶσαν κίνησιν, 182a 1), and not merely with these two (if there are others).

Relying on these conclusions, Plato then has no difficulty in showing that Heracleiteanism, so interpreted, cannot be used to support the doctrine that knowledge and sense perception are identical. He first (182a 2-b 7) recalls the theory of sense-perception of the κομψότεροι (156c 6-c 7), and distinguishes the three processes of becoming that occur in the perceptual situation: the sense-quality (e. g., whiteness or warmth) comes to be between sensing subject and perceived object; the subject becomes a perceiver (αἰσθητικόν), i. e., comes to have, and not to <u>be</u>, a sense perception; the object becomes of a certain quality (e. g., white or hot) but does not come to <u>be</u> that quality. Both sense-qualities and sense-perceptions come to be between subject and object, and are the offspring of their intercommunion (182b 4-7). What Plato now shows is that if, as the Heracleiteans say, <u>everything</u> is in constant flux in every respect, then <u>a fortiori</u> no sense-quality and no sense-perception "remains in itself" (182e 1). The whiteness that comes between subject and object must itself be constantly changing and is therefore no more whiteness than any other color (182d 2-5). Similarly, the correlated seeing that comes to be is no more seeing than any other perception, and the same is true of the other sorts of sense perception as well (e 3-5).[2] The result is that nothing retains its form; so that in defining knowledge as perception κατὰ τὴν τοῦ πάντα κινεῖσθαι μέθοδον we have unwittingly not said anything more relevant to knowledge than to its absence (e 10-11).[3] We have, in fact, not said anything definite and so have made no progress toward defining knowledge. In order to define knowledge as perception, therefore, we have no alternative but to abandon Heracleiteanism.

Now so far, I think, there is no ground on which anyone could disagree with my analysis. It is accepted on all hands that Plato shows in this passage that Heracleitean metaphysics is a faulty basis on which to erect a sense-perception theory of knowledge; it is in fact incompatible with that theory. The disagreement begins when it is asked what, if anything, more than this Plato shows. As I said above, it is my view that in the course of his demonstration that the Heracleitean theory cannot be used to support Theaetetus' definition, Plato shows that the Heracleitean theory is itself an internally faulty metaphysics: it is not only a faulty basis on which to argue the identity of sense-perception and knowledge, but also no good for doing *anything*.

Now even here there would be pretty general agreement; but there is a sharp division over the sense of this further claim. No one doubts that the consequence stated above is a serious attack on the theory itself in whatever connection one intends to use it. Indeed,

Plato not only proves that Heracleiteanism implies the abrogation of the law of non-contradiction (since if everything is in constant flux in every respect no description applies to a thing in preference to any other): he goes further and says (183a 9-b 5) that no use of language whatsoever is permitted if everything is in total flux. He does, then, quite clearly reject at once the flux metaphysics and any appeal to it as a means of supporting Theaetetus' definition.

Some, however, think that the attack on the flux doctrine is aimed at, and valid against, only an unrestricted Heracleiteanism, one which emphasizes the "everything" in "everything is in motion." Plato is represented by these interpreters as arguing the impossibility of a metaphysics which recognizes only things which are in perpetual flux and does not also admit that there are things of which the flux doctrine is an incorrect account. Provided that one goes along with the Heracleiteans only so far as phenomena are concerned, holding that they are subject to eternal flux in every respect but making explicit exemption in favor of Platonic Forms, Plato's argument against the flux doctrine will pose no obstacle and is not intended to do so. Plato himself, in this view, refutes unrestricted Heracleiteanism as a means of recommending restricted Heracleiteanism of just this sort.

Not everyone, however, accepts this interpretation of Plato's argument. Recently Richard Robinson and G. E. L. Owen have argued[4] that Plato shows, and intends to show, that the Heracleitean doctrine about anything, whether phenomenon or Form, is false. He does not merely refute the flux doctrine in the weak sense supposed by the interpretation just mentioned--by proving the truth of its logical contradictory, i.e., by showing that not everything is in constant flux--but proves the stronger contention that nothing is subject to flux of the sort the theory must have in mind. Hence, on this second interpretation, Plato shows that neither of Forms nor of phenomena is a Heracleitean account correct; and from this it must follow that, for Plato at this time, whatever important differences there may be between Forms and sensible things, neither class of entities is changing constantly in every respect.

In interpreting the refutation of Heracleiteanism in 181-183, as these brief remarks indicate, matters of the very first importance for the understanding of Plato's philosophy are at stake. As I shall try to show, there is really no reasonable ground for doubt that some version of the stronger interpretation is correct. The weaker has really, when brought into close connection with the actual text of the passage, nothing to recommend it. The only reason for accepting it is that it has been accepted in the past,[5] and seems the only alternative to far-reaching revisions in the canonical understanding of Plato's philosophical opinions. It is time, however, to realize that it is the argument which must be interpreted, and if the argument cannot be so interpreted as to fit with canonized views, this fact had better be candidly admitted. It is no good to be sure that Plato cannot have argued in a certain way unless you can show that some alternative interpretation fits his actual text. As I shall show, the versions of the weak interpretation so far produced certainly do not fit what Plato actually says; nor do I think any adequate version ever will be produced.

Before turning to the analysis of the refutation itself, however, it is worth pointing out one obstacle confronting the weaker interpretation which is posed by the argument of the pages following the refutation. In this later passage Plato is arguing directly that perception does not amount to knowledge. Now if the traditional interpretation of the refutation of Heracleiteanism is correct, Plato nowhere before the beginning of the final argument rejects the Heracleitean account of phenomena in general or the theory of perception of the κομψότεροι in particular. In fact, in the refutation of the flux doctrine Plato commits himself to the truth of the Heracleitean account of phenomena, and although this does not show that he accepted the theory of perception as well, Cornford, who accepts the traditional view, thinks[6] that he did accept it and even that it is assumed in the final argument disproving the identity of perception and knowledge. Thus those who accept the weaker interpretation of the refutation must interpret what follows in such a way that, even if the <u>full</u> theory of perception of the κομψότεροι is not being accepted, at any rate no assumptions are made about perception and its objects which are incompatible with a Heracleitean account of the phenomenal world. In fact, however, the rejection of the sense-perception theory of knowledge relies upon an argument which flagrantly contradicts the Heracleitean theory.

An essential step in the argument there is the attribution of οὐσία to sense qualities (185a 8-9: we are able to think about color and sound that they both <u>exist</u>). Now though it is true that Plato argues here that it is not by sense-perception that we come to know that these things exist, this fact does not in the least detract from the significance of his allowing that of a sense-quality one can use ἔστι.[7] For the essence of Heracleiteanism, as Plato has expounded and developed it in this dialogue, is the refusal to use any stabilizing word (cf. 157b 5, οὔτε ἄλλο οὐδὲν ὄνομα ὅτι ἂν ἱστῇ) of anything; and the primary culprit in this regard (152d 8, 157b 1) is εἶναι. Therefore if Plato only rejects Heracleiteanism if it implies that *nothing* (including the Forms) is exempt from flux, but not if it asserts merely that no phenomenon has any stability, he must ban εἶναι altogether from any application to phenomena. But in 185a he *does* apply εἶναι to αἰσθητά, and does so not as any merely careless "talking with the vulgar," but with full theoretical awareness of the consequences, since on this attribution he bases his most complete refutation of the identification of knowledge and perception. The inescapable conclusion is that in the final argument he retains nothing of the Heracleitean thesis: not its theory of phenomena, and not its theory of perception. If this is so one will expect to find lying behind the proof that Heracleiteanism is a faulty basis on which to argue the identity of knowledge and perception the further awareness that in itself, and regardless of how far one allows it to extend, Heracleiteanism is a false doctrine. What *cannot* lie behind that proof is the acceptance of Heracleiteanism as a satisfactory basis for a theory of phenomena and perception.

The argument of 182-183 is extremely condensed, but I think that close attention to the detail of what is said will show pretty conclusively that Heracleiteanism is being rejected altogether, and not retained as the correct account of sensible phenomena. The first point to insist upon is that the argument nowhere says or implies that phenomena, if subject to constant flux in every respect, are unsuitable objects of knowledge, on the ground that objects of knowledge must be stable. What it says, is that if everything is in flux nothing can even be _true_, or _perceived_, or (one may add, though Plato does not) _believed_ (183a 4-6). What's wrong, that is to say, with the flux theory is that it makes it impossible for anything to be, or even to become (183a 6-7), X rather than not-X, and thus by denying the law of non-contradiction the flux doctrine renders discourse, and not merely knowledge, impossible.

Plato evidently means this to be a _reductio ad absurdum_ of Heracleitean metaphysics. Now, the absurd consequence Plato deduces from the doctrine of flux is that nothing can be _or become_ X rather than not-X (183a 4-7) (and, as a result, that no use of language is permitted, since words have significance only where the law of non-contradiction holds). Whatever alteration Plato himself would make in the Heracleitean doctrine must therefore have the consequence that phenomena can be said at least to become so rather than not so; the law of contradiction must apply to phenomenal becoming as elsewhere, even if it remains illegitimate to say anything more stabilizing than "becomes so and so" of phenomena. Phenomena must, in short, be subjects of discourse.[8]

Now even this much is enough to refute what appears to be Cornford's version of the weak interpretation of the argument.

Cornford thinks that Plato's purpose is "to point out that, if the objects of perception (to which [the Heracleitean doctrine] does, in his opinion, apply) are taken to be 'all things,' there can be no such thing as knowledge at all, since no statement we make about these perpetually changing things can remain true for two moments together" (p. 97). And he adds (p. 99) that "the conclusion Plato means us to draw is this: [we must] . . . recognize some class of knowable entities exempt from the flux and so capable of standing as the fixed meanings of words." Now if, as Cornford's further silence seems to allow us to infer, this means that phenomena, since they <u>are</u> "perpetually changing things" cannot have words applied to them, but this is possible only for the objects of knowledge, the Forms, then Cornford's interpretation fails. For, as we have seen, Plato implies that the correct metaphysics must make provision for truths about phenomena. Reference to the theory of Forms here can only be justified to the extent that it permits Plato to maintain, what he shows the Heracleiteans cannot, that the law of contradiction holds for phenomena (at <u>least</u> in the attenuated form that only one of "becomes X" and "becomes not-X" can be true of a thing at a given time).[9]

Cherniss' interpretation[10] makes good this deficiency in Cornford's reading of the passage. He argues that the "ontological proof" of the existence of Forms, of which our passage is the main representative, shows that the constant change of phenomena, which Plato took for an evident datum, can only be explained if there are entities exempt from this change. He therefore agrees with Cornford and Aristotle that

Plato always held a Heracleitean view of sensible phenomena and exempted only the Forms (and human souls?) from constant flux; but unlike Cornford he definitely takes Plato to be arguing that Forms are necessary in order to make phenomenal flux intelligible. The argument, as Cherniss reads it, "examines the hypothesis that reality consists in nothing but . . . process, that *all* things are constantly changing, and shows that . . . [it] would not only leave no room for fixed states and determinate processes but must also involve the denial of the law of contradiction. In short the very processes into which all phenomenal existence is resolved by this hypothesis imply the existence of immutable, determinate entities."[11] The result is, according to Cherniss, that Plato recognized here that a condition of saying that all phenomena are in flux in every respect at every moment is that one be able to say of any particular γένεσις *what* γένεσις it is: thus since "the sensible phenomenon is not a definite object (ἐκεῖνο) but always a degree of approximation (τοιοῦτον οἷον ἐκεῖνο) the transient phenomena themselves imply absolute and immutable entities which are the standards and causes of these approximations."[12]

Now Cherniss' version of the argument is by no means so easily understood as his forthright and vigorous exposition of it might make an inattentive reader think. But apparently the idea is this. Flux of *everything* in every respect is a self-refuting notion, since it makes it impossible for any statement--even a statement no more definite than one employing γίγνεσθαι and avoiding εἶναι--to be true. There must, therefore, be some immutable things, namely unchanging Forms or standards by reference to which we are able to distinguish one γένεσις from another; the Forms make this discrimination possible by, as it were, fixing for each γένεσις the <u>direction</u> of its progress (thus one phenomenon is an "approximation" to one Form, another to another). And this function of the Forms is supposed to be carried out on a phenomenal world which, as the Heracleiteans maintained, is constantly <u>changing</u> its characteristics at every moment in every place. The effect of the addition of Forms is to enable us to say " γίγνεται X" rather than not-X: it reinstates the law of contradiction for phenomena without also forcing the reimportation of εἶναι into statements about them.

There are two difficulties in understanding and assessing this view. (1) How in general is the fact that Forms are "fixed standards" to which phenomena are "approximations" to be understood as an answer to the problem of change discussed in the <u>Theaetetus</u>? How, in other words, does Cherniss think this theory meets the objection Plato raises in the <u>Theaetetus</u> against the idea of constant succession altogether without duration of anything? And (2), more narrowly, where exactly in the text of Plato's argument is this theory being argued for as the solution to the problem posed by Plato?

The theory of flux examined in the <u>Theaetetus</u> asserts the constant <u>succession</u> of qualities, and Plato's refutation quite evidently (cf. ἀεὶ λέγοντος [ἡ λευκότης] ὑπεξέρχεται ἅτε δὴ ῥέον, 182d 7) turns on the fact that on such an hypothesis nothing <u>retains</u> any character for any time. He appears to be saying that nothing can really become green if it has no sooner done so than it passes on to another color, at the same time passing on to different places and properties of every other sort as well. Under these circumstances, since it never remains green for any duration however short, it cannot any more rightly be said at any moment to become green than red. Now Cherniss' interpretation, in order to meet this criticism, must be understood in the following way: by introducing the Forms as fixed standards Plato is enabled, as he has argued the flux theorists are not, to say what a thing becomes at a given moment. Because he has the Forms to rely on he can say that a thing becomes green (and not red) at some moment. But according to Cherniss Plato accepts the "fluxers'" view that nothing remains green or any other color for any period. And it seems quite certain that Plato was saying against them that this fact deprived them of the capacity to say that anything becomes green at a given moment. How then does he manage to accept the view which according to him made their theory incoherent, while claiming that under his aegis that view is entirely harmless? Evidently Cherniss must hold that since Plato has the Forms to appeal to as entities exempt from flux, the argument against constant succession is evaded. I do not myself see how this result is to be effected, and Cherniss has certainly not explained his view sufficiently to suggest how he would attempt to argue the point.

In fact, I think he may not have seen clearly that what Plato is discussing under the name of the flux theory is a doctrine of constant succession, and that Plato's argument against the Heracleiteans turns on their attempting to say what something becomes without allowing that anything possesses any character for any time. Cherniss' talk of phenomena as "approximations" to Forms suggests a rather different view of the flux theory and Plato's objection to it.[13] To say that on Plato's view phenomena are approximations to Forms seems to amount to saying that they are always only in process of becoming F without every being F. Forms fix, as I put it above, the direction of any phenomenon's progress at any moment: now it is on its way to being green, now to red, etc., without cease. What the flux theorists lack, on this view, is any means of saying at any given moment that a thing is <u>on its way to</u> green (rather than red or any other color); since they deny that there are any fixed standards they cannot denominate any one such momentary progress a progress of <u>this</u> sort rather than of <u>that</u>. Plato can say what a thing is in process of becoming at any moment, because he has his Forms to appeal to as standards of approximation; but without them neither he nor the flux theorists could describe anything.

The trouble with this view (which, as I say, seems to be the one Cherniss really holds) is that it seems not to conceive at all rightly the criticism Plato makes of the flux theory. For there is, on this interpretation, nothing said about constant succession at all; attention is directed instead to a kind of γένεσις which affects a thing wholly at one moment. The Heracleiteans are represented as wishing to hold, with Plato, that a chair or a table at a given moment is in process of becoming green (or that at that moment it is striving to be such as the Form of Green is, or that it is an approximation to Green), but because they deny that anything is at rest, and therefore reject the theory of Forms as standards, they are debarred from saying ever that a thing is becoming F, rather than not-F. But as I have already said above, I do not find anything in the exposition and criticism of the theory of flux to suggest that it is a theory holding that phenomena are on their way toward green or red or whatever, without ever being it; it is, as Plato's refutation obviously takes it, a theory about the succession of green, red, and the rest. What the theory wishes to say is that things *become green*, then red, and so on; not that they are *in process of becoming green*, then in process of becoming red, and so forth. Hence Cherniss' point about Forms as providing fixed directions of change seems to be relevant to a different theory about change from the one Plato is discussing.

It seems to me, then, that the doctrine of Forms as "fixed standards" fits very ill as an answer to the objection Plato raises against the theory of flux in the *Theaetetus*. But even if it were a satisfactory general point for Plato to have made at this juncture in the argument, it would still be incumbent on Cherniss to show how Plato's actual words can be interpreted as arguing for this view. It is in the other exposition of his interpretation, in his article, "The Philosophical Economy of the Theory of Ideas,"[14] that he shows most clearly how he thinks the text runs. He rightly finds the nub of the argument in the distinction between local and qualitative change and the consequence Plato forces on the Heracleiteans for asserting constant change of everything in both respects. The argument, as he reads it, "attempts to show that the constant flux of phenomena involves alteration as well as local motion but that alteration requires the permanent subsistence of immutable abstract qualities."[15] A little further on these "abstract qualities" become "immutable and immaterial ideas,"[16] so that it is clear that Cherniss takes the argument of 182d 1-7 as showing, *not* that something in the world of becoming must be at rest in some respect, *but* that something "immaterial" and at rest is required in order to defend the assertion that nothing in the world of phenomenal becoming is at rest in any respect. Cherniss therefore represents Plato as arguing in 182d 1-7 that the *abstract quality* whiteness must not be in flux since if *it* were in flux one could not say of any change that it was a whitening or of any "thing" that it was on the way to white, rather than to any other color.

But *is* this what 182d 1-7 says? The first thing to notice is that in this context λευκότης (d 3) is not the name of an *abstract* quality. The whiteness, warmth, etc., which Plato here says to be constantly changing, according to the Heracleiteans' hypothesis, are, as 182a 3-8 reminds us, the offspring of agent and patient in the perceptual situation. They are (cf. 156a 3-c 3) fleeting *instances* of whiteness, warmth, etc. which come-to-be in between agent and patient; they are phenomenal and *sensible* qualities, and not *abstract* at all. They are *what* one sees and not what what one sees is an instance of. They correspond to momentary sense-data and not to the qualities which the sense-data exhibit. It is the constant flux of these color-instances which, as Plato argues in 182d 1-7, the Heracleiteans must in consistency maintain.

And his point is not that the Heracleiteans refute themselves because they maintain that abstract qualities like whiteness keep changing to other qualities, but because on their view no instance of whiteness remains an instance of whiteness for any time. Plato nowhere in his argument mentions abstract qualities and the necessity that they should be fixed; what he does mention are concrete αἰσθητά and the necessity that they should retain their form for some period of time. Hence his conclusion cannot be that for a change to be definitely a change to white there must be a fixed abstract Form White, but must rather be that no change can be a change to white if there succeeds a change to yellow or green without the whiteness having lasted for any period of time however brief.

There is not, then, the slightest reason for accepting Cherniss' view that Plato rejects Heracleiteanism because it makes no provision for Forms as fixed standards. It is patently fixity in the world of phenomena that he argues for, and the argument cannot be interpreted as arguing for fixity elsewhere. The mere introduction of a Form of whiteness, in fact, would be no sort of reply to the objection Plato makes to the flux theory: if phenomena are in flux, no matter how immutable the standard you are provided with, the color you see will not stand still long enough to be classified as an instance falling under one standard rather than another. It is exactly as Plato himself says (182d 3-5): "Since there is a flux of this itself, the whiteness [the αἰσθητόν, cf. 156b 7-c 3, that comes between agent and patient], and a change to another color, in order that it not be caught resting in this respect, can one ever call it any color and be speaking correctly?" There must be rest in the world of becoming in order for it to be talked about at all.

The upshot is that reference to the Forms, even in Cherniss' more sophisticated version of the traditional view, is out of place. The essential thing being argued for, to repeat, is that there must be stability _in_ the world of becoming in order for it, or any part of it, to be a subject of discourse. However changing and shifting it may be it cannot be at _every_ point changing and shifting in _every_ respect. Therefore, even if Plato thought that there had to be Forms and that they were necessarily exempt from flux, he is certainly not arguing that point here. It is constant flux of _anything_ in every respect that he shows to be a self-refuting notion.[18]

When, therefore, Plato sums up his objection against Heracleiteanism in 183a 2-7 we are justified in understanding him to mean not only that not everything is in constant flux but that nothing is. He says, "But, as it seems, if everything is in motion every reply, whatever any one might answer a question about, turns out to be equally correct--both that it is so and that it is not so, or rather, in order not to bring these people to a standstill by our mode of speaking, that it _becomes_ so." This does not mean, as it would mean if Cherniss' reading of the argument were correct, that once _some_ things were allowed to be at rest the law of contradiction would be reinstated for _everything_, but rather that the law of contradiction cannot apply to a thing so long as _it_ is in motion in every respect.

That this is so is indicated not only by the previous argument but also by a passage of Aristotle (*Met.* Γ. 5. 1010a 1-1010b 1) which discusses Heracleiteanism in terms parallel at many points to this discussion in the *Theaetetus*.[19] Aristotle, like Plato, connects Heracleiteanism followed to its logical extreme with the denial of the law of contradiction.[20] In his statement of the ultimate consequence of Heracleiteanism there is no emphasis on the fact that one cannot say anything definite *only* if *everything* is in flux: as he puts it, "of that which is changing nothing is truly asserted, or at any rate it is not possible to make a true assertion about what is everywhere in every respect changing." (1010a 8-9). The consequence of Heracleiteanism, then, as Aristotle sees it, is essentially the same as what in my view Plato also deduced from it: that of *anything* that is in constant flux nothing true can be said. It is true as Cherniss says,[21] that one of the refutations Aristotle goes on (1010a 32-35) to propose for the Heracleiteans involves proving that there is *something* ἀκίνητος. But this cannot be parallel to what Cherniss thinks Plato proves in the *Theaetetus* passage, since to prove that there are unmoved movers of the spheres (which is what Aristotle's ἀκίνητος φύσις must refer to) does not reinstate the law of contradiction for phenomena as Plato's invocation of the Forms in Cherniss' view is supposed to do. Aristotle's appeal to the ἀκίνητος φύσις is on a level with his remark (1010a 25-32) that since only the tiny part of the sensible cosmos nearest to us is constantly coming into being and passing away it would be fairer to acquit our part because of the other than to condemn the whole on account of our part: these are best seen as typically Aristotelian overkill arguments. In any case he also sees quite clearly that to get at the nub of the Heracleiteans' difficulty more is needed than *these* arguments: for he points out that there are good grounds for denying of anything in motion that it is in motion in every respect (1010a 15-25). Thus Aristotle sees that a consistent Heracleitean must deny that the law of contradiction holds of *anything* that is in motion in every respect, and he says nothing to suggest that this was somehow not a correct inference from Heracleitean premisses. So that if this was something he learned from Plato, Plato also saw that to resolve the difficulty the Heracleiteans embroil themselves in it was necessary to introduce stability into the world of change itself, and not enough merely to posit the existence of some things outside of the world of becoming and exempt from flux.

Close analysis of the argument of 182-183 reveals, then, that Plato's rejection of Heracleiteanism as a basis on which to construct a defense of the thesis that knowledge is perception also involves the refutation of Heracleiteanism itself. The inference to this effect drawn from consideration of the final argument of this section (184-186) has therefore been vindicated: Plato implies in 182-183 that both the Heracleitean theory of perception and the Heracleitean theory of phenomena are false.

B. *The Flux Argument in the Cratylus*

In order to consolidate this conclusion it will be useful to consider a passage from the end of the *Cratylus*. The argument of that passage has long been recognized[22] to be closely similar to the present argument from the *Theaetetus*, and it is necessary to show that it can be interpreted in conformity with the general conclusions I wish to elicit from the *Theaetetus*' discussion. The *Cratylus*' argument (439c 7-440d 6), which is also and explicitly directed against Heracleiteanism, turns upon the denial that any mode of description (προσειπεῖν, 439d 8) can be correctly applied to a thing that is subject to constant flux.[23] Various features of the *Theaetetus*' argument, however, are missing in the *Cratylus*'--notably the distinction between local and qualitative change and the consequent sharpening of the paradoxical implications of the flux theory. It is by making this distinction, as I have been interpreting the argument, that Plato is able to show the absurdity of the Heracleitean attempt to banish from discourse about phenomena both "is" and every attributive expression except when explicitly preceded by a verb of becoming. The argument in the *Cratylus* does not have any of this detail,[24] and does not directly confront Heracleiteanism as a doctrine of phenomena, which is what in the *Theaetetus* it is taken to be. Rather, without providing an elaborate and precise interpretation of the doctrine, such as the theory of the κομψότεροι in the *Theaetetus*, the *Cratylus* produces a brief argument to show that flux and constant motion are not essential features of τὰ ὄντα (440c 6, etc., = τὰ πράγματα, 440d 1, and χρήματα, d 2). Two features of the argument stand out: (1) Plato leaves on one side sensible phenomena and introduces αὐτὸ καλὸν καὶ ἀγαθὸν καὶ ἓν ἕκαστον τῶν ὄντων οὕτω (439c 8-9, cf. 440b 5-6), then arguing that *these* things are not like flowing streams; (2) essential to the argument by which he shows this is the point familiar to us from the *Theaetetus*, that a thing that constantly changed could not be described or named because it would become different and slip away even while we were speaking (439d 8-12). The fact that this point is the same as that of the *Theaetetus* (182d-183a) but is used to show *only* that τὸ καλόν *et al* are exempt from flux, and not that phenomena like beautiful faces are exempt as well, has been taken as practically conclusive proof that the intention of the *Theaetetus* is merely to show that *Forms* are not in flux, and not that phenomena are not.[25]

Close attention to the context of the argument and to the detail of its development, however, show this view to be mistaken. First one must take note of the relaxed and consciously undogmatic character of the *Cratylus*. Socrates throughout the dialogue is the same self-consciously agnostic inquirer which he is, for example, in the *Meno*: even when giving (as at 434c-435c) excellent arguments against some philosophical proposition he draws back from announcing a positive result (cf. 435c 6-d 1). So in the final argument of the dialogue we are presented with a *hypothesis* (439c 6-d 7) from which it follows (e 3-5) that some things never change at all; and officially Socrates goes no further than to point out (440c 1 ff., d 2-6) that *if* this hypothesis is correct then it is not true that everything is like a leaking pot or a man with a runny nose, as the flux theory implies. He deliberately avoids committing himself on the question *whether* the hypothesis is correct or whether, perhaps, the Heracleitean theory may be true. By thus limiting the question to whether the Forms, if they exist, are entities that change, Socrates is enabled to keep up his pretense of not having or reaching any positive philosophical conclusions of his own. He could not have done so had he undertaken the direct confrontation of a carefully elaborated Heracleitean theory, as he does in the _Theaetetus_, where, however the argument is interpreted in detail, Heracleiteanism is shown to be self-refuting and (183a-c) a positive result is attained and announced.

The argument of the _Cratylus_ begins by _assuming_ (439c 7-d 1) that there are Forms--αὐτὸ τὸ καλὸν καὶ ἀγαθόν and the rest. About each of these it is further assumed (d 5-7) that it is always such as it is at any time, that is, that whatever character it has at any time belongs to it at every time. The subsequent argument then consists in showing that given this latter assumption about the Forms it cannot be right to say that any Form changes at all. Though this might be thought so obvious as not to need argument, Socrates actually does argue the point; and the argument he gives actually proves much more than he needs. In fact, he really proves not only that Forms do not change at all but that nothing that can be a subject of significant discourse can change in every respect at every moment.

The first and most important point established is that if a thing is constantly changing in every respect it is impossible to apply to it any substantival or any adjectival expression (d 8-9): if it is changing in this way at the time when we assert that it has such-and-such a character it has already passed on and is no longer correctly so characterized. And never having any definite character (e 1-2) it could not be any definite thing (have any substantival expression correctly given to it) either. If, in fact, a thing is ever in any definite state, and can be described as "such and such," during the time when it is in that state it clearly does not change (in that respect at least) (e 2-3). We have, however, assumed that Forms can not only be described as "such and such," but even that every characteristic they have at any time they have at every time: so that, by the foregoing argument, Forms must not change at all (e 3-5). Always being in the same states and having the same substantival expressions truly applicable to them, they never change in any respect.

This argument[26] obviously has the consequence that anything in total flux could not be talked about at all, and therefore that anything that is said to be in motion must also be at rest in some respect. This fact is not the less obvious because the consequence is not explicitly drawn and used as the basis for a direct assault on Heracleitean metaphysics. For Plato clearly does not think that it proves only that Forms must be exempt from flux: the Forms are in the clearest possible way introduced as the extreme special case where not only the possibility of identification and description must be retained, whatever the consequences, but even the same names and descriptions must apply for all time. If, in the special case of the Forms, all motion whatsoever must be denied, this is only because in the general case motion in some respects and at some times must be denied if discourse is to be possible. The fact, therefore, that this argument is specifically applied only to the question whether Forms can be in flux is absolutely no indication that Plato thought that it only had consequences for the Forms; any one who supposes that a thing in motion can be talked about could be shown on the basis of what Plato says here that it cannot be in motion in every respect.

In the subsequent argument of the Cratylus Plato goes on to associate knowledge and the Forms, and it has been thought that his remarks here show that his fundamental argument against Heracleiteanism is that it destroys the possibility of knowledge, because knowledge requires absolutely unchanging objects. We have already seen that in the Theaetetus' refutation of Heracleiteanism, where Cornford attempts to introduce this view into the argument, no such thought is expressed by Plato: it is the impossibility of significant speech, definite perception, and true belief, rather than the impossibility of knowledge, that he has in view there. In the Cratylus, however, having argued that Forms must be exempt from change because they can be talked about, he goes on to add a supplementary argument to the same conclusion drawn from considerations about knowledge.

The Cratylus makes two somewhat separate arguments about knowledge. The first (439e 7-a 5) follows directly on the argument I have just analyzed and, like that one, follows out the consequences of the hypothesis that αὐτὸ τὸ καλόν, etc., exist. Though it was not mentioned when the Forms were introduced at 439c-d, Plato is assuming that these entities can be known; and this first argument shows that if this is so they cannot be in perpetual flux. For, as the previous argument has shown, anything in perpetual flux is in no determinate state at all, but a thing that has no definite character can certainly not be known, since it falls away and changes even while one tries to get to know it. Knowledge requires that things "be somehow." Nothing so far suggests that a thing, in order to be known, must be *always* as it is, and never change in any respect:[27] here, as in the previous argument, the Forms overfulfill the requirement. A Form has always the same properties and therefore, *a fortiori*, it is at any given time in a definite state; but it is the latter fact, and not the former that, according to this argument, makes a Form a possible object of knowledge.

The other argument (440a 6-c 1) is that if knowledge exists it cannot be constantly changing, since it would then never *be* knowledge but would constantly be falling away into some other sort of thing. And similarly for knowing subject and the object of knowledge. Now this argument, like the previous one, appears to be compatible with a view which makes knowledge attainable of anything provided only that it is at rest in some respect; it seems not to require the absolute permanence of whatever is known. On the other hand Plato does imply (ἀεί, b 5) that knowers, and presumably therefore also known objects, exist forever, and this suggests that in fact the view he is taking of knowledge is the canonical Platonic doctrine that knowledge is a matter of eternal souls coming into contact with eternal and unchanging objects. And if this is so, it is necessary to adjust one's understanding of the two arguments about knowledge. But it is important to observe that even if

Plato here is arguing that there cannot be knowledge except of entities that do not change at all, this is perfectly compatible with the view that he at the same time allows phenomena *not* to be in flux. There is no reason why he cannot retain the view that knowledge requires absolutely unchanging objects while recognizing that a phenomenon is at rest in some respects at each moment.

The upshot is that the flux argument in the *Cratylus* in no way contradicts the argument of the *Theaetetus* as I have interpreted it. The fact that the *Cratylus* mentions only the Forms as things exempt from flux does not in any way show that in the *Cratylus* and in the *Theaetetus* Plato means to refute Heracleiteanism by emphasizing the "all" in "All things are in flux" and then proving that there exist non-sensible, absolutely unchanging entities. In the *Theaetetus'* refutation the Forms are not even alluded to, and we have now seen that the *Cratylus'* use of the Forms does not support the traditional interpretation. Socrates introduces the Forms in the *Cratylus* as a hypothesis, and the subsequent argument neither proves, nor attempts to prove, that the Forms must exist, by way of refuting Heracleiteanism. Rather it provides reasons for saying that if the Forms exist, are always such as they are at any time, and can be known, then they do not change at all and Heracleiteanism is not true. Socrates refrains from proving that Heracleiteanism *is* false--which he might have done by proving the truth of the antecedent of the hypothetical proposition just cited, or by proving directly the incoherence of Heracleiteanism itself. This he avoids because he wishes to maintain a discreetly neutral position. Nevertheless, the argument by which he proves the hypothetical proposition does clearly show that he has grasped the essential point which Plato uses in the _Theaetetus_ to prove the incoherence of a Heracleitean account of anything. Hence the differences between the structure and development of the argument of the _Cratylus_ and that of the _Theaetetus_ cannot be used to argue that the _Theaetetus_ intends to be showing _not_ that any changing phenomenon must be at rest in some respect _but_ that, though all phenomena incessantly change in every respect, some non-phenomenal objects exist that do not change.

C. _Results_

With this result now firmly achieved we can return to the _Theaetetus_ and assess the consequences of the refutation of Heracleiteanism provided there. According to my interpretation Plato shows that if Theaetetus accepts the Heracleitean banishment of εἶναι from the world of phenomena then he cannot support his definition of knowledge as perception, since Heracleiteanism implies that anything you call perception has as much right to be called not-perception as perception, so that by identifying knowing as perceiving Theaetetus has not advanced his case even one step. More important than this embarrassment to Theaetetus is the consequence of Heracleiteanism to the Heracleiteans themselves: they end up by denying the law of contradiction and cannot even permit themselves the "both so and not-so" which that denial would seem to allow them. In fact, no use of language is left to them at all.[28] As I have argued, Plato, in showing here that universal flux is self-refuting, means to be proving that of anything, phenomena as well as whatever else there might be, one must be prepared to use some εἶναι description: one <u>cannot</u> restrict himself exclusively to γίγνεσθαι expressions in describing anything. In short, there must be οὐσία and στάσις <u>in</u> the world of phenomena and not merely outside it.

Now in reaching these conclusions Plato definitively rejects the Heracleiteans' attempt to avoid every use of εἶναι and to limit themselves to γίγνεσθαι. But, as I showed in discussing the introduction of Heracleiteanism in the *Theaetetus* (152d-e), this attempt was something Plato himself contemplated making: the metaphysics of the *Timaeus* rests explicitly on the banishment of εἶναι from the realm of γένεσις. It therefore follows from my understanding of the refutation of the flux doctrine that in Plato's view this metaphysics is incoherent. As I have already indicated, the fact that Plato goes on, in the subsequent refutation of Theaetetus' sense-perception theory of knowledge, to speak of sense qualities as having οὐσία shows that he evidently drew this moral from his earlier argument. I shall not discuss the possible ways in which this conflict between the *Theaetetus* and the *Timaeus* might be taken account of, nor shall I attempt to trace evidences in later dialogues, such as *Sophist* and *Philebus*, of the same conflict. It is enough to have shown, as I think I have shown, that the conflict is really there and cannot be wished away as currently fashionable interpretations think it can.

CHAPTER IV

THE REFUTATION OF THE SENSE-PERCEPTION THEORY OF KNOWLEDGE (184b-186e)

Having shown that the equation of knowledge with perception cannot be defended κατὰ τὴν τοῦ πάντα κινεῖσθαι μέθοδον (183c 2-3), Plato turns at last to consider the merits of the equation in its pure state, without admixture of Heracleiteanism. The conclusion of his argument (186e 9-10) leaves no doubt that in his view perception, with or without the aid of Heracleitean metaphysics, cannot be equated with knowledge.. But in the interpretation of the argument by which he reaches this conclusion, as we have seen is also the case in the interpretation of his refutation of Heracleiteanism itself, there are enormously wide divergences of opinion.[1]

Some think that Plato in effect appeals to the existence of certain things which are not objects of perception but which we are nevertheless acquainted with. These he calls κοινά, or "common terms," instancing existence, non-existence, similarity, dissimilarity, sameness, difference, number (185c 9 ff.), honorable, disgraceful, good, and bad (186a 8). According to these interpreters he then argues that the soul in and by itself contemplates[2] (ἐπισκοπεῖν, 185e 2) these objects, since, being common to all things, they are not the objects of any of the special senses of sight, hearing, and the like. Each of the senses acquaints us with its proper objects (the so-called "internal objects"), but with nothing else, and anything which we are not acquainted with through some <u>one</u> of the special senses does not come to us through the senses at all. Now, as one of the common objects which the soul contemplates all by itself and not through any of the senses is οὐσία (existence), it follows not only that <u>some</u> things we are acquainted with are not known by sense-perception but even that none of what is conveyed to us through the senses is in itself knowledge. For (cf. 152c 5, 186c 7 ff.) there cannot be knowledge or even truth where οὐσία is not attained to-- οὐσία being now understood to mean "permanent, pure, really real existence," and not just existence. But as Plato has shown οὐσία is not conveyed through any of the senses but is rather grasped by the soul in its activity independent of the body. Therefore no sense perception amounts to knowledge.

Much in this train of reasoning is obscure and could be questioned; but at any rate the outline of the argument is tolerably clear. According to these interpreters Plato's argument moves in two stages. (1) We are acquainted with the κοινά by some faculty other than sense perception; but (2) since one of the κοινά is οὐσία and there is no knowledge where οὐσία is not attained to, it is in the exercise of the faculty which apprehends and contemplates the κοινά that knowledge consists.

Those who read the argument in this way sometimes go on to point out that in concluding thus that no sense-perception conveys knowledge Plato is assigning to the senses just the same role as that which in the <u>Republic</u> (522e 5-524d 6) they play in the process of acquiring knowledge.[3] In the Republic, it will be recalled, Plato distinguishes between those sense-perceptions that do not call upon the faculty of intuition (νόησις) to investigate them, since they are judged adequately by the senses, and those which do call upon νόησις for inspection and investigation, since the senses themselves in these cases produce nothing trustworthy. The unsound perceptions here in question are those which even while reporting one sense quality to the soul at the same time report the contradictory sensation (523b 9-c 4). One example Plato gives (524a 1-4) is the perception of hardness; in this case, he says, the sense of touch reports to the soul that "the same thing is both hard and soft when it perceives it." Plato's point is that the senses play the role of stimulating, by their confusion and contradictoriness, the faculty of νόησις into operation; and what νόησις does is to turn the soul's gaze away from sense-particulars, which are inadequate and confused instances of largeness or smallness or softness or oneness, and toward (intelligible) objects which are clear and adequate instances of these concepts. In turning toward the intelligible world the soul is then enabled to give an answer to the question what is the large, the hard, the soft, etc., which reflection on our sense perceptions naturally makes us ask, but which we are unable to answer so long as we rely on the reports of sense alone (524c 10-11). And in thus becoming acquainted with intelligible objects the soul is exercising intelligence and for the first time acquiring knowledge. In the Theaetetus, it is alleged, the senses perform this same preliminary and stimulative function, while knowledge is located entirely in the contemplation of intelligible objects-- οὐσία, sameness, and the rest--just as in the Republic knowledge consists in the contemplation of the intelligible instances of largeness, smallness, oneness, and other such objects.

This interpretation, favored by Cherniss and Cornford, and indeed most commentators, has, and is intended to have, the virtue of making Plato's objections to perception as a source of knowledge issue, at all stages of his maturity, from a single harmonious theory of knowledge. But whatever the ultimate truth about Plato's philosophical development or lack of it, I think it can be shown that in their zeal to prove the consistency of the Theaetetus' argument against sense perception with the Republic's two-world ontology and epistemology, the interpreters whose views I have just been expounding have failed to understand the direction and force of the Theaetetus' refutation. The argument of the Theaetetus is not a re-run of Republic VII: it does not assign to perception the same role as the Republic does, and it does not restrict knowledge to an intelligible world as the Republic (in the passage considered) does. The assertion of the Theaetetus that sense perception cannot be knowledge because it does not attain to οὐσία and truth is not tantamount to saying that the objects of sense perception do not have οὐσία and are not "unchangingly real" but always becoming and always changing.[4] Even if the κοινά are Forms, this argument in the Theaetetus does not restrict knowledge to the contemplation of them and things like them.

Before beginning the examination of the Theaetetus' argument, however, it will be useful to recall the state of the argument of the dialogue as a whole at the point where the final refutation is given. As I have argued above, Plato has already refuted Heracleiteanism, whether it is taken in an unrestricted sense, as denying stability to anything, or in the restricted version which holds merely that nothing in the world of sense has any stability. Hence the argument of 184-186 is totally disengaged from the flux theory, and, in particular, from the theory of perception allegedly constructed on Heracleitean principles. We may not assume any particular theory of perception at all; only whatever is needed in order to make Theaetetus' original equation of sense-perception with knowledge (151e) a plausible definition can correctly be even provisionally assumed. It is fair, then, to assume two things about perception and perceptual judgments: (1) judgments of perception are being taken to be irrefutable by appeal to any other person's experiences or judgments, and (2) a perception is something private to a single percipient. These claims have underlain the whole preceding discussion, and to maintain them it is not necessary to accept either Protagoreanism or Heracleiteanism. Evidently in maintaining that perception is knowledge Theaetetus would wish to defend these two propositions. Plato's refutation, as I construe it, grants him these two claims but still refuses to allow that what one apprehends by means of perception alone is ever a case of knowledge, and even goes so far as to deny that perceptions themselves are ever true.

He begins his argument by introducing the notion of elementary sense perception. If the claim of perception to be knowledge is to be tested it is essential to have as test cases instances of pure perception and not hybrids where not only perception but also other faculties of soul are combined. To show that such a hybrid was or was not a case of knowledge would leave in doubt the fundamental question about the status of perception, taken in itself. The first thing Plato does, therefore, is to indicate what, speaking quite strictly, are pure reports of perception (184b 4-185a 3). He then contrasts certain types of judgment which, even though they are judgments <u>about</u> the objects of perception, are not made merely on the basis of perception of them (185a 3-e 2) and are therefore not perceptual reports. After a brief recapitulation (185e 3-186c 6) of the distinction and contrast which has just been drawn, he goes on to argue (186c 7-e 10) that, since judgments wielding the concept of existence (judgments asserting the existence or non-existence of something) belong to the second, and never to the first, group, and since there cannot be knowledge or even truth where there is not existence, judgments of the second group contain all our knowledge, and purely perceptual reports never express knowledge at all.

The first stage of the argument is introduced by the preliminary distinction between the soul and its sense-faculties. The distinction between the organs and faculties of sense and the man or the soul which has them was not taken notice of earlier in the theory of perception propounded by the Heracleiteans (156-157), and its introduction here makes possible the isolation of perception from other functions of the soul which Plato is anxious to effect. The eyes and ears are in fact the organs <u>through</u> which perceptible things reach the soul; it is by means of the soul that men are able to perceive, and not, as it were, directly by means of the organs and the individual sense faculties. Our perceptions are all reported, so to speak, to a single agency which takes cognizance not only of colors, but also of sounds, tastes, smells, and tactile sensations. Each sense faculty, however, is involved in reports of only one class of perceptibles: colors are reported by sight, sounds by hearing, and so on. But about its peculiar objects each sense is uniquely qualified to judge; what is perceived through sight cannot also be perceived through hearing, for example. Whenever, therefore, a single elementary sense quality is being reported to the soul the only faculty of soul which is employed is the one sense faculty to which the quality peculiarly belongs. It is only in such cases that perception can be seen in isolation from other faculties of soul, and accordingly the question whether perception is knowledge reduces to the question whether the sensing of peculiar sensibles is a case of knowledge.

Now it follows from the fact that each sense faculty is restricted to reporting to the soul sense qualities peculiar to it that if the soul in a _single_ act ever addresses itself to objects peculiar to _two_ senses then it is engaged not merely in perceiving them but in some further mental operation. For if it were merely perceiving it would have to be employing some one sense faculty; but as we have seen no sense faculty has any capacity to report objects of any other sense. Hence operations involving at once two disparate sense objects necessarily go beyond pure perception. Plato gives the example of the soul thinking something about two different sense qualities (185a): it cannot then be merely perceiving something about them. And there really are, Theaetetus agrees (185a 10), actions of the soul in which it does consider together two disparate sense-qualities, as when it thinks and judges about sound and color that they both exist (ὅτι ἀμφοτέρω ἐστόν). Likewise one can think that sound and color are different from one another, that each of them is identical with itself, that they are like or unlike one another, that together they are two and separately each is one: in all these cases the soul concerns itself at once about objects of two senses, and therefore none of them is a perceptual judgment.

They are all in fact, as Plato goes on to argue (185b 7-186c 5), judgments rendered by the soul by her own agency and without the medium of any sense faculty or any special organ. In judging that something exists or is identical with itself, the soul is not perceiving anything but rather comparing, reasoning, judging, and concluding something about what the senses have reported. Now it is important to see that this is what Plato is saying in this passage about the soul's relation to the "common terms" existence, sameness, difference, etc. For though his point here concerns what the soul is doing when it applies these concepts to the objects of perception, commentators usually take the argument to turn, rather, on how the soul becomes acquainted with the common notions. A detailed analysis of the passage 185b 7-e 2 will show beyond question that this popular conception is in error.

But before turning to this analysis, it will be useful to consider more closely what the nature of the distinction is which Plato has been drawing between perception and the activity of the soul in which it reasons, by itself and not through the medium of a sense, about the qualities reported to it by the senses. The distinction is sometimes taken to be simply that between sensation and judgment; Plato is thought here to have restricted perception, strictly conceived, to sensation without judgment.[5] Judgment is the province of the soul, the central faculty to which sensory reports are made, and though in formulating judgments the soul operates upon the data of sense no judgment is ever simply a matter of sensation (and therefore of perception). Now though there are grounds for thinking that this is Plato's meaning,[6] I think it is doubtful whether this is the main point he has in mind. The distinction between sensation and judgment is presumably just that the former is not responsible for the formulation of statements, but merely, as it were, provides (some of) the raw material for statements, which it is then the task of the soul to construct by operating without the aid of any organ. If so, then, although Plato does apparently disqualify perception from making judgments, this is not his main concern.

Plato seems willing to grant that elementary perceptual reports--reports of sensations of heat, particular colors, sounds, and the like--are carried out without calling into play any higher faculty of the soul than sense perception itself: and though the report of the presence of a certain color, say red, in one's visual field need not take the form of a statement, I think the contrast Plato means to be indicating between perception and thought is not fundamentally affected if one thinks of perceptual reports as minimal judgments. He evidently does not think that in order to apply a perceptual predicate like "red" to some experience[7] one requires to engage the faculty of thought which is called into play when one makes judgments of existence, difference, similarity, and the like. In naming a sense-content "red," or asserting "I seem to be seeing something red," though the one is a statement and the other is not, Plato seems content to refer merely to sense perception. The contrasting case, where reasoning and comparison of things with one another (186a 10-b 1, b 8, c 2-3) are invoked, clearly does not envisage the faculty of thought being brought into play in order to label sense-contents red or hard or loud. Thus though it seems evident that in applying any concept--red no less than existence--such faculties as memory, comparison, association, etc., are involved, the most important thing to notice about Plato's argument is that he grants to sense perception itself the ability to register and label elementary sense contents (i.e, single colors, smells, sounds, tastes and sensations of warmth and resistance). Plato's contrast seems therefore to be a contrast between minimally and purely perceptual judgments, on the one hand, and judgments of another sort, on the other, rather than between sensation and judgments in general.

What then does the contrast between perceptual reports and judgments of existence, difference, and the rest come to? Further explanation is best put off until we have examined the passage where Plato argues that these other judgments are not and cannot be mere perceptual reports. He has already obtained Theaetetus' admission that we not only notice colors and tastes and the like but also make judgments about the existence of sounds and colors. He next (185b 7-

186c 5) asks how these judgments are made. Since they do not lie within the province of any of the special senses, through what faculty, if any, are they made? His answer, briefly put, is that there is no sense faculty and no special organ through which we perceive that a thing is identical with itself, or that it exists, etc., but these judgments are made by the soul itself without the mediation of any sense. It is very important, however, to see clearly that this and *only* this is what Plato is saying in this passage. Commentators, as I have already remarked, make it appear that he is discussing the mode of our acquisition of the concepts of existence, identity, etc., and of our knowledge of the entities Existence and Identity, but they are able to do so only by translating these concerns into Plato's text, where they demonstrably do not belong.

The passage opens at 185b 7 with the question, "Through what do you think all these [i. e., the so-called common attributes] about them [viz., about sound and color]?" As he goes on to explain, he has in mind that if you perceive that something is red, or sweet-flavored, you perceive these things through the medium of a sense and a sense-organ; and he wants to know whether one perceives something's existence or self-identity or unity through any analogous organ. At c 7-8, having proffered this explanation of his question he repeats it: τούτοις πᾶσι ποῖα ἀποδώσεις ὄργανα δι' ὧν αἰσθάνεται ἡμῶν τὸ αἰσθανόμενον ἕκαστα; ("What sort of organs do you assign for all of these, through which our sense-perceptory part perceives them?") Now it is here that commentators begin to translate and comment as if what were in question was, "How do we become acquainted with the entities Existence, Identity, Unity, etc.?" But it is evident that the question in Plato's text merely restates the question at b 7 and that therefore nothing is said about our becoming acquainted with Existence, but rather about our perceiving or judging <u>about</u> the existence of a thing or quality. This is overlooked only because the restatement omits the phrase περὶ ἀμφοῖν which would make it clear that it is not a question of becoming acquainted with the meanings of these common terms,[8] but rather one of perceiving or judging <u>that</u> they do or do not apply to something.

That the περί clause is to be understood with the restatement at c 7-8 is made certain by Theaetetus' reply: he adds in his answer the περὶ αὐτῶν (d 1) which was only implicit in the question. But he then goes on to omit the phrase, in the same idiomatic way, later in his reply when he in turn reformulates the question: διὰ τίνος ποτὲ τῶν τοῦ σώματος τῇ ψυχῇ αἰσθανόμεθα [αυτά]; (d 3-4). And here again translators omit the περί phrase and misunderstand Theaetetus to be asking himself whether we become acquainted with Existence and the rest, in themselves, through any agency of the body. Cornford compounds this error by misconstruing in Theaetetus' subsequent answer (d 7-e 2) the force of the phrase περὶ πάντων which Theaetetus again reimports. Theaetetus says, "The soul itself through itself, as it appears to me, examines for every object [whether it possesses] these common attributes" (αὐτὴ δι' αὐτῆς ἡ ψυχὴ τὰ κοινά μοι φαίνεται περὶ πάντων ἐπισκοπεῖν). But Cornford takes the περὶ πάντων with τὰ κοινά, and translates "the common terms that apply to everything," presumably thinking the phrase a variation of τὸ ἐπὶ πᾶσι κοινόν above (c 4-5); but even if this is possible Greek, which seems doubtful, it is obvious that περὶ πάντων ἐπισκοπεῖν is grammatically parallel to περὶ αὐτοῖν διανοῇ in the original statement of the question (b 7).[9] Other translators (e.g., Diès) take the περὶ πάντων with the verb, as by position it would most naturally be construed, but they have not, I think, seen the consequence of so doing. The consequence, to repeat, is that Theaetetus says nothing about how we become **acquainted with** Existence and Sameness, but rather tells us that judgments of the existence and identity of a sense-quality are not made by the agency of any sense but by the soul without the aid of any organ.

Having reached this conclusion Plato pauses to consolidate his position by running through the list of κοινά and obtaining Theaetetus' agreement that the soul by itself makes judgments applying each of these to the objects of the senses. Here again translators confuse the issue by taking Plato to be discussing how we arrive at our acquaintance with these common entities; and again there are very clear signs that nothing of the sort is in question.[10] Thus when Socrates inquires whether καλὸν καὶ αἰσχρὸν καὶ ἀγαθὸν καὶ κακόν are among the κοινά about which the soul judges all by itself, Theaetetus replies in the affirmative (186a 9-b 1). But he goes on to add that when the soul judges about these things it calculates within itself past and present events and things against future ones. Now this is a pretty good brief account of how one judges whether a particular person or action or situation is good or bad or honorable or disgraceful: one does have to weigh past experience and present circumstances in order to get a reasonable judgment as to a person's future behavior or the consequences of an action and so on. But it is surely precisely the wrong sort of thing to do in order to become acquainted with the existence and nature of a Platonic Form. Consideration of phenomena and phenomenal events is notoriously the main obstacle to becoming acquainted with these. It seems clear, therefore, that Socrates and Theaetetus are not discussing the question how we arrive at our knowledge of the Forms Honorableness, Disgracefulness, and the like; they are, rather, inquiring how one goes about making particular judgments about the goodness or badness, etc., of particular things.

That this is so is proved by Socrates' final remark in the discussion of the κοινά: there (186b 11-c 5) he contrasts simple perceptual judgments, which according to him any one can make from birth on, with reasonings about the οὐσία and ὠφέλεια of these sense-qualities. The ability to engage in the latter activity is only acquired later and with difficulty. Again it is only too clear that acquaintance with thought-entities is not the point at issue. The contrast is between two sorts of judgments about sense-qualities (and other sense objects), and not one sort of judgment about sense-qualities and another sort about something else.[11]

What exactly are the two sorts of judgment referred to? The

perceptual side is perhaps clear enough, but what does Plato mean by judgments where ἀναλογίσματα are involved? I think the contrast he has in mind is that between subjective reports of purely private experiences and objectively grounded assertions about the existence, probable effects, moral and esthetic properties, and the like, of the qualities perceived. All of these are questions where not merely the subject's private experience is in question: the experiences and opinions of others are also relevant to the truth of what is asserted. That this is the contrast is shown, I think, by the evident reference[12] in Theaetetus' reply at 186a 9-b 1 to the refutation of Protagoras, and in the use to which Socrates puts Theaetetus' remark. We have already seen how Protagoras' claim that whatever any one thinks is true was refuted: whenever what a man thinks involves *prediction* objective standards are introduced which are incompatible with the claim of universal truth (178a-179b). Here Theaetetus answers Socrates' question about how one judges about the honorableness or goodness of something by again appealing to the fact that prediction, which is involved here, requires reflection about what will in *fact* turn out to be the case; the soul's activity of reflection by itself and without the aid of sense faculties is therefore connected in this case with objective standards by reference to which the judgments it delivers are to be assessed. Socrates takes up this point and links together judgments of existence and usefulness, in both of which the soul delivers judgments independently of sense faculties and makes assertions involving a reference to objective conditions. To perceive the hardness of something hard, he says, involves no more than perception, and is therefore merely a subjective report. But to judge that the hardness <u>exists</u>, that there really <u>is</u> something hard to be perceived, requires thought because it requires prediction and reference to the behavior of something in an objective world. Likewise it is an objective fact, and not a matter of any one's impressions, that hard and soft are contraries, or that the hardness you perceive is the contrary of the softness you perceive. And so, in general, reasonings of the soul with respect to οὐσία and ὠφέλεια (186c 2-5) go beyond sense perception and involve a reference to objective conditions, and this is why experience and education are required before the ability to engage in them is acquired.

In sum, then, Plato is arguing that it is only in reports of the presence of the elementary sense-qualities in one's private experience that the soul functions with the aid of the senses without any higher faculty; and only here is true subjectivity to be found. As soon as one goes beyond this, and introduces concepts like goodness, identity, difference, and number, other powers of the soul are brought in, and with them comes reasoning involving a reference to objective facts, standards, and conditions. Foremost among the concepts which the soul applies by thinking, and not merely by perceiving, is existence, and in the final stage of the argument refuting the claim of sense perception to be knowledge this fact is crucial. As I remarked above, Plato argues that not only is sense perception not the whole of knowledge, it is not in any case knowledge at all.

He argues this (186c 7-e 12) by reaffirming that knowledge must have οὐσία and truth as its content, and showing, on the basis of his foregoing analysis of judgments involving κοινά, that sense perception does not have these for its content. To understand his meaning all we need do is attend carefully to the analysis just produced of judgments of existence. When he says that sense perception *per se* is unable to arrive at οὐσία he just means that sense perception, being the purely private recording of private and fleeting sense-contents, does not judge or assume anything about the existence in an objective world of any of the things it perceives. By restricting itself to judgments of the appearances actually present to consciousness it declares itself incompetent to decide any question to which any one else's experiences or opinions have any relevance. But by so doing it necessarily fails to make any objectively valid judgments. Knowledge, however, is always of what *is* the case, regardless of who discovers or thinks *that* it is the case. Therefore purely private sense reports, however irrefutable, do not constitute knowledge at all.

It is interesting to notice that Plato says not only that sense reports fail to attain to οὐσία but even that they fail to attain to truth. He does not explain this remark, but it is perhaps not impossible, in light of the argument as I have construed it so far, to venture an interpretation of his meaning. Inasmuch as he associates truth and οὐσία, saying (186c 7) that there can only be truth where there is οὐσία, it seems reasonable to conclude that he is restricting the concept of truth to assertions of objective fact. He does not mean that all perceptual judgments are false, but rather that they are hardly either true or false, since they do not make any objective assertions. Since elementary sense reports cannot be wrong, it is not correct to say that they are always right, either. Nothing can be true which might not also have been false.

I said above[13] that the fact that Plato denies here that in perception one can "grasp truth" is some ground for taking his distinction between perceiving, on the one hand, and reasoning, comparing, and thinking, on the other hand, as a contrast between sensing and judging. To be sensibly affected is not to assert anything, hence not to attain the level of truth and falsehood at all; truth and falsehood reside in the reasonings we do on the basis of our sensations. This would imply that the judgment that something appears to me now green involves reasoning (comparing this sensory impression with others, for example), and I have already indicated that the sort of reasoning to which Plato appeals as contrast to sense perception seems to involve more than the minimum required for judging. For this reason I have not interpreted his argument as aimed primarily at using the sensing-judging distinction to refute the claim of perception to be knowledge. Now that I have gone through Plato's argument as a whole this decision can be defended by appeal to a further consideration.

If Plato's rejection of the claim of perception to be knowledge were based on the distinction between sensing and judging his argument would run as follows: Perception cannot be knowledge because, properly construed and isolated from factors of the soul which are not part of perception itself, perceiving is just the having of sense-impressions, and having sense-impressions is not even thinking anything, much less knowing anything. But here we must ask ourselves what his opponent, his knuckles thus rapped, would be able to reply. Evidently any one who claimed that perceiving was knowing would have in mind, as Theaetetus clearly did (152b-c), that what appears to some one in perception is true and is known by him to be true: in short, such a theory holds that such utterances as "It appears to me now that something green is before me" are true if sincere, and express knowledge. But Plato's refutation, construed as importing the sensing-judging distinction, not only does not show this to be false, but if anything implies that he would accept it: the example just cited is a case of judgment, and it is in judgment by contrast to sensation that knowledge is to be found. All his argument shows, therefore, is that any one who wishes to maintain the substance of the traditional claim that perception is knowledge will have to alter his way of speaking and hold that perceptual judgments express knowledge. And this seems not a very happy conclusion to leave Plato with.

By contrast, the interpretation I have adopted, in addition to granting to perception the use of the perceptual concepts which Plato evidently allows it, provides a stronger refutation of perception's claim to be knowledge. For on my view it is precisely the minimal perceptual judgments recording colors, tastes, sounds, etc., as objects of immediate perception which are denied to be expressing knowledge. A report of immediate experience does not express knowledge because it says nothing about any objective facts and has no implications concerning what is happening, or will happen, or is the case in the world at large. As Plato puts it (186d 2-5) in summing up the results of his argument against sense perception: "Therefore knowledge is not to be found in sensory experiences, but in reasoning about them; for, as it seems, in the latter it is possible to grasp existence and truth, but in the former this is impossible."[14] We have now seen that the reference to existence and truth is not, as Cornford thought it was, an oblique indication that knowledge requires to be about unchangingly real objects, the Forms; if my interpretation is correct, the reference is rather to objectivity, without prejudice to the kind of thing which has it.[15]

But if this is so, what are we to make of the passage from the *Republic* (522e 1-524d) so often cited as parallel to this argument of the *Theaetetus*? Surely the resemblances between the two show that I have been misinterpreting the *Theaetetus* passage? To this I shall not have much to say; detailed comparison of the two passages, now that I have explained what I take to be the true meaning of the argument from the *Theaetetus*, can be left to any one interested in pursuing the question. A few remarks may, however, serve to indicate what any one who undertakes the task will find.

The first thing to notice about the *Republic* passage is that it knows nothing of the strict interpretation of sense perception according to which, as we saw the *Theaetetus* holds, only simple sense-qualities are objects of sense perception. The *Republic* speaks indiscriminately of sense perception of a finger (523c 11 ff.); of perception that the same thing is both hard and soft (524a 3), which seems to involve a judgment of identity and so is not a perceptual judgment at all in the Theaetetus' use of this term; of perception of something as a unit (524d 9-e 6), which appears to break the Theaetetus' canon that judgments of number are altogether beyond the scope of sense perception even to attempt. In fact, the Republic envisages (523a 10-b 4) sense perception as making a practically unlimited range of judgments; the distinction it draws (523b 9-c 4) is between those judgments based on perception which are clear and satisfactory and those which are not clear but rather confused and even contradictory. But the Theaetetus says nothing about the senses attempting to make judgments of existence or identity or number or usefulness, but necessarily failing; its point is not that such judgments, when the senses make them, are not trustworthy, whereas when made by νόησις and applied to the right kind of objects numerical judgments, for example, are clear and even necessarily true (cf. 524e 6-525a 2).

Furthermore, the Theaetetus positively attributes to the soul in sense perception the ability to judge without recourse so long as it limits itself to reports of its proper objects; but in the Republic's different scheme the contrast being pursued does not allow to perception even this. For among the perceptual judgments which in the Republic Plato says call νόησις into play are the perception of τὸ κοῦφον and that of τὸ σκληρόν (524a 8). These perceptions, he maintains, always are reported together with perceptions of their opposites; in sense-reports each of a pair of opposites comes συγκεχυμένον (524c 3-4) with the other, and this means that the senses are incapable of judging adequately of lightness and heaviness and hardness and softness. They strictly do not know what they are saying (524a 6-8) when they say "Hardness appears here now." If one wants to know what hardness is one will have to abandon sense-reports altogether and attempt to separate hardness from its opposite, and discover some intelligible object which can serve as an instance of hardness which is not in any respect ever also soft. But, as against this, the _Theaetetus_ (184e 4-6) happily allows the senses to report hard things and light things, without any hint that they convey nothing trustworthy in this regard. The _Theaetetus'_ contrast is not drawn between trustworthy and untrustworthy sense reports, but between sense reports, strictly conceived, on the one hand, and judgments passed by altogether a different faculty, on the other hand.

These few remarks should be sufficient to dissociate the argument of the _Republic_ from that of the _Theaetetus_. The _Theaetetus'_ argument is certainly no pale rehash of arguments to be found in the _Republic_. It marks, in fact, if my construction is correct, the earliest expression of the far more important and far more interesting point that knowledge is essentially bound up with objectivity. Perceptual reports may be infallible but they do not constitute knowledge because they say nothing that appeal to the facts about anything in the common world could have any tendency to show to be false. This conclusion, though not of course the arguments adduced to prove it, bears a certain obvious similarity to Kant's and Wittgenstein's views about subjectivity and knowledge, and this affinity seems to me a far more interesting outcome of the final argument of the first part of the *Theaetetus* than the orthodox attempt to make the *Theaetetus* merely repeat things said already in the *Republic*.

CHAPTER V

FALSE BELIEF

A. Introduction

In the course of his refutation of Theaetetus' first attempt at a definition of knowledge, Socrates reaches the conclusion that knowledge must reside not in mere perceptual awareness--mere παθήματα--but in the reasoning we do on the basis of our experience (186d 2-5). As I argued above this in fact suggests an account of empirical knowledge which takes Plato far beyond the old over-simple dichotomy, found in the Republic, between knowledge concerned with the Forms and (mere) belief about empirical matters. In the sequel, however, we find Plato disappointingly not pursuing this suggestion; instead Theaetetus takes up a hint prepared for him by Socrates and proposes as a new definition that knowledge is identical with true reasoning or true belief (ἀληθὴς δόξα). This definition is hardly more promising than the one just disposed of, and in fact when Socrates at length (201a-c) undertakes to test its adequacy, he is able to refute it with as much ease as one would expect: obviously some true judgments are made by luck or by guessing or in some other way fail to display knowledge of the matters at hand.

It is obvious, however--as our experience in the first part of the dialogue has already forewarned us--that Plato's interests in the Theaetetus are hardly restricted to the consideration and rejection of various definitions of knowledge. In the first part, in fact, the definition of knowledge as perception was only faced at 184-186, where it was overturned with relative ease: the other thirty Stephanus pages were taken up with the far more important tasks of expounding and refuting the Protagorean theory of truth and the Heracleitean theory of reality. So here Theaetetus has hardly offered his new definition of knowledge before Socrates introduces (187c 7) a different, though no doubt related, question for discussion: how is false belief possible? With the exception of the very brief argument already alluded to (201a-c), the second part of the dialogue is wholly concerned with this question about false belief.

The question how false belief is possible is one which plays a prominent part in three other dialogues of Plato: *Euthydemus*, *Cratylus*, and *Sophist*. As I shall try to show, the arguments of the *Theaetetus* about false belief are to be understood in the closest possible connection with the remarks and theories about false belief in those other dialogues. In effect, the *Theaetetus* shows that on the theory of meaning which dominates the discussions of the *Euthydemus* and *Cratylus*, and which is otherwise certainly not a wholly unnatural theory, there really cannot be any beliefs that are not true. In the third part of the *Theaetetus*, in the guise of a dream, Socrates produces (201e-202b) a theory of *logos* (account, explanation) which seems to contain also a pretty explicit version of the theory of meaning underlying these discussions, and in the subsequent criticism of it he puts his finger more or less explicitly on the feature of the theory which both makes it a bad account of what a sentence or complete thought is and causes the difficulty in understanding how false belief or judgment is possible. It is then up to the _Sophist_ to formulate a new and better positive account of what a complete thought is and how false thinking is possible. The discussion of false belief in the _Theaetetus_ and the criticism of the dream theory, then, together bring out quite clearly certain basic inadequacies of the theory of meaning in question and prepare the way for the _Sophist_'s different theory.

To show in detail how all this is so, we will have first of all to consider briefly the statement of the difficulty about false belief in the _Euthydemus_ and the ultimate solution provided by the _Sophist_: to see the origin and solution of the problem will facilitate a (relatively) smooth analysis of the _Theaetetus_' difficult arguments. But before beginning the analysis and exposition of this part of the dialogue something should be said to forestall two likely objections against the attempt to construe the _Theaetetus_' discussion as thus concerned with the same problem which the _Sophist_ finally solves (to Plato's satisfaction, at any rate).

The problem about false belief which Socrates introduces in the _Theaetetus_ involves a difficulty in understanding what can be going on in some one's mind when he accepts a false belief. In entertaining a belief he must have some objects before his mind. But as there are only two classes of objects, those he knows and those he does not know, it is impossible to see how he can be believing something which yet is false: for things he doesn't know he cannot entertain any thought about

(i. e., he cannot have them before his mind), but since he knows all the things which he ever has before his mind there seems no room for error. He certainly cannot, if he really knows a thing, confuse it with or mistake it for something else which he also really knows; and in that case there seems no room for him to be doing anything that could result in false belief. Now, obscure though this puzzle is, it evidently turns upon making false beliefs involve the apparent impossibility that one both know and not know some objects. And in the subsequent discussion Socrates and Theaetetus accept the terms of the argument as laid down here, and direct their efforts toward discovering some acceptable sense in which a person can in fact both know and not know the objects before his mind in belief, so as to make believing falsely a real possibility.

Now these facts might be taken as showing that the problem pursued in the *Theaetetus* is a problem about the psychology of belief, and that therefore it is not the same problem as the one raised and solved in the *Sophist*. The *Sophist*'s problem, in fact, is alluded to in the *Theaetetus*, but only to be put aside in favor of the difficulty just referred to. The two problems proceed respectively κατὰ τὸ εἰδέναι καὶ μὴ εἰδέναι and κατὰ τὸ εἶναι καὶ μή, and are obviously not flatly identical. The difficulty κατὰ τὸ εἶναι καὶ μή, which the *Sophist* treats, is just a deeper version of the familiar sophists' conundrum that anyone who really has a belief has to be believing *something*, which therefore exists; but if what some one believes exists, his belief is true. False belief is impossible because a belief that was not true would be one that had no content: a belief, thought, or statement is true if significant, and the false is swallowed up in the meaningless. In dealing with the difficulties involving the *objects* of false beliefs the *Sophist* apparently ignores the other side of the question, the subjective or psychological aspect: i.e., the problem how anyone comes to make a mistake in his thinking. These other difficulties, then, are independent and require an independent treatment; the discussions of the *Theaetetus*, which treat this topic, should therefore be understood independently of the *Sophist* and its solution to its different problem.

This attitude is one which various writers have, more or less implicitly and vaguely, been inclined to take.[1] But while it is no doubt correct to say that two problems are involved, and even that one of them is in some sense psychological, the other ontological and semantical, it is a mistake to think of them as independent questions requiring separate treatment and solution. For, as the obvious example of Wittgenstein shows, philosophical theories of meaning and philosophical theories of mental operations are often mutually implicated, so that a theory of meaning and a theory of thinking form in reality a single philosophical doctrine springing from one and the same original insight or basic idea. Whenever this is so we may expect weaknesses or difficulties in the two parts of the theory to be interconnected in such a way that showing the inadequacy of the one at the same time casts doubt on the other; and to reject, say, the theory of meaning in favor of a different account will at the same time amount to the rejection of the associated theory of thinking. That this is the situation with the discussions of the Theaetetus and the Sophist will be shown in detail later on; but here one indication can profitably be brought forward.

In Socrates' exposition of the difficulty κατὰ τὸ εἰδέναι καὶ μή, discussed briefly above, it is suggested or assumed that a false belief must involve the misidentification or confusion together of certain things known to the believer: the whole subsequent discussion treats this as a fixed point and attempts merely to provide a means of avoiding the apparent contradiction that one should know a thing and yet fail to recognize it for itself. But why should anyone think that false beliefs, as a general thing, must involve such mistaken identifications? For example, if I suppose wrongly that Plato was a wily Roman, instead of a wily Greek, what possible reason is there for thinking that what must be going on in my mind is the confusion of one thing with another? What can Socrates be thinking that makes him so sure that this is what some one has to do in order to hold a false belief? Obviously the range of things that a philosopher can recognize as going wrong in such a case is dependent at least in part upon the conception of the meaning of a sentence or statement which he is working with. Suppose, for example, that in analyzing the statement given above you distinguish a subject-term with corresponding thing meant, a predicate-expression standing for an attribute (being a wily Roman) and a relation between thing and attribute indicated by the "was." Then you will be likely to think that the falsity of the belief consists in getting the relation between Plato and the attribute of being a wily Roman wrong: and this may have happened in various ways, and not merely on account of a mistaken identification of some person or attribute. But suppose your theory of meaning mentions only two things in its analysis of the statement, leaving out the relation. Then this account will be unavailable to you, and you will have to search for the cause of the falsity in the subject-term and the predicate-term and their relations to their designata. Without going further, it should be obvious that different analyses of the meaning of a statement pose different restrictions on the range of things that can go wrong and result in a false belief. And this is enough to suggest that when Socrates assumes that false belief must involve mistaken identification of something he is working with a theory of meaning which restricts, or seems to restrict, the range of possible sources of error in just this way. If so, then however psychological the treatment of false belief in the *Theaetetus* may be, it may yet be part and parcel of the problems of meaning involved in the sophists' conundrum and Plato's analysis in the *Sophist*.

Similar considerations answer the second objection I promised to consider. Noticing the *Theaetetus*' concern with mistakes of identification, in the passage already considered and indeed throughout the discussion, one might get the idea that what is bothering Plato is not something about false beliefs in general, but only something about false identity judgments.[2] To make such a judgment appears to involve knowing the designata of both terms of the identity (else the speaker does not know what he's saying), yet at the same time requires not knowing the designata (since he fails to recognize and identify them properly). Clearly enough the difficulty here concerns the notion of recognition and the connection between knowing something and the ability to recognize it; and there does not seem to be such a link between this and the problem discussed and solved in the *Sophist* that the position attained by Plato in the later dialogue dissolves the difficulties of the *Theaetetus*. The *Sophist* propounds a theory of *predicative* judgments, which defends the possibility of false predications against the difficulties raised by the sophists' conundrum about thinking what is not; but surely some one who saw how it is possible to say falsely that Theaetetus is flying might balk over "Theaetetus is Theodorus." He might, in short, raise once again the difficulty cited above and go on to worry, in the same vein as the middle section of the *Theaetetus*, about how knowing and not knowing can be combined in the way they seem to be in false identity judgments. And if that is so then the *Theaetetus* must surely be read as a separate discussion of a separate problem from the problem of false belief raised elsewhere in Plato's writings.

The idea that the *Theaetetus* is concerned only with the analysis of false identity judgments is a very interesting way of approaching the argument of this part of the dialogue; not the least of its merits in comparison with other views often taken is that it makes a serious effort to construe the argument as directed at some recognizable and interesting philosophical nexus. But two considerations show, I think, quite conclusively that the *Theaetetus* is not raising difficulties only about false identity judgments. First, there is the fact that nowhere in the discussion is it indicated in any way that only some but not all false judgments involve the difficulties alleged. As we have seen, Socrates begins the discussion by, to all appearances, assuming that false belief *in general* requires taking one thing for another. And this impression is reinforced at several points in the subsequent development: thus at 189b 12 and 190e 1-3 "taking one thing for another" is given as the *definition* of false belief. And in the same context it is evident that not merely false judgments of the type of "Socrates is Plato" are being analyzed: such a sentence as "The Taj Mahal is ugly" is also being thought of (189c 5-6) as involving the mistake of saying "ugly" when you should have said "beautiful," and this is in turn evidently (though obscurely) conceived of (190b 2-4) as involving the erroneous identification of the ugly (i.e., the thing meant by "ugly") with the beautiful. It therefore appears that *all* false judgments, predicative as well as overtly identifying judgments, are being thought of as at bottom just mistaken identifications. If so, then the prominence of identity judgments should not be taken to imply that *Plato's* problem in the *Theaetetus* is different from that of the *Sophist*: as I remarked above, the idea that every false belief *must* involve a mistaken identification is likely to be the result of an overly restrictive theory of meaning. And the *Sophist*, in substituting a less restrictive account of meaning, may very well deprive the *Theaetetus'* problems about false identity judgments of their interest for Plato.

Of course, it might be said, even if this is so the *Sophist* has not rebutted the *Theaetetus'* arguments against the possibility of false identifications: though it reduces the area in which these arguments can cause trouble, it does nothing to alleviate the fundamental difficulty obstructing the understanding of identity judgments. To this extent, then, it appears that the *Theaetetus* is concerned with a different philosophical problem from that of the *Sophist*, and one which is not affected by the *Sophist*'s account of predicative judgments. This *may* I think be true. It is certainly true that much of the argument of this part of the dialogue takes as examples such mistakes as thinking that Theodorus is Theaetetus, and if the discussion raises any serious problems about this kind of mistake, then such problems would remain for anyone who has the *Sophist*'s account of predicative judgments. On the other hand, if I am right that Plato's real interest is in the kind of mistaken identity judgment which he takes to be involved in accepting such a false belief as that the Prudential Center is beautiful, there is no guarantee that the difficulties one might discover in the misidentification of persons and ordinary objects are the ones he is really concerning himself with. Mistaking Theaetetus for Theodorus is a rather different kind of thing from mistaking the beautiful for the ugly, and the difficulties Plato has in mind when he talks about knowing and yet not knowing a thing must be interpreted with the latter mistake primarily in mind. By following after the more ordinary kind of false identity judgment one may well misunderstand what is really at issue. It may turn out that there is really no general problem about false identity judgments raised at all, but only one about the special kind of misidentification involved in mistaking the beautiful for the ugly, whatever that turns out to be.

In any event, neither the concern with a "psychological"

difficulty about knowing and not knowing nor the interest in false identity judgments has any tendency to show that the *Theaetetus'* worries about false belief are not bound up most intimately with those of the *Sophist*. So far I have only given hints as to how the argument of the *Theaetetus* has to do with problems about the theory of meaning; now it is time to consider this question more directly.

B. *Euthydemus and Sophist*

The *Euthydemus*, as I remarked above, is the earliest of Plato's dialogues in which the problem of false belief arises. The argument Euthydemus invokes (283e 7-a 8) to prove that falsehood is impossible can be put as follows:[4]

Premiss (1): Anyone who says anything says some one definite thing, one of the things that are (ἓν τῶν ὄντων) and something different from the other ὄντα. He λέγει τὸ ὄν.

Premiss (2): To say what is (λέγειν τὸ ὄν) is to speak truly.

The conclusion follows immediately: to speak at all (and not merely remain silent or emit inarticulate noises) is to speak the truth.

Now as it stands this argument is evidently invalid because it involves a fallacy of equivocation. In order for the conclusion to follow the "saying what is" of the first premiss must have the same meaning as the "saying what is" of the second premiss. But this condition is palpably not met: premiss (2) employs a sense of τὸ ὄν or τὰ ὄντα which means "what *is the case*," while premiss (1) evidently means by τὸ ὄν "something that exists," "something that there is to say." The equivocation is even more obvious when the argument is put negatively, with the conclusion that speaking falsely must really be equivalent to not speaking at all. For when one defines false speaking as τὸ τὰ μὴ ὄντα λέγειν the meaning is "saying what is not the case," but this phrase has to be taken to mean "saying what doesn't exist" in order to make false speaking seem the same as saying nothing.

It was presumably this consideration which led Shorey to refer to the sophist's argument, both as it appears here and as Plato develops and refutes it in later dialogues, including the Sophist, as "the μὴ ὄν quibble."[5] But even in the Euthydemus there are signs that such a simple reply as the one just given is not satisfactory. For, obviously enough, the distinction between two senses of λέγειν τὸ ὄν will not dissolve the paradox for anyone whose view of what it is to say something meaningful commits him to holding that anyone who says anything, in saying τὸ ὄν (= "what exists"), also must say τὸ ὄν (= "what is the case"). Thus it may be that there is nothing more in Euthydemus' argument than the mere equivocation,[6] while nevertheless much more is at stake.[7] In Dionysodorus' argument against the possibility of contradiction, which follows immediately in the Euthydemus (285d 7-286b 6), the larger trouble can be seen arising.

Dionysodorus argues as follows: Contradiction evidently involves making two different and conflicting statements about one and the same thing. But this is impossible: either the λόγος I assert expresses the same πρᾶγμα as your λόγος, in which case we are saying the <u>same</u> thing; or else they express different πράγματα, in which case, so far from contradicting me you have merely changed the subject. How could I, who say a certain thing, be contradicted by you when you are not saying that thing at all?[8]

Now it is obvious that here, as earlier (283e 9) at the outset of Euthydemus' refutation of falsehood,[9] the thing that a statement is about is being thought of as specified not by the subject-expression alone but rather by the statement as a whole. Thus "Socrates is standing" and "Socrates is not standing" are not about one and the same thing, Socrates, and do not say different things about the same thing. Inasmuch as "standing" and "not standing" have different meanings, stand for different things, the two λόγοι are about different things. Socrates-plus-standing is a different thing from Socrates-plus-not-standing or Socrates-plus-sitting, and therefore any two λόγοι that differ in meaning are <u>about</u> different things; and since they are about different things no two statements ever <u>meet</u> each other so as to be conflicting or contradictory. In this way Dionysodorus is conflating the thing a statement <u>says</u> with the thing it is <u>about</u>.

Now let us go back to Euthydemus' argument about falsehood and consider it again, bearing in mind the conception of λόγος which emerges in Dionysodorus' denial of contradiction. Does that argument crumble when the distinction between being <u>the case</u> and being <u>in existence</u> is drawn? Obviously not. Any λόγος which is significant (and so says "things that exist") is correlated with a πρᾶγμα specified by the totality of the meaningful parts of the λόγος in question; if, however, this is so, any λόγος must be true since there is no truth about just the thing it expresses which it <u>can</u> contradict. And if it doesn't conflict with the truth, it must be true. Every meaningful λόγος has its πρᾶγμα, and no λόγος can do anything more than indicate its <u>own</u> object; so where is there room for falsehood, even granted that λέγειν τὸ ὄν is an ambiguous expression? Evidently the ambiguity of τὸ ὄν is not the real root of the most stringent denial of the possibility of falsehood.

It may be said that nevertheless there is nothing more to the argument than a superficial fallacy. For by appealing to Dionysodorus' denial of contradiction I have only retreated from the equivocation on τὸ ὄν to the further palpable confusion of thinking that the thing a statement says is what it is about. For it is only too evident that it is the subject-expression alone whose role in the sentence it is to pick out the thing talked about; the predicate-expression does the talking, and does nothing to fix the subject of discourse. Two sentences can be contradictory just because they can have the same subject-expressions, and their predicates can be such that nothing that has the one can have the other. It is only by ignoring these obvious points and conflating the two "things" in question that Dionysodorus is able to "prove" his point.

It should be observed that this reply has resorted to a thumbnail sketch of a theory of sentence-meaning and truth, replete with discriminations of role and talk of logical incompatibilities. Any one who attempts this reply must admit that in order to give a fully satisfactory answer to the argument, taken together with its farthest ramifications, one must engage in philosophical semantics. It requires an explicit theory of sentence-meaning to get fully clear of the problem of falsehood which the sophists have raised. This, of course, is exactly what Plato finally recognized in the *Sophist*, and his own theory of meaning there is, as we shall see below, very similar in intent and effect to the sketch given just above. That it was no *palpable* confusion which he had to overcome is testified to by the *Cratylus*' and *Theaetetus*' earnest and concentrated wrestlings with the old theory of meaning lying behind Dionysodorus' denial of contradiction. What this theory is it is now time to inquire.

As we have seen, Dionysodorus thinks that a sentence as a whole, and not merely its subject, determines what thing or things it is about. He is evidently assigning to each of the parts of a sentence the same role as that which is in fact performed by the subject: designation. It therefore suggests itself that behind his argument against the possibility of contradiction there lies a theory of the sentence whose main features are the two assertions: (a) A sentence contains a lot of *names* and (b) Names are simply strung together in order to make a sentence. Now, as we shall see, this conception of what it is to say something lies behind a number of passages in Plato's dialogues, but there is only one place where it is anything like explicitly stated. This is in Socrates' dream, which introduces the final section of the *Theaetetus* (201e 1-202b 5). The theory which Socrates expounds as something he has dreamed has sometimes been taken to be itself a theory of logos (= statement)[10] which exhibits the two features mentioned just above.

But it seems, in fact, that it is primarily a theory of logos in the sense of account or explanation and not a theory of statement _per se_. All the same, within the dream there is to be found not only the idea that naming is the fundamental linguistic operation but also an overt statement that a sentence is in effect just a collection of names.

The dream theory supposes that ordinary physical objects are collections of discrete parts and that the simple parts into which any such complex can be analyzed can be named but cannot be expressed by any more complex expression. It is possible to give a logos or account of a complex thing by listing its simple parts, but the parts themselves, being simple, have no such logos. Now about the simple elements Plato says not only that they cannot be analyzed into simpler parts but also that if they could be analyzed then they could not only be _named_ but also _said_ (202a 6-b 2). That is, the explanation or account of a thing which consists in listing its smallest parts by name is being thought of as simultaneously explaining the thing and _saying_ it: δεῖν δέ, εἴπερ . . . εἶχεν οἰκεῖον αὑτοῦ λόγον, ἄνευ τῶν ἄλλων ἁπάντων λέγεσθαι (202a 6-7). It appears, then, that the list of names constituting the explanation or account of a thing also makes up a statement in which the thing is _said_ (and not merely named); and, in fact, Plato goes on to avow the principle lying behind this view, namely that to put together several names is to utter a statement (ὀνομάτων γὰρ συμπλοκὴν εἶναι λόγου οὐσίαν, 202b 4-5). Saying something is here being identified with the successive naming of some things, and the mere fact that more than one name is uttered is apparently being thought of as sufficient to make the difference between a name and a statement.

Now it is most important to observe what is meant by "putting together" in this context. The actual formulation (just quoted) of the theory of statement held by Socrates' dreamed personages is closely similar to the form of words which expresses Plato's own later theory in the *Sophist* (cf. *Soph*. 262d 2-6, 263d 2-3). The *Sophist* does indeed mention both names and "saying parts" (ῥήματα, usually translated "verbs," but evidently intended to cover predicates in general[11]), whereas the *Theaetetus* refers only to names. But this omission is, of itself, of no consequence: even if the *Theaetetus* had mentioned both parts of the sentence, as the *Cratylus* seems to do in a similar context,[12] it would not have effected any essential difference in the theory. For it is the differentiation of function that is important, as we shall see in considering the *Sophist*, and the crucial fact about the *Theaetetus'* theory is that each meaningful part of the sentence is thought of as doing exactly the same thing--designating something. Συμπλοκή here means no more than juxtaposition, adding together, whereas in the *Sophist* it means really "interweaving" in a very strong sense implied by the explicit differentiation of function introduced there.

According to this theory, then, a statement is the result of adding one name to another; a complete thought is the thinking together of two (or more) objects. Thus the thought that Albertine was a boy is to be analyzed as the compound thought *Albertine*-*boy*, the substantive words of the sentence each being taken as the name of some object. To think such an object is to understand what the word in question means, and to think together the class of objects meant by the words of a given sentence is to understand the statement expressed by that sentence. Here, then, we find both a theory of sentence meaning and a theory of thinking and understanding so implicated with each other that to hold the one is tantamount to holding the other.

This theory, simple as it is, can easily be made very seductive. Suppose you begin by asking what are the likely causes of some one's misunderstanding something you say. If you say "Albertine was a boy," the most likely cause of misunderstanding or failure of understanding is your hearer's not knowing what Albertine is being referred to. If then you explain that you mean the character in Proust, and give your interlocutor the necessary page references in _Remembrance of Things Past_ so that he can acquaint himself with Albertine, and he does so, he will then understand the name "Albertine." His understanding of this name, one may say, will amount to his ability to think of just that character in Proust when you say "Albertine": in this sense, his understanding amounts to his having Albertine before his mind's eye when you say "Albertine."

But now supposing he has understood "Albertine" but still does not understand what you have said, what can have gone wrong? The only remaining source of error would appear to be failure to understand "boy." To teach the meaning of the word "boy" you then show him a succession of boys of all varieties, pronouncing the word on each occasion. He will come to understand the word when he grasps the common property exhibited in all these instances; and then his understanding of the word will be his ability to think just that property when the word "boy" is pronounced.

Suppose then he understands both substantive parts of the sentence. Can he now misunderstand or fail to understand? It seems not. To be sure, there are still "was" and "a"; but these are very pale things compared with "Albertine" and "boy," and even if one doesn't know about tenses and articles he will still get along pretty well. Particularly when one has primarily in mind the simplest predicative judgments--statements of the form "X is A" or "X is an A"--the importance of the "X" and the "A" so overshadow everything else that much of the time you could actually get along without knowing anything about the little words that come between. "A," "is," etc., are moreover, as Plato calls them, περιτρέχοντα (*Tht*. 202a 5) which attach to everything, and the fact that they turn up in connection with *everything* might be taken, in conjunction with currently fashionable theories about meaning, to show that they cannot be contributing anything to the meaning of the sentence. If a word can be attached to anything, it might be said, it cannot have any definite meaning, since to mean something definite is to exclude application to some things, as much as it is to imply application to others: anything that attaches to everything of every variety must indeed be pale and content-less. Some such implicit view as this may partly explain the neglect of the connector words and the exclusive interest in the substantive words of a sentence.

Naive as these notions are, they do have a certain plausibility;

and in any case once attention is focussed too exclusively on the more substantive words of the sentence, whether by the reasoning just given or by some other means, the theory of meaning found in the *Theaetetus'* dream follows naturally. If understanding and misunderstanding a sentence is a matter of knowing or not knowing the objects referred to in it, the meaning of a sentence (what it says) must just be the sum of its references. And it is easy to see how this view of the sentence could cause Dionysodorus' failure to understand contradiction. For since in this theory no distinction is marked between subject and predicate it is inevitable that changing *any* (substantive) word in a sentence should be regarded as changing the subject altogether, and from this the denial of contradiction follows.

It is worth noticing here how certain of Plato's own habits would make this theory both interesting and attractive to him. The two most striking features of the foregoing analysis are found also in much of Plato's own philosophizing in the middle period dialogues. These are (a) an emphasis on the substantive parts of the sentence to the exclusion of the others, and (b) the tendency to think of understanding a word, whether verb, adjective, proper noun, or common noun, as directing one's thought toward some *object*. The theory of Forms in the middle period dialogues exhibits both these tendencies in Plato's thinking. It was the preoccupation with adjectives, verbs, and nouns which, as they appeared in their ordinary contexts applied to the ordinary furniture of the world, seemed to be problematical, that led him to formulate the theory of Forms. Thus in the passage from *Republic*

VII already referred to (523a-524d) such a word as "hard" is said to turn out to be used in ordinary contexts with no clear meaning, since the perception which reports something to be hard also reports the same thing at the same time to be soft (524a 6 ff.). In order to find out what the senses can possibly be saying in such a case one has to concentrate on this word "hard" and ask what _it_ means--and not look closer at what the senses report to you _as_ hard To find out about _hard_ one requires to get at it all by itself, and the trouble about things judged by the senses is that by that route one always gets at _hard_ and _soft_ at once, to the detriment of one's understanding of either. In this way by concentrating on some such substantive words one ends by searching out some object to which one can direct his attention in order to satisfy the desire to isolate _hard_ just by itself. Whether or not Plato in the middle period dialogues had any firm theory which erected Forms for every adjective and common noun,[13] it is only too obvious that difficulties about the meanings of (at least some) such words occupied the forefront of his philosophical activity at this period; and it is no less obvious that he found the solution to these problems by thinking of these words as denoting certain objects such that to know them was to understand the words in question.

The theory of meaning, then, which is present in Socrates' dream in the _Theaetetus_ has certain essential features which would necessarily have struck a sympathetic cord in Plato himself, whatever its actual origin. And even to other people it can perhaps be made to seem natural, by some such reasoning as the one offered two paragraphs back. But consider what happens when it is pressed in a couple of places. There are, first, a number of obvious difficulties about syntax. The theory apparently says that a sentence is meaningful if and only if it consists of two or more meaningful "names." And this clearly fails to discriminate between "Socrates is a philosopher" and "walks rides," to say nothing of the more subtle semantically odd but not ungrammatical word-strings such as "Colorless green ideas sleep furiously."[14] One thing that Plato does in the Sophist is to introduce a rudimentary syntactical theory, involving the explicit recognition that a sentence must contain at least one noun (or "naming part") and one verb (or "saying part"): two nouns or two verbs do not yet make a sentence nor does one in pronouncing them in succession say anything. We need not, however, refuse to grant the atomistic theory explained above some measure of recognition of such syntactical elements in the meaning of a statement. We can imagine, for example, that such an atomistic account applies only within certain previously demarcated limits: syntactical requirements must be met before any string of words can be adjudged to have a meaning, but once this stipulation is fulfilled the meaning of a string of words is identical with the combined meanings of the substantive words it contains. Thus the crucial point is that the atomistic theory does not see any philosophical importance in the fact of syntactical restrictions; in recognizing them at all it must regard them as arbitrary and uninteresting from the point of view of philosophical semantics.

A second difficulty goes deeper. In considering the argument of the Euthydemus denying the possibility of contradiction I said that, in effect, Dionysodorus was confusing the thing a statement says with the thing it is about. How, on the atomistic theory just expounded, can this confusion be avoided? If the thing designated by the subject-expression is singled out as what the sentence is about, it must equally be admitted that the predicate has been assigned the function of designation; hence there would seem to be no ground for saying that "Albertine was a boy" and "Albertine was a girl" are about the same thing that is not also a ground for saying the same about "Girls are nice" and "Boys are nice." Furthermore, the atomistic theory has in effect made the sentence as a whole a kind of name, designating the compound object which has as parts the things designated by the individual words. This means that the sentence as a whole is doing exactly the same thing as an individual proper name; and if the criterion of two sentences being about different things is that different things are named in them, then any two non-identical sentences are about different things. By thinking of the meaning of a word as the object it designates, and of the meaning of a sentence as the combined designations of its words, this theory seems firmly committed to precisely the confusion which lay at the root of Dionysodorus' argument. What looks like contradiction is really a change of subject.

This same difficulty can obviously be carried further to show that atomism threatens to abolish falsehood. Clearly if a statement is false there must be another statement which expresses the truth about the matter in question and which the false statement contradicts. But as on atomistic principles there is no contradiction there is no falsehood either. The same point can be made more directly. Since the atomistic theory makes all sentences into (complex) names, and a name succeeds in performing its task if it manages to refer to something, all significant sentences must do successfully what they are intended to do: every significant sentence has its object, so wherein lies its defect? It appears that alleged false statements, no less than true, do designate something that _exists_, and it is not easy to see what more the true ones do to merit that title. Hence the atomistic theory appears to leave no room for false statements.

Faced with this difficulty a convinced atomist would have only one place to look to find room in his theory for falsehood. Falsehood must somehow consist in error in some one or more of the constituent names of a sentence. To have a false sentence you must somehow have a false name--a name which designates an object but does so less well ("falsely") than another name, which, were it used instead, would make the sentence true. Thus "Albertine was a boy" somehow says the same thing as "Albertine was a girl" (the same object, _Albertine-boy_, is referred to by both) but "boy" is the true name for _boy_ while "girl" is false, so that the first sentence expresses a truth, whereas the latter is false Some attempt along this line seems the only possible way of avoiding the untoward consequences just elicited from the theory. If naming is the only operation recognized by the theory some appeal to false names must be made in order to allow false saying. And the difficulty about contradiction can only be evaded by having _both_ statements somehow say the same thing (one of them well or truly, the other badly or falsely): otherwise there is no avoiding the consequence that so-called contradiction is just changing the subject.

We shall see in a moment that the *Cratylus'* concern with the notion of a false name is directed precisely at this problem: the *Cratylus* intends to develop a clear conception of false naming in order to invoke false names as the groundwork of a theory of false assertions. And the *Theaetetus'* idea that false statements must all reduce to false identity judgments is just the convinced atomist's attempt to save his theory by appealing to error in the mode of designating some part of the sentence's meaning--that is, to *mis-naming*, or (what comes to the same) misrecognition.

It will be useful, however, before turning to these further developments, to have in view the theory of meaning produced in the *Sophist*, on the basis of which Plato finally puts forward an account of falsehood that has some chance of being acceptable. I have at various places above referred to the main features of the new theory of meaning, but it will be useful to collect them here so as to see clearly the places where the atomistic theory was finally found deficient. The *Sophist* has been much studied and commented on, but, while acutely aware of the very great difficulties in understanding what Plato says there, I think commentators have not generally seen the importance of Plato's recognition of syntactical elements in the meaning of a sentence.[15] It is important to get this straight in order to show the bearing of the *Sophist's* discussion on the atomistic theory which, as I have been contending, is the main reason for Plato's interest in the sophists' argument against falsehood.

In the Sophist (260b 10-263d 5), the Eleatic Stranger, having argued at length the intercommunion of Forms and the consequent existence of not-being, at least under the aspect of the non-identity of any Form with any other, undertakes to show that statement and belief are such as to admit of not-being and hence of falsehood. At the beginning of the philosophical part of the dialogue (237a ff.) he has confessed the necessity of finding some analysis which will permit a logos to say τὰ μὴ ὄντα without implying that it says nothing at all: the sophists, as we have seen from the Euthydemus, can show that falsehood is impossible unless in saying what is not a logos nevertheless says something that exists (that there is to say). Here he turns, at last, to this task.

It may seem puzzling that, having shown the existence of what is not in a sense that does not give rise to any paradox, the Stranger should think his job still far from complete. But of course he must not only show that "what is not" is ambiguous, and does not always mean (if it could mean this at all) "what has no being whatsoever": he must show that when a statement is said to be false, and to say "what is not," the sense of "what is not" is an innocuous one which does not imply that saying nothing is saying something. Therefore, as he says (260a 7-8), he and Theaetetus must reach an agreement as to what logos is in order to refute the sophists once and for all. Once the nature of logos is understood the question can be faced whether, and if so how, logos "has a share in τὸ μὴ ὄν" (260d 6-8).

The argument therefore proceeds in two stages: first the Stranger asks the question what it is to say something, and then he shows how, given this analysis of statement, it is possible to say something false, something that "is not." Put very roughly, and subject to further clarification, he draws a sharp distinction between naming and saying something, and emphasizes the fact that in a statement something gets asserted of something else, and that this is not and cannot be a matter of naming merely. And falsehood then emerges as the assertion of one thing of another, where the thing asserted is not (not in the sense of non-existence, but in the sense of difference) any of the things to which the subject does in fact stand related as the statement represents them. There is, neither in true nor in false statements, anything non-existent being talked about or asserted of anything, since saying is not just naming; each part of the sentence, and the sentence as a whole, can be meaningful and yet what is said may be false.

The stranger's first move is, then, to propound a theory of logos. Here his crucial advance over the atomistic theory is in allowing more to be accomplished in a sentence than the designation of some existent things.[16] As I put it above, sentences also assert something of something. How do they manage to do this? The Stranger's exposition of his theory is very brief, and it will require a certain amount of interpretation to produce a clear answer to the question.

The Stranger begins immediately (261c ff.) by suggesting that not every meaningful word will fit together in a sentence with every other meaningful word. There are, in fact, two distinct <u>kinds</u> of words, ὀνόματα (or naming-words) and ῥήματα (literally "verbs" but probably including describing-words generally).[17] However meaningful any two individual words may be they do not when pronounced in succession necessarily constitute a logos that itself has any meaning: a succession of nouns, for example, or a succession of verbs, though meaningful in its parts, has no meaning as a <u>whole</u>. Any meaningful logos requires (at least) <u>one</u> naming-part and <u>one</u> describing-part: two such words fit together (262c 5-6) to form a new entity, the logos, whereas words not chosen according to this rule fail to combine and remain nothing more than individual names (or other words) with no more meaning than the meanings of each individual word. A logos, however, because of the fact that it consists of disparate parts performing different functions does succeed in meaning more than the meanings of its parts: anyone who pronounces in succession words that fit together in this way "indicates something about what is or comes to be or came to be or is about to be, and doesn't merely name something, but gets somewhere by weaving together descriptions with names" (262d 2-4). The effect, that is to say, of naming someone and then pronouncing a word meaning an action (262b 5-6) is that you assert that just that person is performing just that action: this you could not have done if the two words were merely juxtaposed and not really <u>fitted together</u>. The syntactical requirement about nouns and verbs (descriptions), which enables this interweaving and fitting together, turns out not to be the arbitrary and uninteresting thing which the atomistic theory assumed it to be, insofar as it took notice of it at all. For behind the syntactical requirement lies the essence of the logos, its ability to assert something, to get somewhere (περαίνειν τι) and do more than name something.

How, then, according to this theory, does a sentence manage to assert something? Plato says that the successive utterance of words does not indicate any fact or event until descriptions are mingled with names; and the ability of a stream of words of this sort to say something is put down to the fact that noun and description fit together (262c 5). What does this come to? The first point to notice is that the descriptions in Plato's examples (βαδίζει, τρέχει, καθεύδει) are all finite verbs, and not for example infinitives or (if he were speaking English) gerunds. "To walk" and "walking" are, as it were, names of verbs, and Plato might have constructed his list of verbs with infinitives or gerunds: walking, running, and sleeping, or to walk, to run, to sleep. I think it is crucial to the theory he means to adopt that his descriptions are all finite verbs and not infinitives or gerunds. For although "to walk" is as much a δήλωμα ἐπὶ ταῖς πράξεσιν (262a 3) as "walks," and perhaps more so, only the finite verb form comes with its function in the sentence already clearly marked. "Walks" demands to be completed by the addition of a name before it; its describing role is already fixed, whereas an infinitive, though perhaps a purer δήλωμα of an action, is for that very reason not a good candidate for the mixed role that descriptions play in sentences. Like "to walk," "walks" expresses the concept of walking (let us say), but unlike the infinitive the finite form is adapted to the additional function of fitting together with a noun so as to apply that concept to it. Plato's use of finite forms therefore suggests that the important part of his theory is the descriptive function which he assigns to ῥήματα, and not the fact (262a 1-7) that both a person and an action must appear in any complete sentence. The important point is the fitting together of name and action-word.

A statement, then, asserts something (and does not merely name or indicate some things that exist) because it contains a part whose function it is not only to indicate some object (say *walking*) but also to describe the object named by the subject of the sentence as performing the action indicated. By contrast with the atomistic conception set out above, this theory explicitly observes the difference between a name and a description and assigns to the parts of a sentence two separate functions. A sentence is to be regarded not as the sum of words which, taken in isolation, perform their linguistic role just as fully as when they are taken together in a sentence. By itself "Theaetetus" names Theaetetus, but by itself "walks," though perhaps it indicates *walking* and so has a meaning in isolation, does not actually perform its job of describing. It is only within the sentence that a finite verb accomplishes its task of describing something, and therefore a sentence cannot be regarded (as the atomistic theory regarded it) as an aggregate of words which could function just as effectively all by themselves. Though it is "flies" in "Theaetetus flies" which describes Theaetetus, "flies" taken by itself does not describe anything.

The Stranger's theory of logos therefore rejects the two central features of the atomistic account of the sentence. There are other fundamental linguistic operations than naming, and a sentence is not merely a collection of words functioning in complete independence of one another. It is obvious, of course, that the new theory, as explained by the Stranger and expounded above, is incomplete. It takes no ingenuity to think up examples for which it does not work. Word-order is not mentioned, nor is any account taken of semantical sources of meaninglessness. But it does accurately record the essential fact about a statement, that in it an <u>assertion</u> is made. The importance of this achievement overshadows all these other inadequacies: for Plato was the first person to reach explicit philosophical awareness of this absolutely fundamental fact about language and thought. That commentators have not given him credit for this accomplishment is due to the fact that they have not appreciated rightly the nature of the atomistic theory which Plato had to fight his way through.

The new theory of logos is, however, only part, though the absolutely essential part, of the Stranger's task. He must now show how, on this understanding of logos, false statements are possible in which however there is no attempt to name or refer to what is nothing at all. The subsequent explanation of falsehood (262e-263d) is extremely brief and difficult to interpret in detail with any assurance. What the Stranger wants to show is that sentences can convey falsehoods even though they meet all the requirements of meaningfulness, including the requirement that nothing non-existent be mentioned. He therefore points out, taking as examples "Theaetetus sits (is sitting)" and "Theaetetus is flying," two facts: (1) each sentence meets the syntactical requirement for saying something meaningful, as laid down above (262e 12-13), and (2) both the constituent words of each sentence have individually a meaning, i. e., they indicate something that exists (263c 7-11, b 11-12) Theaetetus, flying and sitting are definite somethings, and not nothings. Both sentences are meaningful, whether by the standards of the sophists or by those of the Stranger himself.

But in what consists the falsity of "Theaetetus is flying"? It is in deciding what Plato's answer to this question is that difficulties arise. The crucial lines (263b 4-12) read (omitting Theaetetus' responses):

(1) The true statement says things that are as they are in your case.

(2) While, then, the false says other things than the things that are

(3) So it says things that are not as if they were.

(4) Things that are, then, but things other than the things that are in your case. For we said that there are indeed in the case of each thing many things that are, and many that are not.

This specification of how falsehood comes about evidently employs the notion of otherness in some way. The usual view has been that Plato here explains falsehood as predicating of a thing something that is <u>not identical with</u> any of the things which it participates in.[18] The reason for thinking that this is Plato's view is presumably to be found in (2), taken together with the supposition that in thus associating the not-being of falsehood with otherness Plato means to be appealing to the sense of not-being as otherness established in the discussion of the communion of Forms earlier in the dialogue (252-259). And, though that discussion is in places quite obscure, there are grounds for thinking that the only kind of not-being which is there proved to exist is non-identity. Hence, it is thought, Plato must be saying that a false statement predicates something that is not identical with any of the things that the thing in question does in fact participate in.

Now I think myself that the traditional view is very probably correct; very likely, the sense of otherness Plato relies on in explaining how a false statement is meaningful and yet says "what is not" is the sense of non-identity. It is nevertheless true, as Moravcsik has argued,[19] that Plato's discussion of negation in 257b-258c, is not easily understandable as operating with a notion of non-identity exclusively; thus Plato says that τὸ μὴ καλόν is other than nothing else than τὸ καλόν (257d 10-11), while nevertheless recognizing (e. g., 259b) that everything is other than (not identical with) everything else. To go into the analysis of this very difficult passage of the <u>Sophist</u> would take us too far from our main concern, which is with the notions of saying and meaning and their connection with Plato's problem about falsehood. Nor shall I discuss the view about otherness which Moravcsik attempts to extract from the passage and apply to the analysis of falsehood in 262-263. But whatever sense of otherness 257-258 operates with, it is certain that otherness as non-identity is recognized by Plato; and I think it can be shown that this conception is all one needs in order to make Plato's analysis of falsehood both cogent in itself and persuasive against the sophists whom his discussion is mainly designed to placate. To show this much is enough for my purposes, since my interests here lie mainly in Plato's theory of meaning and statement and how this theory contributes to the solution of the problem of falsehood, and not in the detail of the analysis of negation and falsehood for their own sakes.

Moravcsik has argued[20] that the analysis of falsehood in terms of non-identity is a very faulty explanation. For if saying something false is saying something that is different from any of the things that are true in the particular case in question, it follows, he thinks, that in order to know that what someone has said is false one must know that the predicate expressed is different from all the predicates the subject does in fact bear. And surely this means that in order to know something to be false one must know all the truths there are to know about the thing. But in requiring that the predicate be non-identical with _any_ _and_ _all_ the predicates which the subject actually bears the proposed analysis appears to place an absurdly severe restriction on our ability to know any statement to be false.[21]

But does the analysis really require that finding out that something is false must entail this Herculean task? Moravcsik's criticism seems to involve the notion that in analyzing a concept one is providing rules for its application: thus if falsehood is analyzed as saying something different from anything that is true of the subject, Moravcsik concludes that on this analysis to determine that something is false one must acquire a list of all the things that are true of the subject and then establish that none of them is identical with what was asserted of it. But I think this misconceives the purpose of philosophical analysis in general and the aim of Plato's analysis of falsehood in particular. An analysis of a concept must, in general, at least provide for the extensional equivalence of *analysans* and *analysandum*, and in some cases perhaps identity of intension as well; but in no case must it provide rules for the application of a concept. Provided that the meaning of a word is not the same as the method of verifying that it applies to something, then to analyze a concept even in the sense of providing an intensional equivalent will not be the same as giving rules for its application. What it means to say that a sentence is false will then be distinct from how one shows it to be false, and there is no reason to expect that an analysis of falsehood should have anything specially to do with methods of verification. The methods for testing the falsehood of a statement, whatever they may be, will also, given the evident extensional equivalence of the analysis in terms of non-identity, be methods for testing whether the statement asserts something different from anything that is the case. Hence the analysis does not restrict methods of verification in any way in which they were not restricted before the provision of the analysis, and anyone who accepts it is free to employ any test of truth and falsehood which anyone else might use.

It is worth bearing in mind also that philosophical analyses are offered in a particular context and for a particular purpose. Plato's purpose in giving an analysis of falsehood, it should be recalled, is to show how, in the face of the sophists' objections, a false statement can be meaningful. For this purpose he needs only invoke notions which the sophists have no difficulty understanding and show how they are sufficient basis for vindicating the existence of meaningful falsehood. Hence he need not claim that "X is false" <u>means the same as</u> "X asserts something different . . . ," but only that if the sophists grant him, as he has argued they must, the concept of difference, he can show that meaningful falsehood exists. For this purpose the extensional equivalence of falsehood and his analysis in terms of difference is sufficient: in allowing the possibility of saying something meaningful where the predicate expression indicates something different from any of the things that are the case for a given subject, the sophists also admit falsehood.

It seems to me, then, that the analysis of falsehood in terms of non-identity which Plato is usually thought to have proposed is both cogent in itself and well-suited to his particular purposes. Hence although it is possible that 257-258 contains a different sense of otherness from this, and though the analysis of falsehood may, on close examination, turn out to employ the sense of otherness found there, Plato's argument can be made intelligible and satisfying on the basis of the fully-accredited sense of otherness as non-identity.

If then we assume that only the notion of non-identity is invoked, in addition to the account of statement already explained, the brief passage (263b 4-12), translated above, in which the theory of falsehood is explained has the following import. (1) Both true and false statements assert something of a subject. The true statement, that Theaetetus is sitting, asserts of Theaetetus that he is sitting, and one of the things that is the case about Theaetetus is that he is sitting. There is nothing in the text implying any particular analysis of the fact that Theaetetus is sitting--not, for example, an analysis in terms of participation in a Form Sitting, though I see no harm in thinking of the matter in this way. Whether one thinks of sitting as a Form in which Theaetetus participates, or just as an action he is performing, the important point is that the Form or the action is not just indicated by some word in the sentence, but is *asserted of* the subject by means of the fitting together of finite verb and name. (2) The false statement likewise asserts something, but what it asserts is not any of the things that are the case about Theaetetus. Given that the sophists understand what assertion is and what it is for something to be true of a subject, and given that they allow assertions of non-identity, they have no ground for objection to this. (3-4) Hence false statements say "Things that are not," but as we have now seen there is nothing to be feared in this. The things said are not nothing, they are merely different from some other things; but because these other things are all the truths about the given subject we have by this method introduced falsehood.

This theory of truth and falsehood is, roughly speaking, a theory of correspondence of statement to fact. Thus we may think of the true statement as asserting a relation between Theaetetus and Sitting which does in fact obtain, and the false statement then asserts a relation between Theaetetus and Flying which does not correspond to the facts.

But it is important to notice exactly how the correspondence or lack of it is conceived of. Wittgenstein in the Tractatus, for example, thought that correspondence (for elementary propositions) was a matter of similarity of structure in fact and proposition; the names in the proposition were in a certain order or arrangement and the objects named were similarly related, so that in effect the proposition pictured the fact. A false proposition was a picture of a possible state of affairs which just happened not to exist. Now it should be observed that a theory of this type, though more sophisticated than the type of atomism expounded above (since it introduces the idea of structure or ordering of elements), fails to get round the sophists' difficulties with falsehood. For if in general a proposition has three parts, two names and a relation between them, and one thinks of falsehood as the relating of elements of language in a way in which the correlated elements of reality are not related, the sophist seems free to raise his old objection against the possibility of indicating something non-existent. For though the two names might have existent objects, the relation between them would have nothing to correspond to and would therefore be indicating something non-existent. Plato's theory, as I have interpreted it, evades the difficulty because it differentiates between the function of indicating (standing for, referring to) and the function of describing; there is no third thing in a sentence, the relation between the elements, which either corresponds or fails to correspond to a relation between elements of reality. It is the finite verb itself, or in general the predicate, which, put together with a name, does the job of assertion, and assertion is not reduced to any kind of indicating or standing for. Hence there is no room for the sophist to object that a false sentence, or any part of it, refers to or stands for or indicates (or pictures) something non-existent.

Plato's theory of meaning in the *Sophist*, then, is an important advance over the naive theory lying behind the sophists' objections to falsehood. Without it the sophists' denial of falsehood could not have been rebutted. Not even the notion of not-being as non-identity would be of any use in the absence of the Stranger's theory of statement. It would not help to be able meaningfully to say that sitting is not identical with flying (*et al*) if one did not see how "Theaetetus is flying" *affirms* something of Theaetetus. In the *Cratylus* and *Theaetetus*, to which we must now turn, we shall see some of the difficulties which arise if one fails to see that asserting is as fundamental and necessary a linguistic operation as naming.

C. *Cratylus and Theaetetus*

In the *Cratylus* Socrates is called upon to adjudicate the dispute which has broken out between Hermogenes and Cratylus over the question of the origin of names. Do words come to have their meanings by convention, as Hermogenes holds, or do they have their meanings, as Cratylus believes, somehow by nature, by some natural relation (e.g., that of resemblance) to the things they name? In the course of this discussion many different points are made which bear on a number of different topics in which Plato was interested.[22] One topic that figures prominently is the relation of naming to saying and the problem how falsehood is possible.

In the course of the dialogue Socrates manages to embroil both Hermogenes and Cratylus--the former unwillingly, the latter willingly--in the denial of falsehood. In order to do this he obtains their assent to a version of the atomistic theory I have expounded above and represents them as failing to, or refusing to, distinguish between what a name means (refers to) and what a particular speaker may mean (refer to) by it. The effect of the failure to make this distinction is to prevent both naturalism and conventionalism from maintaining the existence of "false" names (names which refer but do so badly); and this result, coupled with the atomistic conception of the meaning of a sentence, effectively stops either from granting the possibility of falsehood. Socrates himself then builds upon Cratylus' theory that a name has meaning by somehow resembling the thing it names, in order to draw the distinction between what a name means and what a particular person means by it (applies it to); and having done this he proposes a theory of falsehood which continues to construe a sentence as merely a collection of names but attempts to permit some names to be false so that logoi may be false as well. Thus the whole discussion, including Socrates' positive contribution, operates within the framework of the old theory of meaning, and the only advance Socrates makes over Hermogenes and Cratylus is in his recognition of two functions of a name when actually used by somebody, as naming the thing the person uses it as a name of and naming the thing it is itself a name of. One may use a name as the name of something that it does not in fact name; and falsehood of a sentence is construed as falsehood of this sort in one or more of its constituent names.

Hermogenes has hardly enunciated his theory of conventionalism before Socrates finds in it a threat to the existence of falsehood. Hermogenes has said (384d 2-4) that any one can establish any name he pleases as meaning anything he wishes, and can change his conventions whenever he is so inclined; and it has been emphasized (385a 4-10) that *each* person has the right to whatever use of words he pleases, whether or not it agrees with any one else's. This is taken to mean that "whatever name any one says a thing has" (ὃ ἂν φῇ τῳ ὄνομα εἶναι) really belongs to it (385d 1-2), and this already suggests that no name can be false For if I use "horse" to refer to an animal standing before me, and the names I use refer to whatever I take them to, then "horse" is the correct name (now, for me) for this animal. No one can ever misuse a name because to use it at all is to name something with it, and Hermogenes' conventionalist views commit him to the thesis that whatever any one decides to use a name as the name of is correctly designated by that name.

It is important to realize that Hermogenes thinks of all words as names, as expressions which denote or refer to something; and his extreme conventionalism therefore amounts to the thesis that any one can refer to anything he pleases by whatever name he pleases. And from this it is a short step to the denial of falsehood (misuse of names) which Socrates attempts to force on him. Hermogenes ought, of course, to have resisted the inference by insisting that his conventionalism is a theory entirely about how names are *introduced* or *coined* as names of things; and since falsehood involves the misuse of a name once its reference is fixed, which his theory does nothing to disallow, he has not said anything implying that there are no false statements.

This reply insists merely upon the difference between naming something x (= baptizing it) and calling something X (referring to it by X), and Hermogenes certainly intends to be holding just the theory that baptisms all take place by convention (385d 7-9). Socrates is able to browbeat him into half-admitting that his theory denies the possibility of falsehood because both baptizing something and using a name to refer to a thing are naming it; this enables Socrates to slide from Hermogenes' claim that no baptism is truer or more correct than any other to the claim that no application of a name is more right than any other Of course, had Hermogenes' conventionalism included a distinction between naming and describing this confusion would have been more easily prevented. For, to take Hermogenes' examples of "horse" and "man," when I call something a man I am not naming him at all, but describing him; "man" is a name for a species or a concept or whatever, and in giving the word a meaning, on conventionalist assumptions, one establishes it as a name for that concept (say), which it then conventionally expresses. And thereafter, on occasions when it is used, it is used to describe (etc.), correctly or incorrectly, the things to which it is applied, and not to name them. Hence given these distinctions Hermogenes could straightway deny Socrates the means of collapsing his conventionalism into a denial of falsehood.

But Hermogenes is determined to think of all use of words, as well as all introduction of words, as simply naming or referring to things. Even so, however, he has the means of admitting the possibility of a false name, provided that he recognizes the distinction between what a name names (has been introduced to name) and what a person on a particular occasion names by it. The universal correctness of the former sort of naming does not imply the universal correctness of the latter sort.

Hermogenes is however not permitted even this distinction: Socrates will invoke it later on his own account, but neither Hermogenes nor Cratylus is permitted to appropriate it to his own use. Hence Hermogenes is stuck with the consequence that no name can be false, that is to say, not the name of the thing the speaker uses it to refer to. If this is so, Socrates at once argues, then no statement can be false. For a true logos is one in which all the constituent names are true (385c), and a false logos has necessarily a false element. But since, as Hermogenes' theories seem to imply, no name can ever be false, no logos can ever be false either. Hence conventionalism does away with falsehood and makes everything true.

Socrates here manifestly invokes a theory of logos that is fundamentally the same as that which is to be found in the _Theaetetus_ (201-202). The _Theaetetus_ has a theory of simple elements of reality with corresponding simple names which is lacking in the _Cratylus_ passage, but it also contains the view, as we have seen, that a statement is a collection of names each of which performs the single function of designation; and this theory pretty clearly lies behind Socrates' view about falsehood in the _Cratylus_ passage. For if he thinks that the only possible source of falsehood in a logos is falsehood in some one or more of its constituent names, he evidently ignores or fails to notice the contribution made to the sentence by everything other than the names it contains, taken one by one. That this is what he has in mind becomes explicit later in the dialogue in his examination of Cratylus' naturalist doctrine.

Cratylus holds the view that each word comes to name a thing by some natural process and altogether without any convention or decision on the part of any man. Like Hermogenes he regards his theory primarily as an account of how words come to have the meanings they do have, and therefore his main contention should involve something about how one word is fit to express a certain _concept_ and another another, or how one word is appropriate to one _type_ of object. But, again like Hermogenes, he fails to draw the distinctions necessary to permit him to state this doctrine clearly. Just as Hermogenes' conventionalism turns out to prohibit not only false names in the sense of names not suited to express the meanings they do express, but also false names in the sense of names wrongly applied to particular things, so naturalism as upheld by Cratylus makes it impossible for a name to be false in either of these ways. If a name has its meaning by nature--say by resembling the thing it names--then its meaning is fixed; no matter what use you may try to put it to _it_ continues to refer to whatever it resembles. Hence "Hermogenes" (meaning "sprung from Hermes") is not the name of Hermogenes, who has not the correct character, but of someone else whom the name fits (429b 12-c 4). And if any one tries to refer by this name to someone to whom it does not by nature belong he will simply not have performed any language-act at all: it will be as if he made an empty motion like striking a gong (430a 4-5). All names, then, according to Cratylus, which are really (meaningful) <u>names</u>, are correct (429b 10-11). And this is taken to mean that either a speaker means by a name what <u>it</u> means or he means nothing: in apparently naming a donkey standing before me a "horse" I either perform no significant act of speech or else I in fact refer to something else, viz., whatever "horse" correctly names. Whereas for Hermogenes a name always means what I mean by it, Cratylus' doctrine maintains that I always mean (if anything) what the name I utter means.

Socrates is quick to see that Cratylus' theory commits him to the denial of falsehood. Cratylus in fact happily admits that he thinks falsehood impossible and supports this conviction by direct appeal to the impossibility of saying what is not (429d 4-6). But it is evident that his views commit him to the denial more indirectly as well: if as Socrates has argued a false logos must contain a false name then given Cratylus' view that all names are correct all logoi must be true (or else meaningless). The denial of the possibility of falsehood therefore results for Cratylus, as it resulted for Hermogenes, from a combination of two theses, or rather one thesis and the failure to draw a distinction: the thesis that a logos is the sum of its constituent names and the failure to permit that while a name may itself name one thing a person may refer by it to another.

In the sequel (430a 6-433b 7) Socrates reaffirms the theory of logos while attempting to draw upon the possibility of mis-naming to show how false logoi can occur. He begins by recalling the theory he has earlier proposed (422a-424a), that fundamentally the meaning of words is due to their being copies or imitations of the things they mean. Cratylus not unreasonably accepts (430a 10-b 2) this theory as a plausible interpretation of his own otherwise unexplained[23] contention that names have a meaning grounded in nature. Socrates presses the notion of a copy to show (430a-431b) that, just as when one has two pictures of different people it is possible to take the picture of A to be a picture of B, so if names are copies of the things they designate it is possible to mistake the name of one thing for that of another, and when this happens one gets a <u>false</u> name. The effect of Socrates' argument here is to distinguish, at last, between what the name actually is the name of and what someone may mistakenly use it to designate. For in taking the name of A for that of B and using the name "A" to refer to B, I make a mistake--just as if someone should take a picture of A and hold it up to B, thinking it a picture of him (430e 3-431a 5). In either case a mistake is made, and in the case of names we say that <u>false</u> naming has occurred, as well as mistaken attribution (430d 2-7).

Plato is often taken[24] to have given in this comparison of a false name with a wrong attribution of a picture, a brief but quite adequate explanation of falsehood. No doubt the ground for thinking this is that Socrates seems to say that falsehood results when one <u>misdescribes</u> a person as a man or a woman, just as it is an error to take a picture of a man as resembling a woman. This impression is reinforced by the fact that at a crucial point in the passage (430e 9-431a 5) Socrates shifts from talking about pictures and names of just <u>one</u> individual (portraits and proper names) and talks instead as if the misappropriation of names involved saying of a particular man that he is <u>a</u> woman. And this appears to show that misdescription or false predication is what he has in view. But the very fact that he shifts so freely from proper names and portraits to general terms is proof that he is thinking of the general term "man" as being a kind of proper name of all the men, taken separately; and the false naming he envisages amounts to referring to something as a "woman" which yet is not identical with any of the things which "woman" properly names. Hence the false naming is not misdescribing and the view of the falsehood of a name which Socrates recommends is not so adequate as it at first might appear.

At any rate the account of sentence-falsehood Socrates goes on to develop on the basis of mis-naming has nothing in common with the theory of falsehood of the <u>Sophist</u>, in which misdescribing is the very nub of the explanation. For he immediately argues that if a name can be misapplied in the way explained so can a ῥῆμα. He gives no illustration of what he means by ῥῆμα here or what he thinks the parallel mistake about ῥήματα would be. But, even if one supposes him to mean "verb" by ῥῆμα,[25] the mistake he has in mind is presumably that one could use "riding" to say what someone is doing when he is in fact walking, and such a mistake would amount to taking walking for riding. In any case from the fact that names and "verbs" can be false he infers that statements as well, since they are merely collections of names and verbs, can be false (431b 5-c 1). It is obvious that here Socrates assumes that the truth or falsehood of a statement is the result of the rightness or wrongness of its individual words taken in isolation from one another and from the logos. "Man," "walks," etc., each refer to something (or some things), and if a person uses "man" to refer to that thing (or one of those things), and likewise uses "walks" correctly, and so on for each word in a group, then what he has said is true; the only thing that can make what he says false is the misuse of some one or more of the individual words.

This account of falsehood is amplified and further defended in the passage immediately following (431c 4-433b 5). Socrates begins by discussing a point quite different from the one he has just been making, and the relevance of what he says to the possibility of false naming appealed to above only emerges towards the end of the passage. A portrait is well made, Socrates urges, when it contains the proper colors and shapes, etc.; but it does not cease to be a portrait just as soon as a wrong color is introduced. It is still a portrait, only a bad one. Likewise for names: "Hermogenes" is just a faulty copy of Hermogenes, it doesn't fail altogether to copy him, or become a copy of someone else. If its letters fail to correspond exactly to Hermogenes' basic character, that does not make it not Hermogenes' name, any more than a few incorrect colors or lines in a portrait make it cease to be a picture of the person represented. In fact, Cratylus is quite wrong to insist that every name that *truly* names anything must be correct, because since names are imitations of their *nominata* it *must* be possible for the imitation someone produces to be a bad one. It is of the essence of an ὄνομα that it should be a *copy* and not an exact replica, corresponding in every single detail to its original: a "copy" that differed not at all from its original would not be a copy at all, but a re-creation of it. Cratylus and his picture must be two different things, original and copy, and not two of the same thing: one does not want in making a picture or statue of Cratylus to end up with *two* Cratyluses (432a 8-c 5). Hence a name, as copy, must fall short in a variety of ways, and in varying degrees, of its original. The very basis of the theory of natural naming, therefore, requires that there be room for some names to be well made and others badly made; if to name something is to imitate it in letters and syllables (μιμεῖσθαι γράμμασί τε καὶ συλλαβαῖς, 423e 7-8) then one can perform this task with varying degrees of competence, and names can be both well and badly made

Now this further elaboration of the copy-theory of names is in the first instance directed not to our problem, the possibility of *using* a name on some occasion to indicate something which the name itself does not indicate, but to the quite different question whether there are grounds for distinguishing between a better and a worse established *usage*. Socrates himself speaks of νομοθέται here, and is at least part of the time talking about the formation of names and the assignment to them of their meanings (εἰκόνας ἐργάζεται, 431c 12).

In the preceding discussion of true and false naming and true and false statement, he has been talking not about the making of a name or a picture but of the use one may make of these εἰκόνες once they have been constructed. His point there was that one can misuse an εἰκών and thus falsely name something; here he is showing that one εἰκών can be better than another at imitating its original, and yet both are εἰκόνες of the same thing. Hence there is room for bad or wrong names in two senses: names which are the established names for certain kinds of things (or certain individual things) but which are πονηραὶ εἰκόνες of them, and names which are on particular occasions used as the names of certain things of which they are not εἰκόνες at all. Both name-creators and name-users can go wrong, in their different ways.

But though the ways in which they err are different, there is a close analogy between what happens in the two cases, and Socrates emphasizes (432d 11-433b 5) the parallels between them. A name is a collection of letters, just as a logos is a collection of names. What makes a name not a good name, as we saw, is its containing some wrong letters, i. e., letters which do not correspond to the nature of the thing being named. Likewise, Socrates now tells us, a logos can have some wrong names in it, i. e., names which do not correctly name the thing to which they are referred. But we have now seen that even when a name is not the best or fully correct name for a thing it nevertheless does name it, if it is copied after it. So also a logos that contains false names, and is therefore false, does not fail to refer to a thing or fact (in which case it would be meaningless) or just have a different subject matter from the true statement which it is thought to contradict: it states the same things as the true statement, only not so well, since some part of the things or facts reported are mis-named and so badly referred to. Thus a statement with wrong names in it does have a meaning (just as a bad name is notwithstanding a name), and nevertheless containing false names as it does, what it says is false.

It is important to see exactly what Socrates is suggesting here. His point can be put in the following way. Suppose two sentences which differ only with respect to some one word: e g , "The cat is on the mat" and "The cat is on the pillow " Very likely when these sentences are simultaneously affirmed only one of them will be true. Now we saw in the Euthydemus that when, for example, the cat is in fact on the mat, the statement asserting this fact is true, it λέγει τὸ πρᾶγμα περὶ οὗ ἂν ὁ λόγος ᾖ (283e 9). And the trouble then arose what to do with the statement that the cat is on the pillow. It appeared that just because the one statement said "pillow" where the other said "mat," they were simply talking about different things, stating different facts, not possibly incompatible (286b 3-5). The one stated the fact that the cat is on the mat, the other just didn't state that fact at all (b 5-6); hence, so far as their difference goes both might be true. Here, in the Cratylus, however, Socrates thinks this view too simple. It is not true that the false statement doesn't say the same πράγματα as the true one. Because we have introduced the notion of false reference we are in a position now to see how the two statements can be both stating, in a way, the same facts: in the false statement "pillow" does not name something different from what "mat" does in the true one. They name the same thing (the mat), only one is its true name, the other a false one. Hence in the false statement μηδὲν ἧττον ὀνομάζεσθαι τὸ πρᾶγμα καὶ λέγεσθαι (432e 5-6); since the sentences are otherwise identical they are similar enough to state the same group of things (just as two different but similar names can be allowed to name the same thing), ἕως ἂν ὁ τύπος ἐνῇ τοῦ πράγματος περὶ οὗ ἂν ὁ λόγος ᾖ (e 6-7). Under these circumstances λέξεταί γε τὸ πρᾶγμα, but κακῶς (433a 5-6). Thus the introduction of the notion of a false name has enabled Socrates to get round the old objection to falsehood and contradiction by making both true and false statements say, in a way, the <u>same</u> things. Falsehood is due to the fact that, though all the things in question are said, one (at least) is given a false name.[26]

The upshot, as Socrates says, is that so long as Cratylus accepts the theory of natural naming he cannot consistently deny that falsehood is possible in names and logoi, nor can he insist that every word expresses perfectly whatever meaning it has. But Socrates in what follows also shows pretty clearly that no such theory of natural naming as the one he has earlier constructed with an eye to Cratylus' thesis can be true: as the example of σκληρότης ("hardness") proves, those who so pronounce the word certainly do not mean the thing any less or more effectively than the Eretrians, who say σκληροτήρ--and this despite the fact that ρ and σ have by no means the same force according to a naturalist account (434c-435c). The ability of words to do their jobs effectively, or more and less effectively, is certainly not a result of their resembling more or less closely the things meant. Does Socrates' belated rejection of his theory of natural naming mean that the account of falsehood just explained goes by the board as well, as merely the best one can do on a naturalist basis and therefore nothing Socrates is either committed to or ultimately attracted by?

I have already remarked that, aside from details drawn from the copy theory, Socrates relies upon two theses in constructing his theory of falsehood: the distinction between what someone uses a name to designate and what the name itself names, and the view that the meaning of a sentence is the sum of the meanings of its constituent words. Now neither of these two features of the account of falsehood is in any way withdrawn or, in the case of the theory of logos, even questioned anywhere in the *Cratylus*. Obviously they are at least as much the property of Socrates as they are Hermogenes' or Cratylus'. If, therefore, only this distinction and the theory of logos figure essentially in the account of falsehood, there is no reason to conclude that Socrates in the end rejects that account or that he only intended it as a theory appropriate to the doctrine of natural naming. And in fact it is easy to see that what Socrates says nowhere depends essentially upon the conception of names as copies of things. The possibility of misnaming for which he argues at 430a-431a obviously remains a possibility however words come to have established meanings, whether by nature or by convention or in any other way you like. So long as it is legitimate to argue that though a name does in fact name one thing it can be made to refer to something else, this part of the theory remains intact. The copy-theory here only provides a concrete illustration of the general point. Likewise, and even more obviously, the theory of logos which makes a mistake in naming result in a mis-statement is entirely independent of the copy-theory.

There remains only one part of the account where some close reliance upon the copy-theory may be looked for. This is the comparison of the badly made name and the false statement For here Socrates implies that what enables a true and a false statement to contradict one another is the fact that they are sufficiently alike so that each can be referred to the same things and thus both can, in a way, be reporting the same facts And he implies that what connects a sentence as a whole with the set of things it means or says is its resemblance to them, just as an individual name has its meaning by resemblance. A wrong letter here or there does not do away with the overall resemblance of name to thing, and similarly a wrong name or two in a sentence doesn't prevent it from being a report of the same facts or things as a sentence with no wrong names in it. As he says, even in the false statement the τύπος of the fact referred to remains (432e 6), and this is as much as to say that the false sentence doesn't altogether fail to resemble the facts. The notion of meaning and reference by imitation thus plays an important part in the final statement of the theory; it is, in fact, invoked to explain how false and true statements manage to come into conflict by referring to or reporting the same facts

It is true that for any atomistic theory of meaning and any attempt to explain falsehood as misnaming there must be a problem in explaining how the false statement manages to become connected with the facts it reports badly If the fact is that Socrates is walking and I say "Socrates is riding," then for what I say to be false not only must "riding" be the wrong name for what Socrates is doing, but I must also be intending to name what he is doing when I say "riding." My words have to be directed as it were, at just Socrates and the walking; if, for example, "Socrates" is directed at Socrates but "riding" not at Socrates' walking but at some riding being done elsewhere in the vicinity then despite the fact that "riding" is a bad name for walking, which Socrates is doing, what I have said will not be false. When he first introduced the notion of a false name in his examination of Cratylus (430a-431b), Socrates seemed to be thinking that the reference of the false name was made unambiguous by some kind of ostension--he thinks of a speaker approaching Cratylus, pointing to him, and saying "Your name is 'man'" (cf. 430e 9 ff.). He is encouraged in this by his example: since "man" in the predicate of such a judgment as "Cratylus is a man" is thought of as a name of just the same thing as the subject "Cratylus" names, there is no doubt what thing is being named by the word, once the reference of "Cratylus" is fixed. But in more complex judgments where each part names a separate element in the situation (Socrates, the walking) possibilities of ambiguity obviously arise. It seems that the resemblance of statement to facts is intended to cover such cases: because most of the names are correct the statement as a whole is tied by resemblance to a set of facts and the deviant name is thereby given its reference. "Socrates is standing on the chair" is referred to Socrates' standing on the table by the general resemblance of statement and fact, and "chair" is clearly then trying to name the table. The false name is referred, as it were, to the thing in the fact which remains unnamed when all the true names are correlated with their objects.

Now this is obviously very crude, and, in fact, it is just here that the Theaetetus presses the idea that falsehood amounts to misnaming: the notion of the speaker's intention in using his words must be brought in more explicitly, but when it is introduced the Theaetetus has difficulty in understanding how a person can intend to name (e.g.) some walking and yet call it riding instead. In the Cratylus these problems do not yet arise, since the picture-theory effectively slurs them over. But it can now be seen that the picture theory is not an essential part of Socrates' view that the false and the true statement both report the same things or facts: if one has in reserve some such notion as the speaker's intentions then no special resemblance account will be needed to ensure that the false statement is trying, but failing, to name correctly the same πρᾶγμα as the true one. No doubt the conventionalist thesis which Hermogenes should have defended would be able to hold a theory of falsehood in all essentials like the one Socrates expounds in 432e-433a: it needs only assume that a speaker can intend to be reporting a set of things and yet misname one or more of them.

It appears, therefore, that though the theory of falsehood Socrates propounds in 430-433 is tailored for the specific copy-theory constructed by himself earlier and accepted by Cratylus, its truth is nowhere made to depend upon the special thesis that a sentence gets its reference by means of resemblance. Hence when Socrates rejects the copy-theory for the reasons given above, he does not reject the theory of falsehood. Given his continued acceptance of the view of a sentence as a collection of names and his doctrine of false naming, the account of false sentences remains untouched.

It is now time, at last, to return to the *Theaetetus* itself and examine the troubles raised and pursued there concerning the notion of false judgment or belief. If we bear in mind the theory of meaning lying behind the denial of falsehood in the *Euthydemus* and the reply to the *Euthydemus*' arguments which the *Cratylus* constructs on the basis of the same theory, the immediate concerns of the *Theaetetus* easily fall into place.

First of all, the immediate assumptions of Socrates' argument in the *Theaetetus* now have a clear enough sense and direction. First the assumption that false belief must amount to the false identification of one thing with another (188b). As we have now seen, on the theory of meaning with which Plato has been occupied earlier there is hardly room for falsehood of any other sort; and the *Cratylus* has explicitly traced falsehood in sentences involving predication to this kind of error. Socrates' assumption that falsehood must amount to misrecognition therefore alerts us that the old theory of meaning is still on the agenda in the *Theaetetus*.

The other puzzling assumption Socrates introduces holds that for our purposes everything falls into one of two disjoint classes for any person, the things he knows and those he does not know. This does not mean that given any true proposition a man at any given moment either knows it or doesn't know it, but is rather a division of *objects* (broadly conceived as including both persons and, apparently, attributes).[27] And it very soon emerges (188b) that if you don't know a thing you can't have it in your thoughts, so that to be directing your thought to some object is taken as requiring knowledge of it. This in turn seems to imply (188b 3-5) that you cannot be thinking of a thing unless you recognize it. The division of things known and things unknown therefore amounts to a division between what anyone has in his thoughts, recognizing it for itself, and what he does not have in his thoughts at all. Combined with the first assumption this division produces the paradox that false thinking is impossible, since there cannot be any thought of an object which yet mistakes it for something else, and if there are no mistakes of this sort there are no false thoughts at all.

Why then does Socrates assume that to have anything in mind is necessarily to recognize it and therefore not to make a mistake about it? The source of this assumption, like that of the other assumption mentioned above, can be found in the theory of falsehood Socrates sets up in the *Cratylus*. In discussing this theory above I said that any atomistic theory of meaning which makes falsehood a matter of misnaming some part of the things or facts reported must explain how the false name comes to be applied to the thing it is used to name. In some cases, of course, as Socrates in the *Cratylus* recognized, what thing is meant will be obvious from the circumstances--one points and says "horse," or otherwise shows what thing is intended. But in general such external aids are not available, and something else must be brought in and appealed to as establishing the connection between name and thing. Clearly enough what is required is reference to what the speaker intended to name by the word: even where there are such external signs as pointing, it might be said, no amount of gesticulation can make the word name the thing unless the speaker is directing his thought to the same thing as he is pointing to. The *Theaetetus*, in shifting from false *statement* to false *thinking*, takes account of this fact. A false statement requires both false naming and false thinking; false naming involves directing one's thought toward an object, having it before one's mind, and then giving it a wrong name. And just here is where the *Theaetetus'* difficulties with falsehood begin. If one has an object before his mind how can he misname it? To misname it is to fail to recognize it for what it is, to confuse it with something else, and this seems impossible. Suppose for example that you have walking before your mind and say to yourself "sitting." You understand what this word means; sitting is something you know. Hence when you say "sitting" and understand what you are saying, you must have sitting before your mind as well. Then to misname walking as "sitting" is to have two objects before your mind, walking and sitting, while thinking they are one: walking is taken to be sitting. But this seems impossible, because in having these two things in mind you must know _that_ the one is walking, _that_ the other is sitting, and therefore that they are two and not one. If you do not know that it is walking that you have in mind, what justifies any one in saying that by "sitting" you referred falsely to walking? The requirement that you know both what "sitting" means and what thing you are referring to by it seems to end by requiring that you confuse two things together while at the same time knowing them to be perfectly distinct.

The assumption that you must know anything that can be an object of your thought is therefore intimately related to the theories of meaning and falsehood Socrates was working with in the _Cratylus_. Those theories have required that one have a thing in mind and yet not know it for itself; and the _Theaetetus_ begins its examination of falsehood by expressing its puzzlement over how these requirements can be met. And if they cannot, as the _Theaetetus_ immediately sees, then the proposed explanation of falsehood falls to the ground.

Before pursuing the problem further the _Theaetetus_ pauses, as I have already remarked, to consider briefly the problem of falsehood κατὰ τὸ εἶναι καὶ μή. The brief rehearsal of the sophists' puzzle about thinking what is false entailing not thinking at all, is largely ignored in what follows: the only important effect it has on the subsequent argumentation is in the analysis of falsehood as ἀλλοδοξία which is produced in the immediately succeeding passage (189b 10-190e 4). The sophists' argument had alleged that thinking falsely was thinking things that do not exist, and Socrates in supposing that error consists in ἀλλοδοξία explicitly mentions (189c 1-2) that the things which on this account are objects of thought in false belief are all of them ὄντα.

For the rest, the definition of false belief as ἀλλοδοξία seems intended to bring out more fully and explicitly the difficulties already hinted at, somewhat obscurely, in the initial statement of the problem at 187d-188c. According to this definition, the first of three proposals tried in the course of the discussion, whenever any one thinks something false he exchanges in his thought one existing thing for another. False thinking is just mistaking something for something else.

Now this definition is meant to cover all types of false judgment, as indeed any one should see if he bears in mind what is said in the <u>Cratylus</u>. This is made clear immediately (189c 5-7) by Theaetetus' remark that just the kind of exchange which Socrates has in mind does in fact occur when someone thinks ugly instead of beautiful or beautiful instead of ugly and thereby thinks something false. Theaetetus must here be thinking of such mistakes as the judgment that the Prudential Center is beautiful: he thinks that when someone falsely believes such a proposition he has in his thoughts (δοξάζει) (the) beautiful when he should have had (the) ugly. And this is in turn being thought of as ἀλλοδοξία, exchanging one thing for another in one's thoughts.

It is not clear from Theaetetus' remark whether he means that the person who judges wrongly has both the beautiful and the ugly in mind when he asserts his falsehood, at that moment mixing them up, or whether perhaps the only thing in his mind when he makes his mistake is the beautiful, the thing he actually names. Thinking beautiful instead of ugly (ἀντὶ αἰσχροῦ, 189c 6) rather suggests the latter. But it is clear that if he only has in mind the beautiful it will be impossible, on the theory adopted by the *Cratylus*, to convict him of falsehood. For though no doubt he thought beautiful instead of ugly there would be no error in that unless he had himself wanted to name ugly or had intended to state the fact which is correctly reported by "The Prudential Center is ugly." If he wanted to say and think the beautiful, and nothing else, then his thought would appear to be entirely in order and the statement in question true: each part names something correctly, so the whole is true. Everything he has thought is an ὄν and he has not exchanged any ὄν for some other ὄν.

Socrates in his examination of falsehood as ἀλλοδοξία corrects this omission in Theaetetus' understanding of the thesis. He points out (190d 7-10) that if a person has in mind only one of two things he cannot be taking the one for the other; if he isn't even thinking the ugly in any way or to any degree (μηδαμῇ, 190d 8), but has the beautiful in mind simply and straightforwardly, then he can't be confusing the two and thinking the ugly is the beautiful. The mistake requires that both be somehow had in mind.

Suppose, however, that both are had in mind. Then what happens when someone judges falsely that the Prudential Center is beautiful is that he thinks both the beautiful and the ugly and judges that the ugly is the beautiful. What does this judgment that the beautiful is the ugly amount to? Judging, Socrates says, is just internal saying (189e 6-190a 6), so that thinking that the beautiful is the ugly is really saying to yourself "The beautiful [which you have here before your mind] is the ugly [which is there before your mind]." But is this a possible mistake? Socrates thinks not: no one, even in his sleep or in a fit of madness, has ever said to himself that the beautiful is the ugly or the wrong the right, or that odd is even or two is one. If you have two things before your mind and attach to each its own name you cannot then think one is the other; having them in mind in this way precludes, according to Socrates, the kind of mistaking and misrecognizing which ἀλλοδοξία entails. Hence ἀλλοδοξία cannot occur either when a man has just one of two things in mind or when he is thinking both; and we have not made any advance toward understanding how false thinking occurs (190d 11-e 3).

Why does Socrates think that in mistaking the ugly for the beautiful, in the process of saying such a thing as "The Prudential Center is beautiful" instead of "The Prudential Center is ugly," I must be saying to myself "The beautiful is the ugly"? Let us grant him that it is impossible to say this to oneself, understanding what one is saying: this impossibility results from the fact (as I put it just above) that to have the beautiful in mind and attach to it its own proper name is to distinguish it from any other thing similarly had in mind and recognized as itself. Thus we may grant that it is impossible ever to say falsely to oneself "Mr. Jones is Mr. Smith," since so to name them is to mark them off from one another, and one cannot simultaneously hold them apart and collapse them together.[28] But this is not the only way in which I could mistake Mr. Jones for Mr. Smith in my thoughts: I might have Mr. Jones in my thought not by way of his proper name but by some definite description ("the butcher around the corner") and then take this person, who is in fact Mr. Jones, for Mr. Smith (who is perhaps the baker). In order to mistake Mr. Jones for Mr. Smith I need not say to myself "Mr. Jones is Mr. Smith": I may say instead "The butcher around the corner is Mr. Smith." And whereas the former looks very like something it's not possible to say to oneself, the latter doesn't begin to look impossible. Is Socrates, in holding that to think one thing is another is to say to oneself that the one is the other, ignoring the distinction between proper names and definite descriptions and insisting that to say to oneself that one thing is another must be to refer to two things by name and then conflate them?

It is important to notice, I think, that throughout the discussion of ἀλλοδοξία Socrates has in mind the kind of mistake which Theaetetus himself introduced by his example of thinking beautiful instead of ugly. That is to say, he has in mind primarily not mistakes of one person for another but mistakes involving what for lack of a better noncommittal expression I shall call predicate-entities. And the conditions under which such mistakes are supposed to arise are given by the theory of meaning and falsehood I have expounded above. A false statement is represented as saying badly all the same things as some true statement says well, and thinking falsely is thinking of all the same things as make up some true thought but failing to recognize one of them for itself. Now there is no doubt that Socrates thinks this mistake involves naming two different things correctly and yet confusing them; but it is not clear whether this is due to the failure to distinguish proper names from definite descriptions or whether there is some feature of the theory of falsehood which makes it necessary (or seem necessary) that the false thinker have in mind under their proper names all the things which make up the true thought. If so, Socrates' idea that in making such false judgments as that the Prudential is beautiful I must say to myself "The beautiful is the ugly" will show not a confusion about two different types of referring expression but rather a serious difficulty in the theory of meaning and falsehood being accepted in the whole discussion. If on this theory one irretrievably _must_ both correctly name two objects and nevertheless confuse them, then the theory is stuck with the ruinous consequence that falsehood must involve saying to oneself "A is B" in so many words.

Now it does seem to me that there are fairly plausible reasons for thinking that the theory of falsehood as misnaming does require that one be able to confuse two objects which one has in mind in the strong sense that each is given its correct proper name. According to this theory, the false thinker has in mind, is directing his thought toward, the object (say, the beautiful) which the true statement names correctly and which is one constituent of the fact being reported. Can he have the beautiful in mind without knowing that it is the beautiful (and so not the ugly)? Definite descriptions are not so easy to think of for predicate-entities as they are for persons, but they do exist. For example "the quality mentioned second in the title of Burke's book on aesthetics" is a definite description of the beautiful, since the title in question is _Treatise on the Sublime and Beautiful_. Suppose then a man has the beautiful in mind under this description: then he need not know that the object he has in view bears the proper name "the beautiful" and room is left for him to take it for the ugly. But does he in this case have the beautiful in mind in the way required by the theory of falsehood? The fact which he is supposed to be misreporting is (say) the fact that the Taj Mahal is beautiful, and he is supposed to have the objects _Taj Mahal_ and _the beautiful_ in mind in order to do this. Is the fact that the Taj Mahal is beautiful the same fact as the fact that the Taj Mahal has the quality mentioned second in Burke's title? It seems not. One could, to use an old idiom, make the latter fact go out of existence by altering either the appearance of the Taj Mahal or the title of Burke's treatise, but only the first of these changes would have a similar deleterious effect on the fact that the Taj Mahal is beautiful. Because the definite description in question is only contingently related to the beautiful, a pair of propositions which are identical except that where the one has "beautiful" the other has a non-analytic definite description of the beautiful are not the same proposition and do not report the same fact. If this is so (or even plausible), then I think the theory of falsehood as misnaming may in the end require (or come close to requiring) that one misname something he at the same time names correctly. For if the fact that the Taj Mahal is beautiful is a different fact from the fact that the Taj Mahal has the quality in Burke's title, and the false thinker is expressing the former fact, but badly, he must have _that_ fact in mind. And this means that he must have the beautiful, correctly labeled, before his mind when he says or thinks to himself "ugly." Otherwise it is a different fact he is (badly) expressing and different things which he is (badly) naming.

The argument just presented obviously invokes the intentionality of thinking and turns upon the fact that the object of thought is an intentional object. It may be contended that these notions are too sophisticated to have lain behind Plato's idea in the _Theaetetus_ that false thinking must consist in taking one thing, though correctly named, for another, also correctly named. It is certainly true that no such view is anything like explicit in Plato's text; but then neither does any other interpretation come close to being explicitly warranted by the text itself. And the fact that throughout the discussion in 189c-190e it is the mistake of one predicate-entity for another that is giving the trouble must be somehow taken account of.

It is hardly possible to decide at this point why exactly Socrates thinks false identity judgments are of the type "A is B" where "A" and "B" are names. But it is important to have the alternatives clearly in mind before proceeding, so that the subsequent discussion can be considered in the light of each interpretation, hopefully making possible a decision between them. In either case the difficulty about identity judgments arises in the context of the theory of falsehood which makes all false judgments, predicative as well as others, the result of misidentifications. But on the first view discussed the particular puzzle about misidentifications which Plato raises will be a difficulty which might just as well have arisen independently of the theory of falsehood: any one who was not clear about the difference between a name and a description might become puzzled about how false identifications are ever possible, since any false identity judgment, if one ignores the difference between names and descriptions, could be represented as having the form of the impossible judgment "Jones is Smith." On the second view it is no general trouble about false identity judgments and essentially no confusion about names and descriptions that stands in Plato's way. On this view, when Plato implies that making a mistake requires naming a thing correctly and yet misnaming it he is not sliding from "The man on the corner [who is in fact Jones] is Smith" to "Jones is Smith," but taking notice of the fact that on the atomistic theory of meaning, to make a mistake requires getting something into one's thoughts <u>by name</u> and yet misnaming it. In fact, as Socrates' discussion of the wax-tablet model brings out, it is the latter view which seems to be the correct one: but this can only be shown later on.

Before considering the next stage of the argument in detail it will be useful to have in mind the course of development of the whole argument from the rejection of ἀλλοδοξία as an explication of falsehood right through to the abandonment of the topic of false belief.

In what follows Socrates attempts to throw light on the apparently impossible false identity judgments he has uncovered, in the hope that it may yet turn out to be possible to mistake one thing for another without having to recognize both of them in the process. He starts by producing some cases where one can and does mistake one person or thing for another without necessarily also recognizing them, and then constructs a model of the mind's operations which shows how these mistakes can occur. This is the simile of the wax tablet. But the cases he had started with, for which the wax tablet model had been introduced, did not include any mistakes which were wholly in the mind, as the examples which caused the original trouble were. In these examples, and indeed in false belief in general according to the theory being accepted throughout the discussion, one takes one thing he is _thinking_ of for another he is _thinking_ of, and the model of the wax tablet, as Socrates shows, fails to permit such mistakes as these.

He then changes models, introducing the simile of the aviary in the place of the wax tablet. The hope is, evidently, to put to use the lessons learned from the exploration of the type of mistake accounted for on the wax tablet model. These mistakes all involved the misfitting, as Socrates puts it (193c), of perceptions to the memory-impressions which are the objects of thought. The thing perceived, about which the mistake is made, is being referred to and so, in a way, thought about, but not for all that recognized for what it is. What the aviary is expected to do (cf. 199b 1-c 7) is to make room for a similar distancing, as it were, of the object about which the mistake is made from the full recognition which would be entailed by having it as a straightforward object of thought at the time when the mistake is made. Just as the perceived object is being referred to and so in a way had in mind (in perception, not purely in thought), so the aviary provides two modes in which an object can be had in mind: when one is actually thinking about it he has his knowledge of it directly before his mind and then knows it for what it is, but he may also have it in mind in the weaker sense that he has come to know it and therefore has an acquired ability to bring it before his mind when he wishes. The suggestion is that when an object is had in mind in the weaker, but not in the stronger, sense misidentifications can occur. This suggestion is at once rejected (since(having the kind of potential knowledge Socrates has in mind obviously does not by itself enable one to be actually thinking about an object, but a mistake about a thing cannot occur otherwise); and with that the whole investigation is abandoned. There seems no way, given the view of falsehood as misnaming, to avoid the consequence that in the general case thinking falsely requires the impossibility that one should both name two things correctly and yet take the one for the other.

The two models of the mind here introduced are, as the foregoing summary of the argument indicates, intended to be graphic illustrations of the process of misidentification which has been bedevilling the discussion of true and false belief. Their interest is pretty clearly restricted to their usefulness for this purpose. Thus when the wax tablet model turns out not to permit purely mental mistakes Socrates both rejects (196c) the definition of error founded upon it (the misfitting of thought to perception) and, apparently, abandons altogether the model of memory as impressions in a wax-block. The aviary model supersedes, and does not merely supplement, the wax block. Socrates is seeking an explanation of falsehood as involving misidentification which will account at once for _all_ false thinking; and the wax block is not thought of as having satisfactorily explained _some_ errors, leaving only certain others to be catered for by some other model. Neither simile is treated as if it had anything more to recommend it than that it permits or seems to permit in a not implausible way the occurrence of misidentification.

Both models are described in such a way that apparently everything that is in any one's mind or which he can bring before it has been acquired from experience of "external" objects. Does this feature of the account deserve special emphasis? Cornford thinks it does. He thinks that this fact about the two similes is important as showing the limits of the _Theaetetus'_ discussion: the apparatus which is available in the _Theaetetus_ for the solution of the problem of error is restricted to just whatever an "empiricist" could in consistency claim for his own. And in particular the Forms, in which Plato himself believed and which he thought to be the basis of the only alternative epistemology, are being excluded. Indeed, Cornford thinks, the failure to get round the _Theaetetus'_ troubles with false belief is entirely due to the fact that the whole discussion works with the "empiricist assumption" that minds are empty at birth and only "gradually filled with contents derived from sensible experience and learning" (_PTK_, p. 136). When the Forms are brought into view, in the _Sophist_, Cornford thinks, the _Theaetetus'_ problems can be broken through, and a correct analysis of false thinking can be provided.

This is a complete red herring. As we have already seen, it is not even clear that any Forms are introduced into the *Sophist*'s analysis of falsehood, and even if there are the solution of the problem emphatically does not turn upon talk about Forms. Nor is it any inadequacy of "empiricism" that causes the *Theaetetus*' inability to understand false thinking. One can suppose that our aviaries are filled up however you like--by God at or before birth, by acquaintance with Forms, by intuition of transcendental entities, or in any other non-empiricist way any one should propose--and the difficulty alleged by the *Theaetetus* will not be touched. It doesn't matter in the slightest how things get there, so long as in mistaking one for another you take yourself to be nevertheless naming and recognizing them for what they are. And this assumption has, as should be obvious from my discussion so far, *no* essential connection whatsoever with "empiricism," whatever exactly Cornford means by that term.

It is, then, the theory of meaning and not (or not primarily) metaphysics and epistemology to which the *Theaetetus*' discussion of false belief belongs. It does, in fact, appear that both wax block and aviary are assumed (191d 7 ff., 194d 6-7, 197e) to be empty at birth and filled up by ordinary processes of experience.[29] But this is an innocuous assumption and nothing of importance turns on it. None of the details of either simile matter to the argument except insofar as they form part of an account of the type of mistake which Socrates and Theaetetus are interested in.[30]

The wax tablet model is, then, introduced because it promises to give a clue to the understanding of misidentification and misrecognition.

Socrates begins the discussion by indicating that he and Theaetetus must give up one of the assumptions they have made in their prior argument; only so can they avoid the consequence to which they have been led. They have accepted that one cannot know a thing and yet not know and fail to recognize it. Now (191a 8-c 1) Socrates is prepared to deny this, by allowing a group of exceptions. It is still firmly accepted that if one has a thing in mind, giving it its correct name, one cannot take it for any other thing to which one gives its correct name, whether this other thing is had in mind or merely perceived (193a 1-3, d 10-e 4). But when a thing is perceived it can be taken, wrongly, to be something which one has in mind under its correct name: seeing Theodorus, I think Socrates and say wrongly that the man I see is Socrates. In this way one need not be actually knowing both objects, and room is left for error; so perhaps mental errors can be explained by arranging for actual knowledge of just one object, the other being had in mind by some means analogous to perception and not requiring that the correct name be applied to it.

Socrates actually mentions three cases in which error can occur (192c 9-d 1): (1) one can know both Theodorus and Socrates, see one of them and take him to be the other; (2) one can know Socrates, see a total stranger and take him for Socrates; (3) knowing Theodorus and Socrates and seeing them both, one can think Theodorus is Socrates and Socrates Theodorus. According to the terms of the wax tablet simile, knowing Socrates and Theodorus is construed as having an imprint of each on one's wax block; and the misidentifications in question take place when one has a perception of someone and refers it to the wrong impression in the wax. One, as it were, holds the impression up to the perception and thinks they fit together when in fact they do not. (Compare <u>Crat</u>. 430d-431a, and my discussion above, pp. 186 ff.).

Though Socrates mentions these three cases and describes the kind of error and falsehood provided for by the wax block model as παραλλαγὴ διανοίας πρὸς αἴσθησιν (196c 5), which evidently fits all three examples, he in fact concentrates all his attention on the first and third. Thus he chooses to illustrate in detail only the two cases where the object perceived is something also known, and the other case, in which something perceived but not known at all is misfitted into an imprint of something known, is just forgotten about altogether.[31] This is all the more striking when Socrates gives his final résumé of the mistakes now shown to be possible, where he takes account only of the two cases where something known <u>and</u> perceived is misidentified: περὶ δὲ ὧν ἴσμεν τε καὶ αἰσθανόμεθα, ἐν αὐτοῖς τούτοις στρέφεται καὶ ἑλίττεται ἡ δόξα, ψευδὴς καὶ ἀληθὴς γιγνομένη (194b 2-4).

There are several reasons why these facts are worthy of note. First, Socrates himself when introducing the exceptional cases where knowing and not knowing both take place says (191a 8-b 1) that he and Theaetetus were wrong to agree that no one can think things he knows to be <u>things he does not know</u>; and Theaetetus immediately explains this by producing exactly the second case mentioned later by Socrates:

"Sometimes I, knowing Socrates but seeing from a distance someone else whom I do not know, think him to be Socrates whom I do know" (191b 3-5). And for a time Socrates continues to have this type of case in mind in his account of the wax block and the mistakes occurring in connection with it (cf. 191e 6-7, 192e 5-6). But as soon as he begins to illustrate the mistakes in detail the original example is quietly, but completely, dropped.

Secondly, the type of case ignored is in fact the general case of which the other two are specifications, and, what is worse, the third is only a more complex version of the first and in no way independent of it. To know both Theodorus and Socrates and perceive them both, but get the perceptions and the memory impressions misfitted, thereby taking Socrates for Theodorus and Theodorus for Socrates, is obviously only to do twice what in the first type of case happens once: for in this case one sees only Theodorus but misfits the perception of him into the impression of Socrates. And the fact that the person actually seen is also someone you know is a mere minor variation of the pattern. Why then does Socrates ignore the general case, where the essential features of perceptual misidentification might be expected to emerge most clearly, in favor of two sub-cases which not only introduce irrelevancies but are not even basically different from one another?

The answer to this question, and the explanation of Socrates' peculiar treatment of the examples he discusses, is that he is not interested in perceptual misidentification in general, or indeed in failures to recognize something as a general phenomenon. He still has in mind the false beliefs mentioned in the discussion of ἀλλοδοξία, where, as we have seen, it appeared to be required that one know two objects and yet mix them up. So here special and explicit provision is made for the type of perceptual mistake involving two perceptions each belonging to a different known person. And naturally enough the taking of a seen but unknown person for someone you know is largely ignored, since it provides no analogue to anything that can be going on in the set of cases in which Socrates is interested. If you do not have any knowledge of a person at all you cannot have him in your thoughts; so the type of case which Theaetetus and Socrates first mention as allowing both knowledge and not-knowledge is in fact beside the point in which they are interested. So it is not surprising that Socrates concentrates his attention on the cases in which the perceived object is also known, but not recognized.

It might be said, of course, that even so he _ought_ not to have so concentrated his interest: if he had stuck to his initial example of mistaking a perceived stranger for a person whom you know, he would have stood a better chance of seeing that what makes this error possible also makes possible false identity judgments where only mentally conceived objects are concerned. For in the case of perceptual misidentifications the mistake is never of the explicit form "X is Y" where "X" and "Y" are proper names: the example itself shows that only _one_ name is available, since the person perceived is not known by name at all. In fact, as reflection on this example makes clear, the person perceived is not _named_ but identified by means of a definite description, together perhaps with ostension and other aids. This shows that there is a crucial difference between naming something and picking it out by definite description, and that it is the possibility of knowing one, or a limited number, of individuating facts[32] about a person or thing without knowing others and without knowing its name, that makes identity judgments both useful on occasion and liable to innocent falsehood. Thus in the perceptual situation envisaged the speaker says "The man coming up the hill is Socrates," and what makes this statement neither trivially true, if true at all, nor self-contradictory if false, is the fact that the subject has been picked out by means of a definite description. The fact that the description serves to pick him out in a perceptual situation is an unessential part of the example, and cases where only thinking is involved should easily suggest themselves once the perceptual example is seen in its proper light. Plato, by abandoning the general case in favor of the more complex and confusing cases where the person seen is also known, obscures the issues and prevents himself from seeing his own examples in their proper light.

Now this criticism assumes that Plato's difficulty here and throughout the discussion is due to his thinking (e. g.) that if the philosopher who tutored Alexander the Great was Aristotle, and I am thinking of that philosopher, I must be thinking of Aristotle: the difficulty then arises that since I must know what I'm thinking I must know that I'm thinking of Aristotle, so that any statement like "The philosopher who tutored Alexander was Plato" must be unintelligible, as involving the impossible thought that Aristotle was Plato. That is to say, the criticism assumes that Plato is discussing a problem about identity judgments in general; and it is true that in order to understand these judgments it is necessary to see that names and definite descriptions are very different things and that (in typical cases) identity judgments involve descriptions as well as, or instead of, names. We have now, however, arrived at the point in Plato's argument where it becomes clear that this line of reasoning, and the criticism founded upon it, misrepresents the problem Plato is exploring in this part of the dialogue.

At 195b 9-196c 9 Socrates, having analyzed his two favored perceptual mistakes, points out that nothing in the apparatus of the wax tablet as so far explained offers any opening for the misidentification of one thing merely thought of, as something else also merely thought of. It has been part of the apparatus of the wax block that so far as the memory impressions in the block are concerned no mistake is possible: each one comes labelled, as it were, with its name. It was because perceptions do not come labelled with their name that error was possible. But when one makes a mistake entirely in one's thinking it appears that one must be precisely not getting the name of one of the memory-impressions right, and this has been forbidden (192a 2-4, e 8-193a 3). But there certainly are mistakes which involve only thinking: e.g., it is possible to make a mistake in reckoning, and think that 7 + 5 is 11. This false belief amounts, Socrates says (196b 4-6), to thinking that the 12 in your block is the 11, and that seems not a possible mistake to make. So the model of the wax tablet has not yet brought us within sight of the solution to the difficulties about false thinking that have been plaguing us.

It is very important to see clearly just how Socrates is here thinking of the judgment that 7 + 5 is 11. Does he think of it as itself a false identity judgment, or does he think that it merely <u>involves</u> a misidentification (much as "The Prudential is beautiful" was not overtly an identity judgment but involved one)? If the former, then "7 + 5" is being regarded as naming or otherwise picking out the number 12, so that to have <u>the sum of 7 + 5</u> in mind is to have 12 in mind (just as in my former example to have the philosopher who tutored Alexander in mind was to be thinking of Aristotle); and the apparently impossible mistake arises because one takes 12, which one had in mind in having the sum of 7 and 5 in mind, to be 11 which one names and thinks after the "is" or "equals." This is the way one would expect the difficulty about mistakes in thinking to arise again, if the criticism made above of Plato's analysis of perceptual misidentification were correct. For he would then, in effect, have employed the distinction between names and descriptions in the context of perception in order to show misidentifications to be possible, but would still fail to see how the same distinction applies in other contexts.

Unfortunately for this view, however, "7 + 5 = 12" is not treated by Socrates as an identity judgment at all, and "7 + 5" is not being thought of as a name or description of the object 12. Accordingly the false judgment "7 + 5 = 11" is not thought to be impossible on the ground that to have 7 + 5 in mind <u>is</u> to have 12 in mind; the place in the judgment where 12 is mistaken for 11 comes after the "is" or "equals." The true statement is "7 + 5 = 12," and in saying to oneself instead

"7 + 5 = 11" one gets everything right but the "11"; the part of the true statement which the "11" displaces is "12," *ergo* 12 is taken for 11. (Compare "The Prudential is ugly" and "The Prudential is beautiful" and Socrates' view that here the ugly and the beautiful are confused with one another.) The mistaking of 12 for 11 enters the analysis not because the role of definite descriptions is not understood but because the theory of meaning being accepted throughout the discussion seems to require that two things be had in mind by name and yet mistaken for one another.

That this is how the example is understood is clearly indicated in the text. Socrates says (196b 4-6) that when any one thinks that 7 + 5 is 11 he thinks that the 12 in his wax block is 11. But he also says (196a 2-7) that when someone wonders how much 5 and 7 are he has in mind the 5 in his block and the 7 in his block, and wants to know the answer to the question how much they add up to. That is to say, the thought "7 + 5 is 12" contains references to *three* impressions in the block, 7, 5, and 12; and the only place where 12 is introduced into the thought is when it is named. What the part before the "is" introduces is exclusively 7 and 5. And to wonder how much 7 and 5 are is not to wonder what object one has in mind *already* in thinking "7 + 5" but to inquire what number must be named (what impression in the block must be thought of) *after* the "7 + 5," if one is to think something true. Therefore when Socrates says that thinking "7 + 5 = 11" is taking 12 for 11 he cannot mean that because 7 + 5 is the same as 12 one can substitute "12" for "7 + 5" in the false judgment and get "12 = 11" as what the man was really thinking. The view that the atomistic theory of sentence meaning is what is causing the trouble here fits much better the description Socrates actually gives of the mistake he has in mind. For, as I have argued above, this theory of meaning in reducing falsehood to misnaming does seem to require that one know two entities by name and yet use the name of the one to denote the other.

The upshot, then, of this analysis of Socrates' use of the wax tablet model is that he is right to take special notice of the instances of perceptual misidentification where the thing perceived is also known. Since he is attempting to find room for falsehood within the limits permitted by the atomistic theory of meaning, he will have to find some way for a thing in some sense had in mind and known for what it is to be mistaken for something else similarly had in mind and known. The facts about perceptual identification suggest that this can occur when the thing is known by name but not had in mind in the direct and simple way which the discussion of ἀλλοδοξία supposed and which the wax block simile turned out not to avoid in the case of purely mental mistakes: what is needed is a purely mental analogue of perception so that a thing can be had in mind but not actively known for itself.

The analogue suggested is not really a very promising one (though, on the other hand, it has to be admitted that the task Socrates sets himself looks pretty nearly impossible). Socrates introduces (197a 8-c 5) the distinction between active and latent knowledge or, as he puts it, between possessing the knowledge of something and having it (actively in mind). And though one cannot mistake 12 for anything else when one has the knowledge of it actively in mind, i. e., when one is recognizing it and naming it correctly, nothing seems to prevent a mistake about it so long as the knowledge is merely possessed and not being actually consulted, just as one fails to recognize a person he sees because seeing him is not yet having the knowledge of him actually in mind. The distinction between possessing the knowledge of something and actually having it in mind, and the possibility of mental error this seems to introduce, are illustrated by the simile of the aviary. There is a difference between possessing a bird, that is to say, having it in your power because you have locked it up in a cage, and having it in your hand (just as there is a difference between owning a coat and wearing it). Socrates therefore supposes that there is a kind of bird-cage in every mind into which one puts every "bird" he catches, i. e., the knowledge of each thing he gets to know. When, therefore, one has gotten to know Socrates one has a knowledge of him in his bird-cage; but to have this knowledge in the cage is not to be actively knowing Socrates, that is to say, thinking of him and knowing that it is Socrates one is thinking of. To have this kind of knowledge of Socrates is like having taken a bird, which was flying around your aviary, actually into your hands.

The way in which mistakes come about can be illustrated by following up the simile.[33] Just as there are two processes that might be called "hunting birds," the acquisition of birds for the collection in one's cage and the attempt to get hold of a bird already in the aviary, so there are two processes of getting to know. One gets to know a thing in the first instance by acquiring knowledge of it as a permanent possession, and then later may once again get to know this same thing by bringing the knowledge from the back of one's mind to the stage of explicit awareness. This double sense of hunting and getting to know seems to solve the old problem. For example, I may know all the numbers, and have therefore the knowledge of each of them in my aviary, but I need not then have the knowledge of any of them immediately before my mind. When this is my situation I may well ask myself how much 7 and 5 make, and then, in order to complete the judgment "7 + 5 is . . .," I reach into my aviary intending to lay hold of my knowledge of 12, but instead come out with my knowledge of 11.[34] Then, in completing the judgment "7 + 5 is 11" I judge falsely, having mistakenly gotten hold of my knowledge of 11 in place of the knowledge of 12 which I was after. I think wrongly that 11 is 12 because I take the knowledge of 11 which I get hold of to be the knowledge of 12 which I was trying to grab.[35] Hence all false judging in the end comes down to the interchange of one knowledge for another (μεταλλαγὴ τῶν ἐπιστημῶν, 199c 10).

It is patent, of course, as soon as this solution is stated that it won't in the least do, and Socrates immediately declares its inadequacy (199d 1-5). It may very well be that in reaching into the aviary you emerge with your knowledge of 11 and not with your knowledge of 12. And no doubt, since your knowledge of 12 remains freely fluttering in the cage, you are not debarred by the fact that you _know_ 12 from making a mistake about it (cf. 199c 5-7): after all you don't have your knowledge of 12 at hand, just as in perceptual misidentifications you have not brought your knowledge into connection with the thing perceived. But what you _do_ have the knowledge of directly before your mind is _11_: how then can you think you have the knowledge of 12 by you, if it's the _knowledge_ of 11 staring you in the face? It's no good trying the diversionary tactic of emphasizing that 12 isn't, after all, being actively known, since to actively know 11 is _ipso facto_ not to confuse it with any other number. Thus although so far as your knowing _12_ goes nothing in the situation as described prevents you from making a mistake, nevertheless the fact that you know _11_ in the stronger of the two senses distinguished is sufficient to disallow the mistake.

What this argument shows is that so long as the blank in "7 + 5 is . . ." is filled with a reference to something which the speaker knows by name and which he knows he is referring to, no mistake can occur. (Theaetetus tries to evade this consequence, as we shall see in a moment, by making _nothing_ in the situation actively known.) Thus if I say "11" and understand what I am saying then I know I am referring to 11: 11 is before my mind and I know it for 11. It then appears that no error has occurred anywhere in the sentence: 7, 5, and 11 are all correctly named and thought, and there is no other place where the statement could go wrong. Perhaps however I had intended to say "12" and to get 12 into my thoughts so as to complete the sentence correctly: then I have gone wrong in putting 11 in its place; and is that not to mistake 11 for 12? No, comes the answer, for at the time when I get 11 into my thoughts I cannot think that I have 12 there. So long as I know that 11 is what I am referring to, then, no matter what I had started out in search of, I cannot *at that time* think I have something in mind which I do not have in mind (cf. 199b 2-4, ὅταν . . . ἀνθ' ἑτέρας ἑτέραν ἁμαρτὼν λάβῃ, *τότε* ἄρα τὰ ἕνδεκα δώδεκα ᾠήθη εἶναι: the τότε is wrong). And if I do not then make any mistake I am not *then* intending to refer to 12 but in fact referring to 11: I must be both intending to refer to 11 and in fact referring to it, and then no error and no falsehood remain. The fact that I have reached into my aviary intending to say and think 12 does not bring about any mistake in what I *do* end up saying and thinking. *That* could be mistaken only if I simultaneously said and meant "11" and thought I was meaning 12. And if this is impossible the aviary apparatus has done nothing to get round it.

The result is that we find ourselves in the very position we were in after the impossibility of falsehood as simple ἀλλοδοξία had been shown. To think falsely that the Taj Mahal is ugly seemed impossible because in order to do so you had to have both the ugly and the beautiful in mind, knowing each by name, and yet think the ugly where you knew you ought to think the beautiful. The aviary simile has attempted to loosen the knot by, in effect, having you intend to say and think the beautiful without ever getting it fully in mind and therefore without ever naming it correctly: but you must, even on the aviary model, have fully in mind the thing you finally do say and think. And to have the ugly in mind and know it for itself precludes thinking to any extent or in any way that what you have in mind is the beautiful. It appears then that if falsehood is to be explained as involving the mistake of one thing for another the mistake *must* occur at the very moment when the ugly is had in mind. But since at that moment, on the aviary model, only one thing is had in mind there can be no mistaking going on: in order to make a mistake, then, one would have to have two things in mind; but this brings the old impossibility back upon us. The upshot is that the kind of mistake required by the atomistic theory of meaning, if falsehood is to be possible, cannot happen. No one can say "ugly" and think and mean the ugly while also partly thinking and meaning the beautiful; but, on the other hand, if he is not thinking and meaning the beautiful at all then there has been no mistake and therefore *ex hypothesi* no falsehood. And this effectively reduces to absurdity the atomistic theory of meaning which has these unacceptable consequences. When Plato next raises the topic, in the *Sophist*, as we have seen, the idea that falsehood consists in misnaming has been abandoned completely. Though the *Theaetetus* neither announces this as its aim nor declares it as the outcome of its argument, it is clear that its discussion of falsehood does show that misnaming cannot be essentially involved.

Theaetetus makes one last effort to evade this consequence (199e 1-6). If the mistake of 11 for 12 is prevented by the fact that one must know 11 for itself at the time when the mistake, if there is a mistake, must occur, then perhaps we can make room for it by having our false-thinker *not* know 11 at the crucial moment. Perhaps what he has taken from his aviary is not his knowledge of 11 but his ignorance of 11,[36] and in that case nothing prevents him from taking 11 to be 12:

having an ignorance of 11 before him he need not know 11 for itself, though he is in fact thinking of it.

Socrates has no trouble rebutting this final plea (199e 7-200c 5). For the question inevitably arises whether the person who lays hold of his ignorance of 11 knows that it is an ignorance he has gotten in hand. It would seem that he must not know this, since if he knows it is an ignorance he will not trust any judgment he is led to make on the basis of it. But if he does not know that his ignorance is an ignorance, but thinks it is a knowledge, we must complicate the machinery of the aviary further and allow not only the knowledge of 11 and the ignorance of 11 to be flying around in the mind's cage, but also the knowledge of the ignorance of 11 and the ignorance of the ignorance of 11. Then, in effect, when a man mistakes 11 for 12 he gets in hand his ignorance of his ignorance of 11. But obviously there is no stopping here, since if he knows this ignorance for an ignorance he will not on the basis of it judge 11 to be 12; we are off on an infinite regress. We can do no better then than suppose an aviary containing only knowledges; and in that case there seems no room for the kind of mistake required by the theory of falsehood as misnaming.

With this Socrates confesses himself stymied for further ways of attempting to salvage false belief from the objection that has been raised against it. He suggests, in an allusion to the distinction drawn earlier (197a-b) between _having_ knowledge (actually about one) and merely possessing knowledge, that he has failed because he has attempted to reach an understanding of false belief before having understood what knowledge is. In order to get clear of the difficulties tangling up the notion of false belief the correct order of procedure is to explain knowledge first. How exactly Socrates connects these two things is by no means clear. It is true that throughout the discussion, and particularly towards the end, the words ἐπιστήμη and ἐπίστασθαι, etc., are used repeatedly, and true also that the final shipwreck of the argument is due partly to the fact that in any thinking the objects of thought are assumed to be recognized as it were by name. It may be that Socrates here entertains the possibility that the general line of argument being pursued above will finally turn out well if only it can be shown that the knowledge one is required to have of the objects of one's thoughts is somehow compatible with not recognizing them for themselves or by name. But it is obvious that such a result would only give temporary relief to a dying theory; and whatever hope Socrates here entertains it is certain that Plato himself in the *Sophist* takes the more radical line of rejecting altogether the theory of meaning which makes these hopes seem the only way out.

In any event, Socrates' opinion that the first order of business is to find out τί ποτ' ἐστὶν ἐπιστήμη serves the purpose of reminding Theaetetus that his old definition still remains on the agenda, and he confesses himself still satisfied with the statement that true belief is knowledge (200e 4-6).

D. The Refutation of the Second Definition of Knowledge (201a-c)

At this point, for the first time, Socrates faces Theaetetus' second definition, refuting it almost at a glance (201a-c). If true belief and knowledge were identical then every time a juryman becomes persuaded of the truth and makes his decision accordingly, his judgment would be the result of knowledge. But in fact there are many cases where the truth of the matter can only be known by someone who has witnessed the event; and when a juryman becomes convinced of a witness' veracity and accepts his account of what happened he judges truly indeed but, since he was not a witness, he does not have the knowledge which the witness possesses.

The implications of this argument are worth dwelling on for a moment. As Runciman has correctly observed,[37] the validity of the argument depends absolutely upon the truth of the premiss that what the eye-witness has is really knowledge. The contrast between juryman and witness would be wholly without the desired effect if neither ever has real knowledge. Suppose, for example, someone in the vein of *Republic* 477c-478a maintains that since juryman and witness make statements about the same matters they must both, whatever their differences from one another, be exercising the same faculty, that of belief: then true belief will not have been shown not to be identical with knowledge, but, at best, one type of true belief will have been marked off from another. As Runciman says, "if eye-witness knowledge is not knowledge but 'knowledge,' then the argument has only proved that true opinion is not 'knowledge.'" Either, therefore, knowledge has not been shown to be distinct from true belief, or there is such a thing as knowledge of temporal events and states of affairs.[38]

This argument should therefore give pause to those interpreters who think that the purpose of the *Theaetetus* as a whole is to show by indirect arguments that there must be (old, middle-period) Forms, since knowledge cannot be defined by any method except one which identifies the Forms as its objects. That interpreters fail to see this only shows how an *idée fixe* can come to occupy so much of a person's attention that he sees it affirmed even where it is almost expressly denied. Cornford's comment on this passage is an amusing instance of this phenomenon. He says (p. 141, my italics): "*This argument is repeated* in a later dialogue, the *Timaeus* (51d), where the existence of the Forms is said to follow from the distinction between knowledge or rational understanding (νοῦς) and true belief." *The argument* of *Theaetetus* 201a-c is most certainly not repeated anywhere in Plato. What does recur in the *Timaeus* passage Cornford refers to is the routine point that true belief is acquired not by instruction but by persuasion and plausible argument; and even if in the *Theaetetus* the further routine point, found in the *Timaeus* passage and elsewhere, that knowledge implies ability to give an account and explanation, had been added, that would not have made the *argument* any the more identical with the *Timaeus*'. Cornford's *idée fixe* prevents him from observing these elementary distinctions, and forces him to see in the actual argument of the *Theaetetus* a merely "analogous contrast" (p. 142) to that between real knowledge and real true belief.

Others who accept Cornford's general line of interpretation of the argument notice the embarrassing fact that the argument really implies the existence of knowledge that is not awareness of a Form. They evade the embarrassment by finding here, as Stoelzel for example does,[39] a "kleine Ungenauigkeit im Beweise" or perhaps an "Ungeschicklichkeit." That it is no _small_ imprecision my analysis of the argument above shows. Stoelzel, and no doubt Cornford and Cherniss as well, feel confident in not attaching much importance to the real argument of the passage because they think that earlier in the _Theaetetus_ Plato has affirmed his old view that knowledge is directed exclusively toward transcendent entities which can only be thought and never perceived: and, it must be granted, if this were so one would have a strong motive for finding in the argument of 201a-c no more than a case of _Plato dormiens_ (as Stoelzel puts it). But the passage to which Stoelzel refers (184-186) as showing Plato's continued acceptance of the old view is itself another case where _idée fixe_ has blanketed the text. As I have shown above, nothing in the argument of that passage supports the usual view (accepted by Cherniss and Cornford as well as Stoelzel) that knowledge is being located as the activity of the soul by which it contemplates transcendent entities without reliance on the objects of sense. Though there may be transcendent entities in the context their mode of acquisition and the activity of investigating them are found in the text only by misreading it. In fact, knowledge in that passage is knowledge _about_ objects of perception. The argument of 184-186, then, when correctly interpreted provides no reason whatsoever for refusing to accept the argument of 201a-c at face value. Quite the contrary: both the argument of 184-186, which concludes the examination of perception, and that of 201a-c, which concludes the examination of true belief, are in agreement that there is such a thing as knowledge of the things of sense. The argument of 184-186 therefore reinforces the straightforward interpretation of the argument of 201a-c given above. What these two arguments show is that knowledge is not mere perception and that it is not mere true belief. These conclusions express truths; the arguments which lead to them are good arguments. But as they are good arguments only if they are understood to start from the premiss that there is knowledge of things in the empirical world, sound principles of interpretation require that we not ruin the arguments and unsettle the conclusions by pretending that in Plato's view there was no such thing as knowledge of anything in the empirical world.

The final argument, then, of the middle section of the dialogue, and the only refutation Socrates anywhere provides of the definition of knowledge as true belief, clearly implies Plato's acceptance of the common-sense view that sometimes a person knows, and sometimes he does not know, but only believes rightly, a matter of empirical fact. It should not be cause for surprise that he accepts this view; the tendency, rampant in twentieth-century scholarly writings on Plato's philosophy, to deny that he does accept it is entirely attributable to a misguided sense that each dialogue Plato wrote forms part of a preconceived plan of philosophical construction. According to this canon the *Theaetetus'* views about knowledge must, at all costs, be made to be elaborations, defenses, and repetitions of those expressed in the *Republic* and *Timaeus*. We have seen already that one thing the first part of the *Theaetetus* does is to refute the idea, explicit in the *Timaeus* and nearly stated in the *Republic*, that the world of sense is a world of γένεσις devoid of οὐσία. And if, as this argument implies, the objects of perception are ὄντα and not merely γιγνόμενα (in the old sense), one of the chief reasons the *Republic* gave for holding (whatever the view was meant to come to) that αἰσθητά are things about which nothing can ever be known is effectively disarmed. The doctrine that only τὸ ὄν is γνωστόν (*Rep*. 478a-b) now no longer need imply that only Forms and not objects of sense can be known about. Accordingly we find *Theaetetus* 201a-c affirming the possibility of knowledge of the world of sense; this is just as one would expect, given the manifest intentions of the arguments of the first part of the dialogue mentioned above.

CHAPTER VI

KNOWLEDGE AS TRUE BELIEF PLUS LOGOS (201c-210b)

A. Introduction

The last section of the *Theaetetus* (201c 7-210b 3) examines a fresh definition of knowledge. The preceding discussion has shown that true judgment by itself cannot be knowledge, and it occurs to Theaetetus that the old definition is not so much wrong as over-inclusive: knowledge might be defined as true belief or judgment restricted in some way. He remembers having heard it said that knowledge is true belief (judgment) accompanied by λόγος (account, explanation, etc.), and this definition now seems to him a plausible suggestion. In order to put it to work, however, one would have to know more about what might be meant by logos in this context. In the subsequent discussion and examination, therefore, four efforts are made to give a precise sense to this notion; but in each case the concrete definition which results is rejected. Here the matter is dropped: there seems to be nothing beyond the four explanations of logos proposed by Socrates which the person whose theory Theaetetus has adopted might have meant by saying that knowledge is true belief plus logos. The dialogue thereupon closes with a declaration of defeat: knowledge is neither perception nor true belief nor the latter together with logos, and no further likely candidate suggests itself.

The bare bones of the argument thus seem perfectly straightforward. It might appear from my summary that the argument carries on from the refutation of the preceding definition, attempting to get at the feature of the eyewitness' judgment or opinion which distinguishes it from that of the juryman. Nothing, however, in the whole discussion of the final definition even remotely approaches a sense of logos which might be appropriate to this case. And, even worse, for most of the discussion (particularly its closing pages, 206e-210), the sense of δόξα and δοξάζειν is clearly not the same as that which was in play there: both the witness and the judge hold an opinion or belief in the sense that there is some proposition which they accept or some statement which they make; *what* they say or believe is true. Hence ἀληθὴς δόξα could there be translated "true judgment," as it could be in the passage (185a-186e) at the end of the first part of the dialogue which suggested ἀληθὴς δόξα as a likely candidate for knowledge, and which was full of references to the *thought* that two things exist (185a 9), that something is good or bad, etc. (186a). But true and false δόξα as involving assertion, affirmation, statement, etc., is pretty well lost sight of altogether in the final section of the dialogue, and we find the discussion centering instead around objects--a wagon, the sun, Theaetetus, the name "Theaetetus"--and ἀληθεῖς δόξαι of them. Here not "true judgment" nor even "true belief" is anything like appropriate. Cornford translates "true notion," and "right idea" or "correction conception" are other possibilities. To have a right idea of a wagon or Theaetetus' name is apparently to be able to recognize these items upon sight or hearing, or, in general, to have something in one's mind that correctly represents them; and then the discussion apparently takes as its task to say what more one needs to have in order to be correctly said to <u>know</u> the wagon or the name. The suggested definitions of logos are suggestions about what this something more could be. Thus the original suggestion that knowledge was to be found in the area of reasoning and judgment certainly envisaged knowledge as a faculty that makes assertions <u>about</u> things, and the refutation of the simple identification of knowledge and true belief reinforced this presumption; but in the final part of the dialogue knowledge and δόξα seem not to be faculties of judgment so much as apprehension or intuition.

Another oddity that bears mention here is the difference between the first definition of logos and the other three. In the others, logos is something which can be added to the right idea of something: one has the right idea first, then gives it verbal expression (206d 1), or adds an explicit list of its parts (207c 6), or grasps the peculiar feature of it which distinguishes it from others (208c 7). These senses of logos are proposed and criticized as answers to the question, What must be had in addition to a right idea in order to attain knowledge? In short, they are proposed and criticized as attempts to provide <u>sufficient conditions</u> for knowledge. This is just what one is led to expect, given that the final section as a whole is introduced (201c 8-d 2) as an examination of the proposed definition of knowledge as true belief plus logos. For assuming that one has a true belief (and true belief is throughout taken as unproblematical) then on this definition having logos as well, whatever it turns out to be, should be a *sufficient* sign of knowledge.

The first sense of logos, the one which Socrates explains by expounding a dream he has had (201d 8-202c 5), is not so straightforwardly comprehensible. It seems to be concerned to argue both for a sufficient condition of knowledge and also for a *necessary* condition; and Socrates' criticism concerns itself with the necessary condition (and matters associated with it) to the total exclusion of questions concerning the adequacy of the proposed sufficient condition of knowledge. The sufficient condition seems to be just that any one who can produce a list of all the parts of a thing knows it. This idea is never clearly stated in the dream, but it is implicit in the account of a complex object as a collection of simple elements, and is no doubt what is alluded to at the end of the dream where Socrates says that besides having a right idea of a complex thing one must also be able to give its logos in order to know it.[1] This conception of logos is, indeed, briefly touched upon in Socrates' criticism of the dream theory (203a-b); but it recurs later (206e) as the second of the three subsequent definitions of logos, where it is examined on its own account, and does not figure prominently in either the exposition or the criticism of the dream theory itself. The dream and its criticism are rather more concerned with the question whether only complex objects can be known and with the question what the complexity of a complex object consists in. The theory of simple elements (στοιχεῖα) which can be perceived and named but not known, though they can be combined into complexes (συλλαβαί) which, because they are complex, *can* be known, seems primarily intended as proposing a necessary condition for knowledge.

The first sense of logos, then, is not merely concerned to provide something which could be added to true belief so as to make knowledge; and Socrates' interest in and criticism of this account of logos is not directed at its inability to perform this role adequately. The doctrine that knowing requires a complex object and the theory of complexity with which the dream operates are the foci of the discussion and criticism of the theory. Any satisfactory and thorough-going interpretation of the final arguments of the dialogue must explain, so far as possible, how the first theory of logos and its refutation belong together with the other three; and we must also explain why the discussion in the closing pages focuses on the difference between a right idea _of_ a thing and knowledge _of_ it.

Some hope of success is encouraged by the observation that both parts of the discussion continue to accept the atomistic theory of meaning which lies behind the difficulties about false belief as well as certain views about thinking and reference associated with it. Thus the dream theory, in a more or less explicit form,[2] contains the view of statement which is assumed in the discussion of false belief: a sentence is just a collection of names, to make a statement is just to think together a group of objects, and the only sort of _meaning_ there is is _designation_. And it is the conception of complexity which is here assumed--complexity is in effect no more than composition, juxtaposition--to which Socrates subsequently directs his attention. Associated with this account of statement is the idea that mental operations ultimately reduce to simply directing one's thoughts toward an object, having it in mind, and labelling it with its proper name. This view was very much in play in the discussion of false belief; and I believe it is also operative in the final three senses of logos of the last part of the dialogue. Knowing something is a mental operation, so that if knowledge is to be explained on the old theory of meaning, it must be some sort of awareness of an object or objects. What room can be made, then, for a difference between mere awareness of a thing (a right idea of it) and the more thorough-going awareness which the word "knowledge" implies? The final three senses of logos proposed seem to me to be attempts to discover, within the confines of the old theory and therefore without invoking any mental operation other than simple awareness of a properly labelled object, something that goes beyond the mere recognition entailed by the possession of the right idea of a thing.

In my view, then, the last part of the dialogue is explaining and testing further the theories of thinking, meaning, saying, and judging which the middle section was entangled in. Before pursuing the detail of the argument with this thesis in mind, however, notice should be taken of the prevalent interpretation,[3] which approaches this part of the dialogue with a rather different set of questions in mind. On this view, what Plato intends to be showing in the final section is that there cannot be knowledge about phenomena because the only sense of logos in which the ability to give logos is sufficient indication of the possession of knowledge is one which can be applied to a Form and to nothing else. According to this interpretation Plato regards the notion that knowledge always involves ability to give a logos as evidently correct, and what the discussion shows is that no way in which you might try to give the logos of a sensible object can succeed in bestowing knowledge of it. Knowledge and the right kind of logos can only be had for Forms. This view has been effectively undermined by Robinson[4] and I shall not attempt a full-scale review and criticism of it. But it is worth mentioning two points about the form of argument which this view must attribute to Plato in order to extract from the discussion the conclusions it wishes to find in it.

One preliminary clarification requires to be made. The association of knowledge with ability to give a logos and the connection between these two and the theory of Forms appear in several rather different contexts in Plato's writings. Sometimes (as in *Meno* 85b-86a, 97e-98a) it seems that knowledge does not always have Forms for its objects, but that knowledge of anything requires a grasp and understanding of Forms; in this case the logos which knowledge implies is an account explaining how and why the thing alleged to be known is true, and the doctrine is that the ability to do this involves a reference to Forms. In these contexts true beliefs are said to become instances of knowledge when the explanatory account has been acquired in addition. Here the same truths can be either believed or known, and the difference between belief and knowledge is not that knowledge is concerned wholly with objects of a different realm, but that it involves a reference to such objects. On the other hand, in other passages where Plato is preoccupied with rather different questions from these, he espouses the doctrine that knowledge and belief do not overlap one another at all, and that nothing that can be an object of belief can be an object of knowledge (*Rep.*, 447a-d, 479d-e). Here there is no question of accepting a truth and then acquiring a logos of it so as to become possessed of knowledge of the very thing which one earlier only believed truly. To obtain knowledge it is necessary to turn away from belief and its objects altogether (*Rep.*, 523a-c) and direct one's attention to Forms exclusively; it is the understanding of Forms that constitutes knowledge. And in these contexts (cf. *Tim.*, 51d-e) giving a logos not merely includes reference to Forms but is somehow exclusively concerned with them.

Now though the two views about knowledge and logos just referred to might be combined so as to minimize or remove their differences,[5] they should not be forthwith conflated. Commentators who think that the final section of the *Theaetetus* mounts an indirect argument in support of the view that phenomena are not suitable objects of knowledge, though they tend indiscriminately to cite passages belonging to both of the two lines of thought cited above,[6] have mainly in mind the second sort of explanation of how knowledge and Forms are associated. In any case their understanding of the course of the *Theaetetus'* argument is more easily defensible taken in this way: the *Theaetetus'* concentration on knowledge and belief of objects, and not of truths about them, finds an evident parallel in the preoccupation of the *Republic* with Forms as the only objects of γνῶσις. In what follows I assume that, according to the interpretation being considered, it is the *Republic's* bifurcation of knowledge and belief into faculties directed at different objects that is being indirectly supported by the discussion of logos in the *Theaetetus*.

Now Plato might have argued for this thesis directly by showing, as he attempts to do in the *Republic*, that perceptible things are too indefinite to be known: there is nothing which any such thing is, so there is nothing it can be known to be. But, according to these interpreters, in the *Theaetetus* he wishes to suggest this conclusion indirectly, by showing that though knowledge is always accompanied by the ability to give a logos or explanatory account of the thing known, no such account can be given of a perceptible thing. One might expect, nonetheless, that the ultimate reason why no account can be given of a perceptible thing is that it *is* indefinite in the way Plato argues in the *Republic*; but in fact there seems to be no such thought lying behind the criticisms of the various senses of logos proposed in the final section of the dialogue. Nothing is said to suggest that "Theaetetus" isn't really just that one name which we take it to be, or that the sun isn't really as unambiguously as possible the sun. So, in any event, the objection to the hypothesis that the right kind of logos can be given of a perceptible thing is quite a different one from the objections raised in the *Republic* and elsewhere against the supposition that perceptible things can be known.[7]

The argument, as Cornford construes it, attempts to show, for a series of definitions of logos, that the possession of the logos of a perceptible thing in any of those senses is no sufficient sign that the thing is known; and the failure of these definitions is intended to show that there *is* no sense of logos in which to give the logos of a perceptible thing is sufficient to imply the possession of knowledge. To define knowledge and logos one must leave perceptible things to their own devices and attend to Forms. There are two important difficulties which this interpretation faces.

(1) For Cornford's *reductio* argument to be at all convincing one would have to be convinced that there were no other definitions of logos applicable to perceptible things than the ones whose inadequacy the discussion attempts to prove. For if there were others Plato could not conclude that perceptible things cannot be known until he had shown that true belief plus logos in these further senses does not amount to knowledge. Cornford recognizes this and expresses his belief (p. 162) that the three senses of logos considered (the expression of the thing in words, the enumeration of its parts, and the account of how the thing differs from anything else) exhaust the ways in which an account might be given of an individual perceptible thing. But why should one think this? Surely other senses would occur to any stubborn defender of the view (whatever exactly it comes to) that individual perceptible things can be known. For example, there might be a Leibnizian definition of logos as the conjunction of all the true statements about a given thing: though no doubt this would reduce the number of objects anyone knows, and perhaps leave God as the only (real) knower, it appears to be different from any of the three Plato gives. The argument Cornford constructs is thus valid only on the very dubious assumption that there are

no other types of account of sensible things than the ones he mentions. Can Plato really have intended to rest his case on such a weak reed?

Again, if as Cornford thinks there is a fourth sense of logos which is _the_ sense in which it necessarily accompanies knowledge and which, in Plato's view, can be given only of Forms, it is odd that in a _reductio_ of the idea that this logos can be given of sensible particulars, Plato doesn't even mention it (or any analogue of it).[8] If this sense of logos is something that one _could_ attempt to apply to a perceptible thing, then Plato should surely (and would surely) have scrapped his other senses and produced a _good reductio_ by showing that when one tries to apply logos in this sense to phenomena the result is not knowledge. On the other hand, if in its very nature the logos which accompanies knowledge cannot be clearly indicated without referring to Forms, this was hardly the place to attempt an indirect argument at all. Either way, the argument Cornford attributes to Plato is an abortion.

(2) According to the usual view the failure to discover a satisfactory sense of logos for perceptible things shows that phenomena are the wrong sort of objects for knowledge to be of. Plato, however, in giving reasons rejecting the senses of logos proposed seems actually to imply that there _is_ such a thing as knowledge of phenomena. The method Plato uses, at least part of the time, to show that the senses of logos proposed are not satisfactory seems incompatible with the conclusion of the argument as Cornford interprets it.

The method I have in mind is a method of counterexample: it involves appeal to a particular example and to what knowledge of that example would actually be. Here one argues that a certain definition is unsatisfactory because there are cases where one has to do more to attain knowledge than just have a right idea plus logos in the sense defined. By using this method one implies that there is such a thing as knowledge in the cases envisaged, but the definition proposed fails to account for it. Plato follows this method in the refutation of the second sense of logos (207c 6-208b 10). Here Socrates takes the example of the name "Theaetetus," and implies that the proposed definition of knowledge would have the consequence that someone knows this name even though his command of the individual letters is so faulty that when he hears *th* he sometimes thinks he has heard *t* (though in *this* case he has gotten it right). But why should this consequence not be accepted? Why should one *not* say that anyone who recognizes the name when he hears it, and can spell it correctly, *knows* it? Because, Socrates says, that is not, as a matter of fact, what counts as *knowledge* in such a case: it is just a fact that when someone has begun to learn his letters he will for a while get them right some of the time, but on other occasions when he is called upon to spell the same syllable he will insert a wrong letter or leave one out. When this is the situation we do not say he knows the letters and syllables in question, and so not the names either. He does not *yet* (208a 5, b 9) know them; he *will* know them when he ceases to make learner's mistakes of the sort indicated. Now it is essential to notice that the refutation Socrates here constructs would fail altogether if it were *not* possible to know letters, syllables, or names. If the further abilities Socrates implies a man must possess in order to know a name did not have anything to do with knowing anything, then the absence of them could not show the absence of knowledge. The fact is that Socrates, like Theaetetus, naturally assumes that his task here is to explain what it is to know, _inter alia_, perceptible things, and he rejects the proposed explanation because it does not fit evident facts about the knowledge of names. He is not, and cannot be, arguing indirectly that there isn't any such thing as knowledge of names or of perceptible things in general.

It might be replied to this that _Socrates_ (Plato) need not accept the "evident facts" about the knowledge of names; all he requires for the validity of his argument is that these facts be such that anyone who thinks (as Plato does not) that there is such a thing as knowledge of perceptible things cannot deny them. Then any one who thinks that the name "Theaetetus" can be known will have to admit that the proposed definition of logos as analysis into elements fails as an account of knowing a name; for _he_ must grant that one can have logos in this sense and not have what _he_ calls (though of course wrongly) knowledge of "Theaetetus." So the argument will have shown that no one who thinks there is knowledge of perceptible things can accept the proposed definition, and that is enough to refute it.

This defense is not convincing. By what right does Socrates assume that anyone who thinks there is such a thing as knowledge of a name will have to accept his appeal to learner's mistakes as showing that one does not exhibit knowledge of a name merely by spelling it correctly? He certainly could have nothing to say to a person who just denied that one must do more than spell the word correctly at some time in order to know it at that time: Socrates and such an opponent would be in agreement that further abilities (correct spelling on other occasions) have no tendency to show knowledge of anything, so that Socrates, at any rate, would have nothing to which to appeal in order to show the man that his account of knowledge is unsatisfactory. The argument to which Cornford's interpretation is finally reduced in the case of the second sense of logos is thus at best entirely *ad hominem*, and has no effect against any one who does not accept the distinction, to which Socrates appeals, between getting a name right on a single occasion and knowing it. And Socrates, who, on Cornford's interpretation, does not accept this distinction himself, cannot insist that his opponent accept it.

It seems to me, then, that interpreted in the most natural way Plato's refutation of the second sense of logos (206e ff.) implies that he accepted that knowledge of perceptible things is possible. So interpreted the argument is straightforward and cogent, rejecting the definition of knowledge as a right idea of a thing plus an analysis of it into parts for a good reason: there are cases where the conditions of the definition are met which are undoubtedly not instances of knowledge. But if this is Plato's argument here, it cannot be his long-range objective to prove that there is no such thing as knowledge of the objects of the senses. In order to evade this consequence and protect the interpretation which would make this Plato's overall aim in this part of the dialogue, it is necessary to postulate a complicated and unconvincing *ad hominem* argument. I see no reason to attribute the bad and graceless argument to Plato, rather than the neat and effective one, and accordingly I reject the interpretation which would force us to attribute the bad one to him.

To sum up the foregoing discussion: I find Cornford's interpretation of the last section of the *Theaetetus* unconvincing for two reasons. It attributes to Plato a *reductio* argument which is awkward and ineffective; and it requires grotesque distortion of the natural understanding of one part of the passage, and even then produces no very convincing interpretation of what is being argued there. These seem to me good reasons for giving up the idea that the third part of the dialogue intends to show that knowledge has other objects than perceptible things.

This natural conclusion is further supported by the consideration that the correct understanding of the argument of the earlier parts of the *Theaetetus* itself provides very weighty reasons for not expecting Plato to have any such intention in the final section. As I remarked above, the chief reason for accepting Cornford's interpretation, or something like it, is the belief that at the time he wrote the *Theaetetus* Plato's view about knowledge was that it necessarily was directed toward Forms, and that knowledge could not be had of perceptible things. But as I have argued above, the main ground on which this view was accepted in the *Republic*--that phenomenal objects have no existence and no settled character at any moment or for any period of time--is in fact overturned in the *Theaetetus* itself. The supposition that there are two distinct worlds, one of change without permanence and becoming without any being at all, and the other a world of being without any kind of change, has been shown to be absurd. The logic of the concepts of being and becoming does not in fact support such a division, and Plato plainly implies that the segregation of the two must be abandoned. In the subsequent argument he in fact does abandon it (184-186); and therefore when in the final argument of the second section (201a-c) he abandons its corollary, allowing knowledge of matters of empirical fact, he is only being consistent with the patent conclusions of his own arguments. Hence the fact that the last part of the dialogue is, judged internally, not plausibly interpreted as making a rear-guard argument for the old segregation of knowledge and belief, is entirely what one would expect. And, of course, this fact itself gives further support, if support is needed, to the interpretations of the earlier arguments which I have defended. The upshot is that the usual way of reading the final section of the dialogue must be rejected as forcing concerns upon the argument which it does not have; and the way is left open for an attempt to interpret it in a way which is more faithful both to the larger concerns of the dialogue and to the detail of its own development.

B. The Dream and Its Refutation (201c-206b)

As I said above, one must look to the atomistic theory of meaning and the theory of mental operations associated with it in order to develop a more adequate interpretation of the closing pages of the *Theaetetus*. In general, the interpretation I shall advance in what follows treats the dream and its criticism as specially concerned with the central atomistic conception of the sentence as a collection of names; and the examination of the subsequent three senses of logos then explores the possibility of finding room within the atomistic scheme for an adequate conception of knowledge.

I said above (pp. 236-238) that the dream is a theory of logos in the sense of _account_ and that it specially emphasizes the point that a thing, in order to be subject to logos and hence to knowledge, must be _complex_. How can this understanding of the dream, which evidently makes it primarily a theory about knowledge, be squared with the view that the dream and its criticism are specially concerned with atomistic conceptions of the sentence? It is true, of course, that the same word "logos" covers both "sentence" (and "statement") and "account," but by itself this fact proves nothing, since in context the word can obviously bear one meaning to the exclusion of the other, and in the context of the final section of the dialogue "account" is certainly at least its _dominant_ sense. Where in the dream is any theory about statement to be found?

Ryle apparently thought that in the dream logos actually _meant_ statement or sentence.[9] He took the dream, in saying that knowledge must be of a complex object which has a logos, to be adopting the view that what is knowable is the _same thing_ as what is statable. According to Ryle, Plato is here noticing that knowledge requires for its expression a complete sentence, which is a complex structure of elements and not the same as, or reducible to, a mere name. Knowledge is of truths or facts, which are complex, and never of single objects; objects are named, facts are stated, and knowledge is invariably of the latter. This interpretation, interesting and suggestive as it is, cannot, I think, be right. For the general thesis being introduced by the dream is quite clearly (cf. 202c 2-5) the view that to know involves giving an <u>explanation</u>, and though the dream goes on to assert that nothing can have an explanation given of it which is not complex, it does not say that nothing can be known except truths or propositions or statements. The implication, in fact, of the theory of elements and complexes is that ordinary physical objects (e.g., Theaetetus, a wagon) are the things that are known (201e 1-2), and though the theory wishes to think of these as complex, it does not seem to hold that knowing them is the same as knowing some <u>fact</u>. It does not seem possible, then, to interpret the dream's central contention as the general doctrine that truths or facts are the objects of knowledge; and in arguing that anything knowable must be complex because it must have a logos, the dream is not directly expounding a doctrine about statements.

But though the dream theory is not as a whole a theory about statements, I think it contains one. The main thesis urged in the dream, as I have said, is that knowing involves an account and that, since giving an account is a complex activity, nothing can be known which does not have a corresponding complexity. The effect is to draw a sharp line between ἀληθὴς δόξα and knowledge, on the ground that knowledge involves an articulation which places it at an entirely different level from the simple "right idea" which, as I have already remarked, seems to amount to no more than the ability to recognize.

There is, of course, a similar difference between a name and a sentence or proposition: a sentence, because it asserts something, is a complex expression, by contrast with a single name, which performs a simple designating function. I believe that the dream theory, as Plato sets it out in the _Theaetetus_, takes note of this parallel between knowing and saying, on the one hand, and naming and recognizing on the other; and the conception of complexity which the dream operates with, and which attracts the major portion of Plato's interest in the whole theory, is precisely the notion of complexity involved in the atomistic theory which we found bedevilling the discussion of false belief earlier in the dialogue. Therefore, in the subsequent criticism of the dream's conception of complexity, where it is shown that on atomistic assumptions it cannot be maintained that only complexes are knowable, the corresponding thesis about the complexity of statements is also under implicit examination. The account of the complexity of knowledge and that of the complexity of statement stand or fall together.

The two theories are connected in the dream by means of the ambiguity of the key word _logos_, which means both "statement" and "account," "explanation," "definition." The passage expounding the dream reads as follows (201e 2-202b 5):

> Each [simple element] just by itself it is possible only to name, and it is not possible to say anything else about it, neither that it _is_ nor that it _is not_: for that would already add being or not being to it and one _ought_ not to bring in anything extra, if one is to say that one itself alone. Indeed, one ought not even to bring in "that one" nor "itself" nor "each" nor "alone" nor "this one" nor many other such things: for these run about and get applied to everything, and are different things from those to which they are applied, but [a simple] ought, if it were possible for it to be said

> (λέγεσθαι) and it had its own proper logos, to be said (λέγεσθαι) without all the others. But in fact it is impossible for any of the simples to be said (ῥηθῆναι) with a logos: they can only be named, for they have only a name. But as for the complexes made up of them, just as they [the simples] fit together to form them [the complexes], so also their names joined together constitute a logos: for the joining together of names is just what a logos is.

Now much in this passage is obscure. But it seems clear that some things are said not to be susceptible of any account, on the ground that they have no proper parts. An account, or οἰκεῖος λόγος, then, contains a reference to each of the proper parts of a thing, and mentions nothing outside it. (It is unclear here, and, indeed, through the whole subsequent discussion,[10] what form this logos takes: is it "P is Q, R, S, T" or just "Q, R, S, T"? But that the proper logos of a thing mentions each part is clear enough.) The theory is thus that one knows a thing when he can name its smallest parts, and that anything which lacks parts cannot be known. Such a simple object can be named, but it is not subject to the kind of articulation which characterizes the objects of knowledge. Other objects, the complexes or συλλαβαί, are thought to be knowable just on the ground that they contain a plurality of simple parts. Simples and complexes differ in only this one respect.

But the sort of list which constitutes a thing's οἰκεῖος λόγος is not merely an account or definition; it is also, as the last sentence of the passage just translated implies, a statement. For the definition of logos as συμπλοκὴ ὀνομάτων which is here appealed to, occurs in a number of places in Plato, in which it uniformly means "statement."[11] So here the logos in which a complex thing is analyzed, and knowledge of it displayed, is also a statement, since in it several names are joined together and statement consists precisely in the conjunction of several names. It may be hard to believe that Plato should really intend in 202b 2-5 to be saying that the list of the parts of a thing constitutes a statement, but, as I have argued above, both the Cratylus and the Theaetetus itself, in the discussion of false belief, do in fact regard a sentence as no more than a collection of names; and therefore to define or give an account of a thing by naming its parts in succession meets the requirements for stating something.

That the account of a complex thing is a statement is perhaps also implied by what is said earlier in the passage. For at several points, Plato mentions the possibility or impossibility of "saying" an object in a logos (a 2, 7, 8; b 1), and this curious mode of expression may reflect the fact that the dream theory thinks of the logos or account of a thing, which is the primary topic of discussion, as also a statement. For if an account is a statement, the account of a thing is not unnaturally described as "saying" it, while a thing which has no parts and therefore lacks an account is naturally said to be only namable and not "sayable." Of course, this use of λέγειν and ἐρεῖν might be due merely to the fact that λέγειν is the verb cognate to λογος; even though in common usage it corresponds to λόγος in the sense of statement, it could presumably be used to mean no more than "give an account of" in a context where λόγος meant account only. But in view of the introduction of logos in the sense of statement at b 2-5 it seems reasonable to understand λέγειν and ἐρεῖν above in their usual sense, "to say or state."

It seems to me, then, that the dream theory, as Plato presents it, does contain not only a theory of logos or account but also a view of logos or statement; for it assumes that every account is a statement on the ground that an account consists of a conjunction of names. It should be observed that I have not, as Cornford does (PTK, p. 145), asserted the converse, namely, that the theory holds every statement to be an account (or part of an account) in the sense introduced in the dream. Whether the dream adopts the view, which appears in the Parmenides (142b 5-d 5), that to describe a thing is to name some of its parts, seems to me not decidable on the basis of what Plato tells us about the theory. All one may reasonably attribute to it is the conception of a statement as a combination of names--whether the names name parts of the same thing or not. From what Plato says, we are justified in inferring only that those statements which are also accounts restrict themselves to naming parts of a single thing.

But that the dream asserts even the lesser thesis is a very important fact. For in holding that accounts are statements the dream theory gives to statements complexity of just the same type as it attributes to the complex objects which it holds to be knowable, and to the accounts in which such knowledge is exhibited. As I have already said, and as Socrates' criticism of the dream brings out quite clearly, the theory of complexity being accepted in the dream is atomistic in character; in criticizing the dream's conception of complexity Socrates simultaneously criticizes the atomistic view of statement. Here lies the connection between the last part of the dialogue and the discussion of false belief.

Socrates' criticism points out an incoherence in the theory of the dream. The dream has wished to insist that knowledge must be complex, and therefore that it must have a complex object. But the account of complexity to which the dream is committed prevents it, Socrates argues, from making out this claim. Either the account of simples and complexes must be modified, or else it must be granted that simples are knowable even though they can have no account given of them. Likewise, either the relationship of sentences to their constituent words must be conceived differently from the way the dream conceives them, or else it cannot be maintained that sentences, as complex entities, are on a basically different level from single words. Socrates' criticism of the dream theory thus poses a dilemma which goes to the very heart of the difficulties facing an atomistic theory of language.

Socrates has, in fact, two different but related arguments against the dream theory. The first, which is announced at the very outset of his critical examination (202e 3-203a 2) but not actually produced until after the second argument is fully expounded (206a-b), argues that the very example of letter and syllable, in terms of which the doctrine of simplicity and complexity was framed, shows the error of holding complexes to be, but simples not to be, knowable. The second, and more ambitious, argument (203a-205e) attempts to recommend this same moral by pointing out the insufficiency of the dream's conception of complexity to support any doctrine to the effect that knowledge is of complexes exclusively and not also of simple elements.

Together the two arguments show that both Socrates and the imagined theorist of the dream continue to accept an atomistic doctrine of language and reality, and must therefore accept the consequent thesis that there is knowledge of simple objects which can only be named and referred to. Knowledge must ultimately, on this theory, be a species of getting a thing into mind, of recognition or correct mental reference.

The longer argument poses a dilemma, on neither horn of which can the dream theorist come comfortably to rest. If the complex (συλλαβή) is just the same as all its elements (as we have seen a sentence has been taken to be a collection of names), then knowing the complex must be nothing more or less than knowing all its elements. And to know all the members of a certain group is the same as knowing each severally, so that if a complex is a sum of elements, knowledge of a complex requires knowledge of each of the elements as well. On this conception of a complex, then, the dream theorist's thesis cannot be defended.

But if, Socrates continues (203e 2 ff.), the συλλαβή is not the same as the sum of its elements it must be something else, different from the elements, which comes into being when they are collected together. Thus, for example, if the sentence "Socrates is flying" does not mean what "Socrates" and "flying" taken together mean, it must be thought of as meaning something else--not Socrates and flying or their combination, but something new and different, not meant by either or both of these. The meaning of a sentence, if it is not identical with the sum of the meanings of its constituent parts, must be something quite unrelated to the constituent names and their meanings, something that comes to be indicated _when_ the names are conjoined but not _by_ the conjoined names. On this view a συλλαβή has no parts; the thing designated by the word "complex" is something else than the elements, which comes into being when they are put together.[12] But if the complex has no parts, it must be as simple as the elements we are now forbidden to say it consists of. And if this view of complex and element is adopted it turns out straightway that in saying that a complex is knowable the dream theorist has asserted that something simple is knowable; complexes end up being really simples.

Thus in whichever of these two ways one thinks of a complex, complexes are no more knowable than simple elements, and the dream theorist's attempt to associate knowledge with complexity fails. In effect what Socrates does in this argument is to present as exhaustive alternatives two conceptions of the relation of complex to element or whole to part, showing that on either view the theorist's contention cannot be defended. The two conceptions in question are reminiscent of an argument in the _Parmenides_ (145a-e), where the One, which has been shown to be infinitely plural as well as single, is declared to be a whole of parts. The One is, then, _qua_ plural, a lot of parts, and also a whole of parts. But a whole is that which contains or encompasses a lot of parts, so that _qua_ whole the One is outside all the parts and each of them; and _qua_ all the parts the One is contained by the whole. Hence it is agreed that the One is both in itself and in something else, and other contradictory conclusions follow. It appears that the refutation of the dream presents these two conceptions of the relation of a thing to its parts as exhaustive alternatives, arguing that whether a συλλαβή is all its parts or something as it were surrounding the parts, it is not in any case an essentially different type of thing from the parts themselves.

But though the *Theaetetus* does seem to be using the *Parmenides'* two conceptions, it presents them rather differently. In the *Parmenides* the whole is said to be something else besides the parts, which has parts by containing or surrounding them; and a whole is not *ex vi termini* identical with all its parts. Of course because the One is successively identified with the whole and with the sum of its parts, the whole will turn out identical with, as well as different from, all the parts. But the two conceptions of whole and sum of parts are carefully kept distinct. In the *Theaetetus*, however, this distinction is deliberately and forcefully disallowed. Socrates argues very hard (204a 7-205a 7), over Theaetetus' objections, that whole of parts and sum of parts are the same thing; and whereas the *Parmenides* defines a whole as what surrounds and contains the parts, when the *Theaetetus* presses the conception of συλλαβή as something different from the parts, it goes out of its way to *deny* that such a συλλαβή is a *whole*. In other words, where the *Parmenides* uses the word "whole" as the name of the additional thing containing the parts, the *Theaetetus* rejects this usage, substituting instead the sum of the parts as what "whole" names. The fact that the usage of the word "whole" is thus reversed in the *Theaetetus* might be taken to throw doubt on the idea that the *Theaetetus* has the same conception of the relation of a thing to its constituents as the *Parmenides* passage contains.

In any event the difference between the two passages does not affect one chief point of similarity. In both passages the thing that has the parts--the One, a complex (συλλαβή)--can be thought of in either of two ways, as identical with all the parts or as something else outside of and different from the parts.[13] The difference between the two discussions concerns only which of these two conceptions is the conception of the thing (συλλαβή, the One) as a whole: in the Parmenides the whole is the thing conceived as outside the parts, whereas in the Theaetetus the whole is the thing conceived as identical with the parts. And it is, in fact, easy to see why the Theaetetus departs from the Parmenides' usage, when one reflects that in the Theaetetus the συλλαβή as different from the parts is going to be found to be something partless and therefore simple (and indeed must be so found if the refutation of the dream theory is to be successful); for to call the συλλαβή as different from the parts a whole would simply invite the objection that a whole must be a whole of parts, so that if the alternative to thinking of a complex as a sum of parts is to think of it as a whole, then on the second conception to know a complex is neither the same as knowing its several simple parts nor is it to know something in itself simple and partless. In view of the association of whole and part, therefore, Socrates must refuse to distinguish whole from sum, if he is to succeed in reducing knowledge of a complex to knowledge of one or more simples.

But though it is easy to understand why Socrates should want to refuse to distinguish between a whole and a sum of parts, it is questionable whether the refusal can be supported by good reasons. The argument

Socrates actually gives is extremely simple. Taking as his (not very felicitous) example the number six, he argues that six is the sum of its constituent units, and that to talk about all the units is the same thing as talking about the sum of six itself. Hence the sum is made up of its parts (204e 2). Therefore if, as Theaetetus has suggested (204b 2-3), a whole is not just identical with the sum of its parts, a whole must not be made up of its parts at all. But a part is always part of a whole, so that it seems impossible to deny that a whole is made up of parts; and, furthermore, anything that loses one of its parts simultaneously ceases to be both the whole thing it was and the sum that it was. Hence whole and sum seem not to be different conceptions after all (205a 7).

These are, in fact, not very good reasons for identifying the conception of a whole with that of a sum, and it is easy to sympathize with Theaetetus' inclination to balk at the conflation. It does not follow that any whole is the same as a mere sum just because it is (in a way) made up of its parts. For in a sum each part contributes to the total nothing more than what it in isolation already contained; its function in the total is precisely its function in isolation. But in such an ordered whole as a sentence or a syllable, even though it is made up of its elements, the elements do not just perform the job which they perform when taken by themselves. Thus if "runs" taken alone indicates an action, the same word in the sentence "Jones runs" does not only indicate an action; it also describes, or applies to, Jones. Hence even though the whole sentence is made up of two parts, "Jones" and "runs," and even though if one of these were taken away there would no longer be the whole sentence, it still does not follow that the whole is just the sum of its parts.

Theaetetus wants, as I have already mentioned, to maintain that a whole is not identical with a sum, but is rather something which arises when the parts are put together, and which is neither simply reducible to the parts nor totally separate from them (204a 8-9). There are indications, as we shall see directly, that the view Theaetetus is inclined to take is a third alternative, which Plato himself had already envisioned in one place in the Parmenides; and the emphasis with which Socrates denies this third conception to Theaetetus is perhaps a sign that in Plato's view the alternatives Socrates forces on Theaetetus must be rejected in favor of this other conception of whole and part.

But even if this is so, I think it is clear that the atomistic theories within which the whole discussion has been moving have not the means to resist the assimilation of whole to sum. If the parts of a complex are just taken in succession, simply added together, it is indeed impossible to see how a whole could be different from a sum. Socrates' argument to show the identity of whole and sum is therefore reasonable, given the limits of the discussion. Hence when he takes the second conception of a συλλαβή, the one corresponding to the Parmenides' whole-as-container, and argues that on this view a complex is itself partless and therefore simple, he is arguing perfectly fairly. If the meaning of a sentence (for example) does not come piecemeal, word by word (as the conception of συλλαβή as a sum would imply), then it must come all at once upon the juxtaposition of the words. And in that case the complex will be something unitary and not related to the single words as whole to parts.

But the possibility still remains that Theaetetus' disinclination to accept Socrates' dichotomy shows a greater shrewdness on his part. Perhaps Plato is here indicating that, though the dream theory has not the means of distinguishing them, a whole and a sum are really different, and that if one attempts to see how this is so he will discover just where atomism goes wrong. This possibility is enhanced by a comparison of Socrates' argument in the Theaetetus with a second passage of the Parmenides (157b-158b). In the Theaetetus it is supposed that if a συλλαβή is not simply all its στοιχεῖα, it must be μία ἰδέα ἐξ ἑκάστων τῶν συναρμοττόντων στοιχείων γιγνομένη (204a 1-2), and as such not a whole of parts but an altogether new and unitary (μονοειδές τε καὶ ἀμέριστον, 205d 1-2) entity. But the Parmenides passage, in language almost identical to that of the Theaetetus, supposes that when parts are put together into a whole it is the whole, which is in a way the many parts (cf. 157e 4-5), which is also μία τις ἰδέα and ἐξ ἁπάντων ἓν τέλειον γεγονός (157d 8-e 2). In other words, the Parmenides seems in this passage to be recognizing that a whole is precisely not merely the sum of the elements, but a new unity which is not flatly identical with them nor yet quite separate and different from them, as the Theaetetus had tried to make the συλλαβή. Of course the Parmenides does not explain how a whole is such a unity, but the bare fact that it recognizes, in this passage at any rate, the necessity of treating a whole as neither a sum nor as something unitary but separate from the parts, seems to me to suggest that by denying the dream theory this possibility Plato means to be pointing out the direction in which one must begin to think in order to achieve a correct theory of complexity. A συλλαβή must in fact be an ordered whole which is both made up of its parts and yet a new unity not reducible to the sum of the parts taken separately. Though Plato does not firmly attain any satisfactory theory of complexity in the *Theaetetus* or *Parmenides*, when in the *Sophist* (252d-253a) he does finally formulate a better theory it is by taking the *Parmenides'* middle way between the *Theaetetus'* two alternatives.

The *Parmenides*, then, in one place seems to adopt a theory of the relation of whole to part which, if applied to the *Theaetetus'* question about συλλαβή and στοιχεῖα and made fully explicit, would lead to radical adjustments in the account of logos and complexity with which the *Theaetetus'* dream operates And it appears that in pointedly denying the dream this third way of conceiving a συλλαβή, Plato means to be indicating both that it is not available to anyone who thinks of the relations of part to whole and στοιχεῖον to συλλαβή as no more than additive, and that this is a fault in the dream theory. However this may be, Socrates himself in the *Theaetetus* accepts the same assumption as the dream theorist, as I have already remarked and as his further argument (206 a-b) against the dream theory shows: it is not *Socrates'* purpose to point this out as an inadequacy in the theory. He is, rather, arguing that there are only two possible ways of conceiving the relation of συλλαβή to στοιχεῖον, and that on either alternative to know a συλλαβή (whatever that should come to) one must be also knowing one or more στοιχεῖα. And whether or not Plato means us to see that the two alternatives do not in fact exhaust the possibilities, they do exhaust the possibilities open to the dream theory, and therefore Socrates' refutation is a fair one.

Having argued to this conclusion, Socrates clinches his point by taking up his promise to "test the letters and syllables" of words, to see whether or not learning one's letters comes about consistently with the thesis that συλλαβαί in general can be known but not στοιχεῖα. If the dream theory were correct we should only be able to know combinations of letters, and our apprehension of single letters should never amount to knowledge. But in fact, Socrates asserts (206a 5-8), in learning to write and spell, the learner's very object is to become proficient at recognizing and discriminating by sight and hearing each single letter just by itself (αὐτὸ καθ' αὑτὸ ἕκαστον) separating it off from the others with which it appears in combination. Knowing one's letters is precisely knowing each letter; and knowing combinations of letters is simply the result of knowing the individual letters. Hence the knowledge of letters is a more fundamental instance of knowledge than the knowledge of the syllables constructed out of them. To judge, then, from the case of letters and syllables, it must be mere joking paradox to say that complexes are knowable while simple elements are not.

Here Socrates is unmistakably endorsing the view that a complex is no more than a collection of independent parts; and accordingly he makes knowledge of the part fundamental to knowledge of the whole. It is important to see that by knowledge of the individual letter he has in mind a sort of awareness which in no way depends upon knowledge of its role in combinations: knowledge of combinations, in Socrates' view, is logically posterior to knowledge of elements taken just by themselves. Since syllables are only collections of letters, no letter can be doing anything in combination which it does not also do in its isolated state; hence knowledge of one's letters can safely be thought of as fully independent of knowledge of syllables. Naturally enough Socrates thinks of this knowledge as basically a matter of recognition, of singling out and correctly naming a sound or written symbol.

It is worth observing here that in later dialogues this simple view of letters and syllables is completely abandoned. Letters are no longer thought of as simple elements of syllables, and knowledge of letters is accordingly not any kind of simple awareness of isolated elements of language. Thus in the *Philebus* (18c 7) Plato argues that it is not possible to know any one letter without knowing them all, and *Politicus* 278a-c, as its context shows,[14] regards the occurrence of letters in combination not as an unfortunate contingency which merely makes the task of isolating each letter and getting a clear view of it difficult to accomplish (cf. *Tht.*, 206a 7), but as the crucial and essential fact about what each letter *is*: to learn a letter is to know what functions it performs *in syllables* and words, and there is no guarantee that knowing a letter in isolation will involve the knowledge of all these functions. Thus though letters are the elements of syllables, and Plato continues to speak of knowing these elements, they are no longer treated as _simple_ entities in the sense of the _Theaetetus_, and knowledge of them is not the simple type of awareness which the _Theaetetus'_ account implies.

The _Theaetetus_ nowhere espouses this later view, but works entirely within the confines of theories built on the opposite assumption that letters (and other elements) are altogether prior to the syllables (and other complexes) which are made up from them. Hence it is going too far to say, as Professor Ryle several times has come close to saying,[15] that in the dream and its refutation Plato definitely shows himself aware that knowledge is propositional or requires a kind of complexity which a simple object taken in isolation does not have. On the other hand the assumptions and some of the unpleasant consequences of the atomistic theories we have been confronted with in the last half of the dialogue are so clearly set out in the dream and its refutation that it is fair to say that the way is being prepared for later positive doctrines along the lines Ryle has indicated. But if the dream and its refutation provide the necessary food for thought which will, when digested, result in the elaboration of the later theories, this is not the same as rejecting old theories in favor of new. And it does seem clear that the most the examination of the dream does is to work out the consequences of atomism, without more positive conclusions.[16]

The upshot is that the dream theory cannot hold that complexes only can be known. Because it thinks of the relation of a whole to its parts as merely additive, it cannot mark the kind of difference it requires between simple and complex in order to maintain the complexity of knowing and its object. The same argument invoked by Socrates against this effort also shows that on a similarly additive atomistic conception of statement and language in general, saying something is only a matter of naming. Neither can knowledge of complex differ essentially from knowledge of simples, nor can a statement differ from a name, if the kind of atomism which we saw bedevilling the discussion of false belief continues to be affirmed.

C. The Three Subsequent Senses of Logos (206c-210b)

The remainder of the *Theaetetus* does not carry this reasoning forward to any more positive conclusion. Continuing to accept the assumptions which have had these ominous consequences, Socrates goes on to inquire what knowledge can be, given these assumptions and the results attained so far. The effect of his further investigation is to turn his attention from the object of knowledge and the question of its complexity, to the mental operation of knowing and the question what, on atomistic assumptions, knowing can be. As I have already said, the effect of atomism is to break down the distinction between knowing something and merely getting it into mind, recognizing it and naming it: in making knowledge of complexes a matter of knowledge of simples it makes all knowledge a species of mental attention to simple elements. The subsequent argument (206c 1-210b 3) considers the consequences of this.

In this passage Socrates proposes three senses of logos which someone might invoke as what must be had in addition to a right idea in order to possess knowledge. I pointed out above that the dream theory is not criticized as a theory of logos in the sense in which logos is something one gives of or for something of which he has a right idea. I think the first two of the three subsequent senses of logos are in fact applications of the dream theory which make it yield a sense of logos of the sort for which Socrates and Theaetetus were seeking. Thus if, according to the dream theory, things which can be indicated by a plurality of names said in succession have logos, logos might consist just in putting some names into conjunction in speech. Then to have knowledge would just be to have some objects in mind and say their names. "Giving logos" would just be speaking the names of things of which one had previously only a right idea. But obviously merely expressing a right idea in speech is not sufficient to show knowledge: anyone has the power of speech, so that in effect anyone with a right idea would also be able to have knowledge (206d 7-e 2).

But if merely expressing oneself in speech would not show knowledge, though this is one obvious sense of logos suggested by the account of simples and complexes given in the dream, perhaps the dream theory can be made to yield a different sense of logos. Giving logos in the relevant sense might be not just speaking but saying in succession the names of all the <u>elements</u> of a thing: one might have the thing in mind without having all the elements discriminated and explicitly labelled and to this (a right idea) one might add explicit attention to each of the elements, thus acquiring knowledge instead of a mere right idea. On this supposition, knowledge would amount to the ability to analyze an object into its constituent simple parts, and conjoining the names of the elements, i.e., constructing a logos, would be the expression of the knowledge of the complex thing. It would also, of course, show knowledge of the elements, since as we have seen to know a complex just _is_ to know its parts.

We have seen above, (p. 245 f.) how Socrates rejects the definition of knowledge as a right idea of a thing plus an analysis of it into its simple elements. It cannot be right to say that a person knows the first syllable of Theaetetus' name just because he lists correctly its simple parts (208a 9-b 2). Knowing the syllable is knowing the letters, but one such performance on one occasion does not show knowledge of either syllable or letters. At the very least one must correctly list the letters on other occasions when the same syllable turns up, in order to be rightly said to know the letter in question. If you sometimes think that "T" and "E" are the parts of "The," and sometimes "TH"[17] and "E" then you neither know "TH" nor the syllable "THE" of which it is a part, either on the occasion when you get them right or when you get them wrong. Since this is so the ability to provide an analysis of a thing cannot be a sufficient mark of knowledge of it.

Now in this second definition of logos Socrates has allowed the possibility that one could have a right idea of an object without also having in mind and recognizing its parts. Thus he supposes that someone could have the name "Theaetetus" in mind, which would presumably involve the ability to recognize it and pronounce it correctly, without having in mind, at least in the same way, the letters of which the name is made up. It is by relying on this difference that he introduces a distinction between knowledge of the name and its letters, and a mere right idea of the name. But it might be said that since according to the dream theory of complexes, which Socrates accepts, a complex of parts is just identical with its parts, to have even so much as a right idea of a complex is to have also a right idea of its parts. To have in mind and recognize "Theaetetus" is at the same time to have TH in mind recognized for itself, and so on through all the letters of the name. This is in fact the position taken in the third definition and its criticism. According to this definition, knowing a thing is having a right idea of it, plus the ability to express its differentness from other things (208d 6-7). According to the terms of the dream theory, an object (e.g., Theaetetus) is taken to be a complex made up of simple elements;[18] and grasping his difference amounts to getting explicitly into one's thoughts that element or set of elements which belong exclusively to him. The criticism of this theory turns on the insistence that even in having a right idea of Theaetetus one must already have all his simple parts present to the mind and fully recognized.

In explaining this third definition of logos Socrates at first employs the illustration of the sun, which is distinguished from all other things by the fact that it is the brightest body that goes around the earth. But he soon shifts to the example of Theaetetus, which he can more easily handle in accordance with the theory of complexity that is central to the whole discussion. To express Theaetetus' differentness is to have in mind, recognize, and name his peculiar snubness and the other elements proper to him. But here there is a difficulty. According to this account we are to have Theaetetus rightly in mind and then add logos of him in the sense explained. But what does this right idea consist in? It appears, in fact, that any one who has so much as a right idea of Theaetetus must have also in mind those features of him which constitute his differentness. For if only those features which Theaetetus shares with others are present in the idea someone has in mind, it does not seem correct to say that he is thinking of Theaetetus at all, rather than of any of the others who have just those same features. To be really having an idea of Theaetetus one must have in mind all his elements--his peculiar snubness, for example, and his peculiar pop-eyedness. In that case, in having a right idea of Theaetetus one necessarily also has a right idea of his differentness, since having him in mind involves having a right idea of all the elements of which he consists. What then does the third definition of logos come to? Since in having a right idea of a thing we necessarily also have a right idea of its differentness, it cannot mean by the addition of logos the acquisition of a right idea of the differentness. We already have that, and, in any case, having it, as we have seen, is compatible with having no more than a right idea of the thing. On the other hand, if the addition of logos means acquiring _knowledge_ of the thing's distinctive elements, the definition of knowledge as right idea plus logos has turned out to be circular. Knowledge of the thing involves knowledge of its distinctive elements, but one cannot hope to clarify knowledge of the complex by appealing blankly to knowledge of the parts. Hence the third sense of logos cannot be employed to clarify the notion of knowledge.

How are these final two definitions and their refutations to be construed? As is quite clear from my exposition of the argument, they are intimately connected with the theory of language, thought, and complexity in general which the dream theory adopts and which Socrates shares. They treat a complex object as the sum of its parts, and assume that knowing a complex is also knowing its parts. And they show that, whether or not having a right idea of a thing also involves having a right idea of its parts, knowledge of the thing cannot be defined by reference to one's situation vis-à-vis the parts. There is a difference between having a right idea of the parts and knowing them, though what the distinction is the theory cannot say; and appeal to the former is insufficient while appeal to the latter, so long as it is left unexplained, involves a vicious circle.

To obtain a firmer grasp on the argument I think it will be useful to consider again the difficulties that arose in the discussion of false belief. At the outset (188a-b) Socrates assumes that anything anyone can have in his thoughts must be something he knows: if he doesn't know, e. g., Socrates at all then of course he can't entertain any thought of Socrates. And we saw that this assumption was dependent on the idea that to have something in one's thoughts was to have, as it were, an object before one's mind, correctly recognized and labelled. The subsequent discussion attempted various ways of loosening the connection between having a thing in mind and knowing it, but it was accepted throughout that if one is <u>actively</u> engaged in thinking of a thing then one must know what thing is the object of his thought, and this involves naming it correctly (and therefore prevents mistaking it for anything else). Knowing an object is here thought of as a kind of recognition or acquaintance and therefore actively thinking of anything is also knowing it.

Now the fundamental thesis lying behind this whole discussion is, as I have argued, the view that speaking is at bottom no more than naming. Stating a fact is thought of as naming the elements that make it up; saying something about a thing is construed as naming the things in question, and nothing more. Hence thinking about a thing or a fact is just directing one's thoughts toward some objects. Knowledge of facts thus must reduce to knowledge of objects, and there appears to be no room for knowledge except as recognition or acquaintance, since there is no room for any other mental operation than recognizing. Hence in the discussion of false belief even thinking of an object is knowing it. In the third section of the dialogue, however, the distinction between simples and complexes is introduced and, although there is still fundamentally no mental operation except recognition, labelling, acquaintance, and contact (cf. ἐφαπτόμενος, 190c 6), it appears to be possible to distinguish, at least for complexes, between mere having-in-mind and knowing. For if a thing has parts it may be possible to have it in mind, recognized and labelled correctly, without, however, having explicit awareness of its parts.

It is this hypothesis which the final two definitions of logos explore. It takes two forms: to know a thing is either to have it in mind and have also in mind all its simple parts, or to have it in mind and have also in mind that one simple part or set of simple parts which is distinctive of the thing in question. The criticism of the two suggestions shows (a) that even in the case of complexes knowledge requires knowing the parts and (b) that knowing the parts cannot simply be getting them into mind and recognizing them (having a right idea of them). At the very least, knowledge of a simple part (e.g., a letter) requires recognition of it not only on one occasion but as a regular thing. And though in making this point (207d-208a) Socrates appears to think of knowledge of a letter as no more than the ability to grasp or recognize a discrete element (it does not involve the more sophisticated knowledge of function appealed to in the _Philebus_ and _Politicus_), he at least shows that knowledge of a letter cannot be something exhibited on a single occasion without reference to other performances on other occasions: at the very least knowledge is not _mere_ grasping or recognition of a thing or group of things. The point is reinforced when Socrates urges, in his criticism of the third definition, that even to have a right idea of a complex is already to have a right idea of all its elements. For in that case one has done all the grasping and recognizing which there is room for even before there is any question of having acquired knowledge. Both the complex and all its elements have been picked out and correctly recognized and still knowledge has not resulted. What more is there which one could do, on the theory of language and thinking being accepted here, to permit knowledge whether of complex or of simple, to take place? It seems that the notions of recognition, mental touching, and having something in the mind are not sufficient apparatus for understanding knowledge, even knowledge of, as opposed to knowledge about, an object. For though given atomistic assumptions there must be knowledge of simple objects if there is knowledge of anything, the battery of concepts admitted by atomism proves insufficient to distinguish between a right idea and knowledge of simple objects; but, as Socrates shows for two favored cases, there _is_ a difference between knowing a simple object and merely having a right idea of it.

Now I do not wish to say that the argument of the closing pages of the dialogue refutes the atomistic theories of meaning and thinking which have these ultimate consequences. I have already said that I think the tenor of the argument exploratory rather than destructive. But the ground is laid in the final section of the _Theaetetus_ for a destructive criticism of these theories. For the analysis is carried to the point where some explanation of knowledge of a simple object must be provided. And as the explanation must square with the simplicity of the objects in question, it may well be doubted whether any such explanation can be forthcoming. A simple object has (201e 3) only a name; it must be immediately apprehended. One mode of immediate apprehension is the ἀληθὴς δόξα in question throughout the closing pages of the dialogue, which in this context involves recognition, correct naming, and similar capacities. Whether there is room for two different modes of immediate mental awareness seems doubtful. But to the existence of some such additional awareness, somehow deeper or closer than a right idea, atomism is clearly committed.

Whether at the time he wrote the *Theaetetus* Plato saw the necessity of abandoning the atomism to which he had earlier been attracted is not easily decidable. It may be that having reached the conclusions set out just above reflection led him to see that knowledge of elements in general, letters as well as other types of constituents, is in fact not aptly represented on the model of being in contact with something or recognizing something for itself. It is in any case certain that both in his use of the letters-syllables analogy in dialogues certainly later than the *Theaetetus*, and in subsequent remarks about knowing, he clearly does not think of letters or other elements as *simples* in anything like the sense of the *Theaetetus*' dream. Elements, like anything else, are the subjects of judgments and not merely of names, and accordingly knowing them is not having any kind of simple awareness of an object. In the passages from the *Politicus* and *Philebus* already cited (pp. 266-267) the knowledge of letters, whether written symbols or uttered sounds,[19] is not a recognizing and labelling operation. It is knowledge *about* something recognized and named correctly, knowledge that it fits with other letters in certain ways and not in others; that it belongs to certain subgroups among the letters and not to others (cf. *Philebus*, 18b 8-c 5, *Sophist*, 252e 9-253a 7). Knowing about letters is at the same time knowing about syllables.

In concentrating on the atomistic theories at work in the discussion of knowledge in the last part of the *Theaetetus* I have had nothing to say about the theory of Forms (except in connection with what I have taken to be mistaken interpretations of the argument). This was because the problems about saying, thinking, and knowing which occupy Plato's attention throughout the discussion are much more fundamental ones than those which led him, in earlier dialogues, to hold that knowledge of Forms is either the only knowledge there is, or is the preeminent kind, as being implied by knowledge of other types. For whether the objects a person knows are Forms or some other kind of thing, there is the further question how to describe the mental phenomenon which is the knowledge of these objects. And in earlier dialogues Plato either neglects this question or suggests that knowing a thing is a kind of mental touching. In the last half of the _Theaetetus_ this previously neglected or ill-conceived question is brought to the fore and vigorously pursued, as we have seen. It is only natural, therefore, that the Forms are not brought into the discussion.[20]

This does not, however, mean that the discussion does not have very important bearings on the theory of Forms. For if knowledge of an object is not recognitional but essentially a matter of knowing some truths about it, then Forms, in order to be known, must be the kind of thing about which there are truths. Just as letters cannot be _simple_ elements of language, so Forms cannot be _simple_ objects of thought. And the shift in the conception of letters and what it is to know them brings with it a clarification, even if not a radical change, in the conception of Forms and what it is to know them. Thus Plato in the _Philebus_ (16d 5-7), in an evident self-criticism, remarks that it is not enough simply to discern a single Form present in many individuals; all the distinctions to be found within it must also be noticed and given their proper place in the scheme of Forms making up the original unity discerned; and knowing these subordinate Forms, as Plato's illustration about knowledge of letters (17a 8 ff.) shows, involves the discernment of similarities, differences, and other interconnections among Forms, a discernment which is not in any case a matter of fixing attention upon an object regarded as a simple object of apprehension.[21]

In the *Theaetetus*, however, as I have said, nothing of these further developments appears. Letters are simple constituents of syllables, syllables are collections of letters. Saying is naming some objects and thinking is having objects before the mind. The consequences of these views are followed up so far as to show that simple elements must be knowable, and it is then shown that knowing here must consist in something more than recognition or getting the thing into mind, despite the fact that any one who held the views in question would be hard-pressed to say what beyond this knowledge of a simple element could be. With this Socrates and Theaetetus abandon the search for a definition of knowledge: before the discussion can be carried to a more satisfactory conclusion, the atomistic theory of meaning and its associated theory of mental operations must be definitively rejected in favor of more correct ways of thinking about assertion, belief, and knowledge.

FOOTNOTES

(For complete references and explanation of abbreviations, the Bibliography should be consulted.)

NOTES TO INTRODUCTION

1. Cf. Diès, *Notice* to Budé edition of *Tht.*, p. 120.

2. Cf. *The Theaetetus of Plato*, pp. lxi-lxii. (Campbell, however, thought the *dialogue* was composed much later.) Campbell's reasons for rejecting the 369 date for the battle seem to me curiously weak. That Terpsion should have waited 30 years to ask to see Euclides' record of Socrates' conversation with Theaetetus (143a 6-7) seems to me not so much more unusual than that he should have waited 6 or 7; and its implausibility is far less than the implausibility which (if I am right about the memorial character of the dialogus) Campbell is left with, given his belief that the dialogue was written much later than 394. (Cf. also Diès' remarks, *op. cit.* pp. 120-121.)

3. Cf. Shorey, Introduction to Loeb *Republic*, I, pp. xxiv-xxv, and Ross, *Plato's Theory of Ideas*, pp. 5-6.

4. Cf. *op. cit.*, pp. xxii-xxiv.

5. As Socrates' reference at *Tht.* 183e 7 ff. to his youthful encounter with Parmenides seems good reason to think.

6. Cf. G.E.L. Owen, "The Place of the *Timaeus*," *SPM* pp. 313-338. See also below pp. 9 f.

7. Cf. *The Unity of Plato's Thought* and "Recent Platonism in England," AJP 9 (1888), 274-309.

8. Cf. Lutoslawski, *Origin and Growth* pp. 224-5, and Susemihl *Genetische Entwickelung*, I, p. 161.

9. See his articles on "Plato's Later Theory of Ideas," *Journal of Philosophy* 1882-1888; cf. Shorey's attack on Jackson's (and Archer-Hind's) views in his "Recent Platonism".

10. Cf. "Recent Platonism" pp. 279-281.

11. Cf. *Unity* pp. 49 ff., especially pp. 55-56; cf. for

the general point "Recent Platonism" pp. 280-281 (it is one main thesis of his dissertation, *De Platonis Idearum Doctrina*).

12. By G.E.L. Owen, "The Place of the *Timaeus*".

13. And the one most cited as a basis for scepticism about Owen's "redating" of the *Timaeus*: cf. Runciman, "Plato's 'Parmenides'", *SPM* p. 152, and Skemp, *Plato's Statesman* p. 238.

14. *A Commentary on Plato's Timaeus*, p. 4.

15. "The Relation of the *Timaeus* to Plato's Later Dialogues", *SPM* pp. 344, 346.

16. Op. cit., pp. 315-316.

17. Op. cit., p. 345.

NOTES TO CHAPTER I

1. Cf. also 168b 6-7 and 183a 3-4 where the same relation is clearly asserted to hold between Theaetetus' definition and these philosophical theories.

2. I shall never mean by "Protagoras" anything but the opponent Plato presents himself within this dialogue. Such attempts as Cornford's (*PTK*, pp. 33-36), based on an article of Brochard ("Protagore et Démocrite", *Etudes* pp. 23-33) to determine what Protagoras really said may or may not be of interest from other points of view, but for the purpose of understanding Plato they are at best superfluous. (Cornford's excursus here actually seems to mislead him into grossly misunderstanding 172a-b; see my discussion below (pp. 81 ff.). There is no doubt that of the two alternatives Cornford discusses, it is the *second* which *Plato's* Protagoras adopts; so the less said about the first alternative, which Cornford thinks Protagoras actually held, the better.

3. The theory of perception outlined at 156-157, which is presented as the μυστήρια of certain sophisticated thinkers, is pretty clearly likewise an elaboration, of Plato's own devising, of the essential doctrines of Heracleiteanism. Thus both the appeal to the flux doctrine as a general support for Protagoreanism and the detailed exploration of how the doctrine

applies to perception and supports a Protagorean account of perceptual judgements, are clearly marked as contributions of Plato's own to the philosophical analysis of the questions and doctrines concerned.

4. Owen, "Proof", SPM p. 305; cf. with my remarks here Owen's discussion of καθ' αὑτό and πρός τι, pp. 302-309.

5. Not in such places as 518c 9, 525c 5 and 534a 4 where γένεσις occurs as a status word designating the realm of perceptibles. Such casual uses of the term cannot be made to bear any heavy philosophical weight in the absence of explicit arguments in favor of one theory or another.

6. My use of the Tim. here to establish what thesis is asserted in the Tht. does not imply any decision on my part on the question of the relative chronology of Tim. and Tht. I do in fact think it extremely unlikely that the Tim. postdates the Tht. (in view, for example, of Plato's refutation of the doctrine of flux in 181-184). But even those who think that Plato in the Tht. accepts a flux doctrine of sorts (one restricted, as the Tim.'s clearly is, to perceptible things), and only rejects a so-called "unrestricted Heracleiteanism" which, like that announced at Tht. 152d-e, holds that nothing anywhere (here below or in a supposed higher realm) is stable in any respect, will have to grant that the flux doctrine of the Tim. coincides with that of the Tht. for the area of their overlap. I use the Tim. here merely because the doctrine is more fully elaborated there than it is in the Tht.

7. Strictly speaking, some part of the receptacle of becoming; the distinction does not matter for my purposes.

8. Commentary, p. 67; compare Cornford PC p. 25: "it is true that in such 'becoming' something new is always appearing, something old passing away; but the process itself can be conceived as going on perpetually."

9. Commentary, pp. 71-2.

10. I do not wish to imply that the Heracleiteans have a right to this use of εἶναι if they deny themselves the other (indeed Plato argues in 181-184 that they do not), but only that to understand what they wish to maintain one must permit them to retain it at least provisionally without the other use.

11. E.g. *Commentary* pp. 348, 342, 122, 117.

12. The similar argument of *Republic* 524d-e explicitly says ἀεί τι αὐτῷ ἅμα ὁρᾶται ἐναντίωμα: cf. *Phdo*. 74b-c. The *Phaedo* nowhere through this discussion even suggests that it is *change* that makes physical equals unsatisfactory instances of equality.

13. Or, possibly, equal to one observer and not to another (depending on how one takes τῷ μὲν ἴσα ... τῷ δ' οὔ, 74b 8-9: cf. Owen, "Proof", *SPM* p. 306 n. 2).

14. That it becomes fiery at moment *t* is not the same thing as its being in process of becoming fiery at moment *t*. The former (non-continuous) usage is required by the flux theory, the latter (continuous) is apparently required by Taylor's application of the flux theory to the *Phaedo*'s discussion of equality.

15. Cf. Campbell p. 53. Actually it is the first two which conflict with the third. There is no indication here (*pace* Robinson "Forms and Error", p. 29-30, seconded by Runciman *PLE* p. 17 note) that the three propositions are *internally* inconsistent or self-contradictory, but only that they cannot all be true if certain further propositions are accepted: cf. also Cherniss *AJP* 68 (1947) p. 136.

16. This being so I doubt that it is right to say that the analysis of the puzzles about size and number represents an advance on the *Phaedo*'s conception of relations. (Cf. *Soph*. 255c 12-d 1, 256a 10-b 4)

17. *The Theaetetus of Plato*, p. 59 (*ad* 156c 9).

18. So Protagoras is made to say in his reply (166b 8): in the actual exposition (157e-160c) this is never stated bluntly, though it is clearly implied by, e.g., 159e 8 ff.

19. Campbell, p. 74 (*ad* 160e 5).

20. Cf. Campbell p. 71 (*ad* 159e 7): "The intention of these words is to mark the incommunicable individuality of every act of sense; i.e. not *wine* or *bitterness*, but the peculiar bitterness of a particular wine to a particular palate at a particular moment."

21. So apparently Campbell (p. 68, *ad* 159a 6).

22. By Gulley, Plato's Theory of Knowledge, pp. 78-80.

23. It should be observed here that it is not only the argument of 157-160 which is inconsequent, but also that of the puzzles of size and number (154-155); and the theory of perception, as I have already remarked, is hardly a serious Heracleitean theory. In fact, there is nothing of any real importance in the whole course of the amalgamation which is well argued.

24. The Theaetetus of Plato, p. 68.

NOTES TO CHAPTER II

1. So I interpret Socrates' concluding remark, 179c.

2. Or made sincerely. Presumably Protagoras would not wish to deny that a man might lie. In this case one can say that Protagoras' dictum does not make the liar's statement true, because what the liar says is not what really seems to him to be the case: Protagoras' theory carefully maintains only the truth of a man's φαινόμενα.

3. Cf. e.g. 152a 6-8, b 6-7, c 3, 158a 6-7, e 5-6, 160c 7-8, to mention only relevant passages occurring before 161c. There is a tendency to drop the suffixes only when one argues from something's being true to x to its being known by him (knowing a thing being throughout associated with its existence or its being the case, simpliciter): cf. 152c 5-6, 158a 2-3, 160c 8-9.

4. Cornford appears to think (PTK p. 62) that the fact that men have a faculty of thought as well as perception does make a difference, but it obviously does not.

5. Protagoras is here treated not as the mere custodian of Theaetetus' theory, but as if he wished to argue Theaetetus' theory on his own account. THis is one of the places where the earlier reduction of the theories to one another is treated as effected (this despite the fact that in this passage Theaetetus is specifically twitted for carelessly identifying perception and knowledge: later on in the refutation Protagoras himself is given his full view, which does not limit knowledge to sense-perception).

6. PTK pp. 62-3.

7. _PTK_ pp. 67-8. How this result is supposed to follow is not easy to discern. Cornford seems to make Theaetetus' acceptance of the account of perception given above the crucial factor in the argument's validity. But nothing in the argument even suggests that seeing is being thought of as the kind of process the Heracleitean account makes it; nor do I see how the argument gains in cogency by so construing it. As I point out below, it is in fact not a good argument at all, nor do I think it valid against either Theaetetus or Protagoras.

8. _PLE_ p. 13.

9. Even stern Plato wrote the _Euthydemus_. Of course the fact that a dialectical display is primarily meant for amusement does not prevent it from raising _some_ difficulties which would trouble even a philosopher in more sober mood. This is the case with some of the _Euthydemus_' arguments, as well as with the second of these three arguments of the _Theaetetus_.

10. Cornford (_PTK_ p. 63) carelessly says that what this argument shows is that there is a sense of "know" (which occurs in "I know French") which cannot be reduced to knowing as perceiving. But as, according to this sense of "know", I can know something even when I'm asleep and not perceiving anything, it is not quite the sense of "know" at issue in the argument (however related it may be). The correct "sense" of "know" is the one indicated in the text--according to which I know certain sounds just in case I am actually perceiving them and recognizing them as those sounds.

11. I therefore do not see how this argument has whatever validity it does have only (or primarily) in connection with some one who accepts the Heracleitean theory of perception. It manifestly applies for any one who grants that there are two organs of sight.

12. 166b 1-4: undergoing a memory experience is having an experience of a different sort from the original perceptual one (though he does not quite say the memory experience is a kind of _sense_ experience). The extension of perception to include such modes of awareness as remembering is, as Cornford says (_PTK_ p.65), the important result forced by the second argument upon Theaetetus' definition.

13. This reply seems to me directed as much against the seeing-not seeing argument as against the memory argument,

given that the "seeing" argument is just a more extreme version of its predecessor. I agree with Runciman (*PLE* pp. 13-14) that Cornford (*PTK* p. 69), is wrong to take it as a reply *only* to the δεινότατον ἐρώτημα, but I think Runciman himself wrong to think that neither this nor the other replies answers that objection.

14. Cf. *Euthyd.* 287a where a similar view of the sophists Dionysodorus and Euthydemus (though based on Eleatic and not Protagorean grounds) is made to lead to a similar personal embarrassment. It is important to note, however, that Protagoras takes the embarrassment seriously, whereas Dionysodorus does not: the sophistical movement had not the uniformity often attributed to it.

15. I am unimpressed by Cornford's assurances (*PTK* p. 72) that this part of the Defense represents genuine Protagorean doctrine. If Protagoras himself actually held the theory of wisdom attributed to him by Plato, I see no reason for Socrates' caution below (169d-e), where he feels the need of proving from Protagoras' own words that he accepts differences of wisdom of the sort attributed to him in the Defense. Cornford in effect later grants this (p. 77), but without finding any conflict with the interpretation of the Defense he earlier adopts.

16. G. Grote, *Plato and the Other Companions of Socrates*, vol. ii, ch. xxvi (cf. pp. 347-363 of the 2nd ed.).

17. Runciman holds a similar view (*PLE* pp. 26-29). But he thinks that what Plato is out to get in the digression is the "pragmatic interpretation of wisdom" which Protagoras has been upholding. Against this he finds Plato saying that wisdom consists in knowledge of certain "absolute standards". But (a) nowhere in the digression is any emphasis put upon the fact that the man of public affairs is *wise* in Protagoras' sense: he does not change any laws or any one's opinions by "reference to criteria of expediency". His function is rather that of manipulating existing laws to his own best advantage. And (b) the passage which is supposed to give Plato's alternative conception of wisdom and knowledge does not say what Runciman quotes it as saying. The passage (176b 8-c 5) says: "God is nowhere and in no way unrighteous, but as righteous as it is possible to be, and nothing is more like god than that man of us who becomes as righteous as possible. . . . . The knowledge of this fact is wisdom and true virtue." No reference here to "absolute standards" as what one must get in touch with in order to have knowledge.

18. Cornford takes 172b 2-6 to be stating a view about δίκαια, ὅσια, etc. which is at variance with Protagoras' and goes beyond it by denying that any of these has any "objective being" (PTK p. 82) of its own: justice and religious propriety are mere conventions and have φύσει no οὐσία of their own. It is not, however, easy to understand what then Cornford believes Protagoras' view to be, inasmuch as he grants that 172a 1-4 expresses Protagoras' view, and can hardly deny that 177c 8-d 2 resumes that same view: these passages, as well as 167c 4-5, make it quite clear that Protagoras held that all a state has to do to make anything really right for it is to decree that it is so, and the view which denies φύσει οὐσία to τὰ δίκαια, etc., is itself glossed as holding that τὸ κοινῇ δόξαν τοῦτο γίγνεται ἀληθὲς τότε, ὅταν δόξῃ καὶ ὅσον ἂν δοκῇ χρόνον. The two views seem, therefore, to coincide, and Cornford is able to persuade himself that they diverge only because he thinks (cf. n. 2 to ch. I, p.281 above) that Protagoras' view about sense-qualities does not deny their οὐσία in the thing perceived to have them but rather asserts the compresence of all the qualities which any and every one perceives. This is, however, highly conjectural, and in any case the denial of οὐσία to τὰ δίκαια at 172b does not introduce an analogue of the more extreme doctrine about sense-qualities which Cornford canvasses and rejects (pp. 32-36) as an interpretation of Protagoras' view about them. Furthermore, the μείζων λόγος of 172b 8 quite certainly (cf. d 5-6) means "longer discussion" and not "more important theory", as Cornford takes it (so as to support his understanding of the denial of οὐσία φύσει to τὰ δίκαια) (cf. Bischoff Hermes 1939 pp. 104-108). Thirdly, ὅσοι ἂν λέγωσιν (172b 6-7) should be read and interpreted (so Diès in the Budé tr.) to mean that those who do not go all the way with Protagoras willingly admit (as Protagoras does not) that judgements about what is to the advantage of a state may be right or wrong, but agree with Protagoras in holding that whatever any state judges to be right is right. I doubt that, even with the reading ὅσοι γε δὴ ... λέγουσι (Cornford's preference), any other sense could naturally be gotten from the Greek: to say that some one does not argue παντάπασι the same as someone else is to imply that there is some common ground between them, and if Protagoras and these alleged other people do not agree about τὰ δίκαια, it is not clear what they do agree about.

19. 175c 1-6. Cornford sees here a reference to the Moral Forms of the Republic. But the philosopher here in question is not specially a Platonist, as 173b and e prove; no particular theory about how these large questions are answered should be read into the description of them, All that

is said is that the philosopher recognizes these questions in addition to those the legal-minded person asks himself. (Cf. Robinson, "Forms and Error", p. 9).

NOTES TO CHAPTER III

1. Parm. 138b.

2. οὐδέ τιν' ἄλλην αἴσθησιν μᾶλλον ἢ μή must mean (so Diès, cf. Campbell ad loc.) "nor is any other sense-perception any more that one than another", and not (so Cornford) "nor is any other perception entitled to be called perception rather than not-perception". Understanding Plato in Cornford's way here makes for a smoother inference in e 10-11 (cf. Cherniss "Relation of the Timaeus", SPM p. 356: "since sensation is then no more sensation than not sensation and so no more knowledge than not knowledge"), but is quite certainly not what the Greek says: Cornford translates οὐδέ τιν' ἄλλην αἴσθησιν μᾶλλον αἴσθησιν ἢ μή.

3. I believe e 10-11 contains the following inference: (a) Ex hypothesi knowledge = perception and (therefore: cf. 164b 1-2) not-knowledge = not-perception. (b) But according to Heracleiteanism, as we have now seen, nothing is any more entitled to be called perception than not-perception. Ergo, we have not said anything in (a) that in any way distinguishes not-knowledge from knowledge; anything that is knowledge by that definition turns out to be also not-knowledge, so that our definition fits knowledge no better than it does not-knowledge.

4. Robinson, "Forms and Error," pp. 9-10; Owen, "Place of the Timaeus," SPM pp. 323-324.

5. The doctrine it provides for Plato, that αἰσθητά are in flux but the Forms are not, has been taken as canonical Platonic metaphysics since the time of Aristotle: cf. Met. A. 6. 987a 32-b 1. And as Aristotle implies that Plato never gave up his restricted Heracleiteanism, so interpreters often take it for granted that the weak interpretation must be the correct one.

6. PTK, p. 101.

7. Cherniss, SPM p. 357n., quoting Owen, SPM p. 324, says, "it is clear that οὐσία is not 'ascribed to the objects

of perception' as such but is an 'object of thought'." This shows *ignoratio elenchi*: object of thought or no, αἰσθητά *are* said to have οὐσία.

8. Gulley, pp. 73, 84 ff., thinks that Plato's argument at 182-3 does imply that nothing can be said of phenomena, because there are no "determinate sensible characteristics," and yet that he intended this *not* as a *reductio* of the flux doctrine of phenomena but as the correct consequence of a true doctrine. The necessity he then finds himself in (pp. 86-87) of explaining away the argument of 184-6 and its appeal to οὐσία is sufficient proof that Gulley has not got 181-184 right either.

9. It should be further observed that Cornford performs an act of supererogation in introducing into his analysis of this passage a reference to the fact that the Forms are objects of knowledge *and are required if knowledge is to be possible*. All that *this* argument sets out to show is (1) that the equation of knowledge with perception cannot be defended κατὰ τὴν τοῦ πάντα κινεῖσθαι μέθοδον and (2) that Heracleiteanism is false (either wholly or in part). To do these things Forms as objects of knowledge are irrelevant; at the most it is pertinent to introduce Forms as transcendental entities which make possible discourse about phenomena as about other things. It is only in the argument of 184-186, if anywhere, that Forms as objects of knowledge become relevant: for there, when Plato attempts to prove directly that perception is not knowledge, it is at least relevant to mention that objects of perception change whereas knowledge requires unchanging objects. For this reason Hackforth's defense ("Plat. Forms in the *Tht.*" pp. 54-55) of Cornford in the face of Robinson's attack ("Forms and Error" pp. 9-10) cannot help matters: the correct reply to Robinson (though I think not even this could ultimately be defended) is that it *is* correct to infer from the refutation of Heracleiteanism to the existence of Forms because the existence of Forms alone prevents phenomenal processes from being not amenable to truth and falsehood.

10. *ACP* pp. 214-218 (cf. 315-316 and notes 216 and 217), and "Philosophical Economy," *SPM* pp.9-10.

11. *ACP* p. 217.

12. *Ibid.*, p. 218.

13. The idea seems to be the same as that which I said above Taylor sometimes slips into attributing to Plato in the *Timaeus* (See pp. 24 ff. above).

14. *AJP* 1936 (*SPM* pp. 1-12); cf. pp. 9-11 for the argument. That the version here is intended to be the same as that in *ACP* expounded above is evident from, among other things, the identity of the formulation of the conclusion and of the general line of argument.

15. P. 9.

16. P. 10.

17. Cf. *Parm.* 160e 1-2 for a somewhat similar use of an abstract noun for something not an abstract quality in the required sense.

18. This same point refutes Shorey's interpretation (*AJP* vol. 10 (1889) p. 64) of this passage. Shorey says that here and in *Crat.* 439-440 Plato allows to himself τοιοῦτον in describing a phenomenal object, but denies even this much to Heracleiteans; and according to S. he is not inconsistent in so doing, since he has, while the Heracleiteans do not, the Forms to fall back on. Having the Forms is supposed to permit Plato to say οἷα ἄττα ῥεῖ τὰ φερόμενα (182c 10). But as we have seen Plato argues that the condition of being able to say this is that these ἄττα *not* be in motion in *every* respect. So even if he has the Forms he is no more able to allow himself τοιοῦτον than the Heracleiteans are, *if* he agrees with them that no phenomenon is stable in any respect.

19. Cherniss refers to the passage in his discussions of the *Tht.* argument both in *ACP* (p. 217) and in "Economy" (*SPM* p. 10). Cornford (*PTK* p. 99) even quotes it. Cf. also Stoelzel p. 70n. For details of the similarity of Aristotle's argument in Γ.5 as a whole and Plato's refutation of Protagoreanism and Heracleiteanism, cf. Cherniss *ACP* p. 217.

20. Indeed, he limits his criticism of it to this point, whereas as I have already remarked Plato goes further (183a 8-b 5) and points out that the theory does not really imply that anything is *both* large *and* not-large (e.g.), but is denied *all* use of language, this one included.

21. ACP p. 217.

22. Cf. Campbell p. 151, etc.

23. These facts, and the fact that nowhere else in his extant writings does Plato directly confront Heracleiteanism, have plausibly been argued to show the chronological affinity of *Theaetetus* and *Cratylus*: Cf. Warburg, *Zwei Fragen zum Kratylos*, pp. 31-61, especially pp. 55 ff. Cf. also Owen, "Place of the *Timaeus*," *SPM* p. 323 n. 3.

24. Cf. 402a-c and 411b-c where the doctrines of Heracleitus and his followers are put in terms which, if regarded quite strictly, do make the theory quite close to that of the *Theaetetus* (cf. esp. 411b 8, πάντως φέρεσθαι, c 4 μεστὰ πάσης φορᾶς καὶ γενέσεως ἀεί. But in the etymologies which are supposed to exhibit dependence on this theory it is only the idea of motion that is retained, and not that of motion of a thing in every respect. Likewise the final argument against Heracleiteanism, while obviously aware of the self-refuting character of the theory (cf. 439d 8-e 3, 439e 7-440a 4), does not press the point but instead goes on to talk about some hypothesized (cf. 439c 7 ὃ ἔγωγε πολλάκις ὀνειρώττω 440c 1-3, d 2-3) entities that never change in *any* respect.

25. Cf. Gulley pp. 70-76, Cherniss "Relation of the *Timaeus*", *SPM* p. 356. Gulley argues, and Cherniss asserts, that in the *Cratylus* Plato grants that phenomena are in constant flux. Gulley bases this view on two considerations: (1) in 439d 4 the clause καὶ δοκεῖ ταῦτα πάντα ῥεῖν appears not to mean (carrying forward the εἰ of d 3) "[we are not enquiring] whether all these seem to be in flux", but rather (though this is grammatically more difficult) "and all these do seem to be in flux." The latter reading, he thinks (p. 72), makes the clause a "statement by Plato that he accepts the doctrine of flux as true for sensibles". But this is silly. All Plato says, even assuming the doubtful reading G. wants, is that faces and other such things, inasmuch as they obviously do change, lend plausibility to the flux doctrine; it is not straight off obviously false or absurd to say that they are in flux. He does not say he accepts the flux doctrine for them, but only that he's not going to discuss its adequacy as an account of them. (This is only prudent, if my interpretation of the arguments of *Crat.* and *Tht.* is right, since it requires more than one Stephanus page (the extent of the *Cratylus'* argument) to show why Heracleiteanism is not true of phenomena (the *Theaetetus* requires major portions of thirty pages, 152-183, to prepare for and provide the proof)). (2) In his subsequent argument Plato shows that if the flux doctrine is true there can be no significant discourse and no knowledge. But he is not satisfied with making this point abstractly: he mentions as objects of

knowledge the Forms, which he argues must therefore be at rest. Surely his reason for doing this is that he accepted that phenomena are in flux and therefore considered that if there were not some non-sensible entities there would in fact be no knowledge. This is a non-sequitur. Though it is true that Plato implies (440b 4-c 1) that knowledge must be of absolutely unchanging objects, nothing in the argument requires or even suggests that nothing else than the Forms is unchanging in any respect or for any time. Phenomena may very well be exempt from flux without yet being suitable objects of knowledge; this, in fact, seems to be the position at which Plato has arrived by the end of the Cratylus. Neither of Gulley's allegations, then, can stand criticism: Plato does not announce his acceptance of the flux theory for phenomena, and by making Forms the objects of knowledge he does not imply that phenomena are in total flux.

26, It is omitted altogether in Cherniss' paraphrase of these closing pages of the Cratylus, "Relation of the Timaeus" SPM pp. 356-7. C. wishes to say that Plato argues from the possibility of knowledge to the necessity of Forms; even if this is what is argued at 439e 7-440c 1, it is perverse to speak as if that's all the passage argues. It also argues from the possibility of discourse, and not merely of knowledge.

27. Cf. Soph. 249b, which likewise asserts that to know anything it must be at rest in some respects, and denies that the object of knowledge is altogether unmoving (cf. Moravcsik, "Being and Meaning in the Sophist", pp. 39-40). Alternative interpretations of this passage, like that which Cherniss announces with such elan, but does not argue (SPM p. 352), fail for, among others, the reasons cited by Moravcsik against Ross.

28. Unless expressions of the form "not even such-and-such", understood as ἄπειρα λεγόμενα can be employed (183b 4-5). Prof. Owen has suggested to me (what Campbell may be hinting at, p. 272) that Socrates may here have in mind purely negative uses of language, i.e. ones which are not taken in any way to delimit or define in any positive way at all the subject under discussion.

NOTES TO CHAPTER IV

1. Compare, e.g., the brief remarks of Campbell (pp. liii-liv), Ryle ("Plato's *Parmenides*", *SPM* p. 136), and Owen ("Place of the *Timaeus*", *SPM* p. 324), with the interpretations of Cherniss ("Relation of the *Timaeus*", *SPM* p. 357 n., and *ACP* pp. 235-6, n. 141), Cornford (*PTK* p. 108-109) and Stoelzel (pp. 74-76).

2. So Cornford, *PTK* p. 104; cf. Runciman *PLE* p. 15 and my comments below, note 9.

3. So Cherniss, "Relation of the *Timaeus*", *SPM* p. 357 n.; cf. Shorey, *Unity* pp. 33-4 (159-60).

4. Cornford *PTK* p. 109; cf. also Runciman *PLE* p. 15.

5. Cf. Cornford *PTK* pp. 102, 105, 108.

6. Chiefly the fact that (186e) he restricts *truth* to the realm where the soul operates without an organ, thus denying that sense perceptions are true.

7. Throughout here I make no effort to formulate my interpretation of Plato with attention to all the niceties the subject of perception requires on its own account. Plato of course writes in a similarly rough and ready way.

8. So Cornford, *PTK* p. 105.

9. Ἐπισκοπεῖν need not mean "contemplate" (so Cornford, cf. Runciman, *loc.cit.*): cf. ἐπισκέψασθαι, which is the aorist used to meet the defect in ἐπισκοπεῖν, just above, 185b, 5. Cf. also 161d 5, e 7, where both ἐπισκέψασθαι and ἐπισκοπεῖν appear and neither means "contemplate".

10. Only 186a 4 even remotely imports an interest in how we become acquainted with the κοινά, and its immediate sequel is quite evidently concerned not with how to acquire an acquaintance with κοινά but with how to employ it in making judgments about αἰσθητά.

11. This much has been seen by various writers: thus Horn (*Platonstudien*, N.F., pp. 237-238) and Taylor (*PMW* p. 339). But they seem not to have followed out very far its consequences: cf. Horn's reference to the theory of Forms, p. 239.

12. Cf. Campbell, p. 162, Cornford, PTK p. 107n.

13. Cf. p. 126 above and note 6.

14. We have now seen that the reasoning here referred to is reasoning about the existence, similarity, usefulness, etc. of objects of sense: and not (as Cherniss would have it, "Relation of the Timaeus", SPM p. 357n.) the apprehension of Existence, etc. "by the soul functioning without any organ of sense and reasoning about the παθήματα."

15. So, though Cornford (PTK p. 106) may be right to object to Campbell's calling the κοινά "necessary forms of thought, which are as inseparable from perception as from reasoning" (p. liii), the thought Campbell was expressing there comes much closer to Plato's meaning than does Cornford with his reference to the fact that the κοινά are νοητά: this fact, if it is a fact, is not to the point in Plato's argument.

NOTES TO CHAPTER V

1. Shorey (Unity, p. 55) holds this view in a quite explicit form. Cornford says (PTK p. 113) that Socrates' argument at 187c-188c is "psychological rather than logical. ...Logicians might maintain that there is a false proposition ...which has a meaning, though I cannot believe it. With that we are not concerned, but only with judgements and statements that can be actually made and believed by some rational being." Since the whole discussion in the Theaetetus develops and attempts to answer the argument cited, Cornford ought to have concluded forthwith that the Sophist is altogether a different matter. In fact, however, he does not unambiguously draw this consequence: still, part of the time he does think of the Tht. as dealing with a psychological problem (which he thinks arises for any one who accepts "empiricist" assumptions about knowledge). Diès (Budé edition, pp. 140-142) follows Brochard (De l'erreur, pp. 16-20) in distinguishing sharply between "difficultés subjectives" and "objectives", and finds the Theaetetus concerned with the former exclusively: it treats "la difficulté fameuse: peut-on ne pas savoir ce qu'on sait?" (Diès p. 142n.). Now Brochard (cf. pp. 15, 20) at least finds the Tht.'s handling of this sophistical puzzle a preliminary skirmish in the same war whose decisive battle is found in the Sophist; but his suggestion, that the compresence of such contraries as

knowing and not knowing is finally explained by the *Sophist*'s discussion of being and not-being, is certainly obscure. In the absence of any evident connection between the two one should, in the interest of clarity, say roundly that the problems are different. Robinson ("Forms and Error" p. 26) finds that the *Sophist* does nothing to solve the *Theaetetus*' problem because the *Theaetetus* is concerned with "how a false statement can gain anybody's credence".

2. This view was upheld by J.L. Ackrill in a paper read in November 1964 to the Harvard Philosophy Club. Cf. also his reply to Demos, Journal of Philosophy, fall 1964.

3. I assume the order of composition of the works here concerned to be *Euthydemus*, *Cratylus*, *Theaetetus*, and *Sophist*. The only probable disagreement any one might have with the ordering is over the relative positions of *Euthydemus* and *Cratylus*. M. Warburg has given a number of arguments (some good, some bad) for making *Cratylus* close in date to *Theaetetus*. (*Zwei Fragen zum Kratylos*, pp. 31-61): and the state of the problem of false belief in the two dialogues, as well as other matters, shows *Theaetetus* to be later.

4. The same point can be put negatively as well (as Euthydemus himself puts it immediately afterward, 284b 3-c 6): to speak falsely is to say μὴ ὄντα, things that are not; but what is not does not exist, and to what doesn't exist you can't do anything at all; speaking is doing something; hence you can't say what's false. The positive argument is more useful for my purposes.

5. So Shorey regularly calls it, e.g. *Unity* p. 53. Shorey's lamentable inability to see that behind this fallacy lay a deep and difficult theory of meaning, and that it is *this* which the *Sophist* finally overturns, led him to think that, since the argument is a palpable fallacy, Plato could at any time in his career have exposed it, by relying on the arguments of the *Sophist*. (So also Mrs. Sprague, *Plato's Use of Fallacy* pp. 15 and 17.). This view in turn leads him into the following evident mistakes: (1) Plato laughs at the argument in the *Euthyd*. (286c-287c) (as also in the *Crat*. 429d 7), which *shows* he was not baffled by it (p. 55); (2) because Plato knows there is a fallacy in the *Euthyd*.'s argument he must have already known what to say to refute it. In fact the main brunt of Socrates' humor in the *Euthyd*. is not the *argument* at all, but Dionysodorus who propounds it: D. pretends to believe that the argument's conclusion is true but does not limit his behavior in the way he ought

if his view were correct (cf. the objection to Protagoras in Tht. 161d-e). What he ridicules is lack of seriousness and not the argument itself. And if this shows that Plato knew the conclusion to be false (one ought not to have to say) it doesn't follow that he knew what exactly was wrong with the argument. And it certainly doesn't follow that he already had fully in view the theory of meaning he later rejects in the *Sophist*, let alone that he had already worked out the *Sophist*'s new theory of meaning! Only a mode of interpretation which, like Shorey's, pays more attention to surface than to substance (e.g. infers from the presence of certain expressions to that of certain argued doctrines and philosophical conclusions) could be content to argue on this subject as Shorey and his followers do.

6. So Mrs. Sprague, p. 15.

7. Hence Taylor's distinction (*PMW* 85) between a "merely verbal" ambiguity between the two senses of εἶναι cited above, and a "metaphysical" confusion (what is not= "blank nothing" vs. what is "other than a given reality") is a step in the right direction. But Taylor never succeeded, in my opinion, in showing how the metaphysical confusion itself makes it seem impossible to speak falsely; nor do I think that the confusion is the only thing preventing a (more) correct conception of meaning and truth, as Taylor seems to think (*op. cit.* p. 85, 389-391, *Plato: the Sophist and the Statesman*, pp. 66-69).

8. In the foregoing paraphrase I have omitted the flourish which some interpreters think Dionysodorus adds at the very end, where he apparently attempts to reduce ἀντιλέγειν to not speaking at all. (So Rouse, Sprague, Jowett?, and Meridier, who take 286b 6, ὁ δὲ μὴ λέγων τῷ λέγοντι πῶς ἂν ἀντιλέγοι; to contain the reduction.) If this is the correct reading of the last sentence then Dionysodorus produces this result by means of the fallacy of *secundum quid* (i.e., by deducing "X is not speaking", without qualification, from "X is not speaking about Y"); I have omitted this final step in the argument since it is evident that the really damaging consequence, also stated by Dionysodorus (286b 3-5), is that in supposed contradiction one actually changes the subject. The last step, if it is really there at all, is just a dialectical flourish. Apelt, however, takes the last sentence in such a way that this last step is absent from the argument: he understands something like τὸ πρᾶγμα with μὴ λέγων (easily supplied from the preceding sentence), and thereby makes the conclusion of the argument correspond with the conclusion as

I have stated it in the text. However the final sentence is taken the essence of the argument remains as I have given it.

9. That περὶ οὗ ὁ λόγος here means "what (his) sentence or statement is about" and not "object of disagreement" (so, apparently, Rouse) or "subject of discussion" (so, apparently, Méridier's "dont il s'agit" and Apelt's "von der die Rede ist") seems to me shown by the appearance of the identical expression at *Crat*. 432e 5-6, where this meaning is certainly indicated by the context, and by the association of λόγος (statement) and πρᾶγμα just below, *Euthyd*. 285e-286b.

10. Such a view seems to be implicit in various of Professor Ryle's writings on Plato: cf. e.g. "Plato's Parmenides", *SPM* pp. 136 ff. and R. C. Cross's references to an unpublished paper of his in "Logos and Forms" pp. 433 ff.

11. Cf. J. M. E. Moravcsik, "Meaning and Being" pp.62-64, and Stenzel, *Plato's Method of Dialectic* p. 126.

12. *Cratylus* 431b 2-c 1. Comparison of this passage with other places in the *Crat*. where ῥήματα are mentioned (399b, 421b, e, 425a, 426e) in fact suggests that here ῥήματα does not mean "verbs" but rather *phrases*, so that *Crat*. 431b-c would not be even an apparent parallel to the *Sophist*'s requirement that a sentence have both a name and a verb. But even if it does here mention both names and verbs as sentence parts it does not share the *Sophist*'s theory of logos. For the *Crat*., having mentioned both parts of the logos can go on (432e) to give an account of the falsehood of a logos which utilizes only ὀνόματα: obviously no essential differentiation of roles has yet been recognized. It would be inconceivable for Plato, after the explicit theory of *Soph*. 261e-262d, to speak of a logos as if it contained *only* names, as *Crat*. 385c-d and 432e do, and the fuller statements of 424e-425a and 431b-c do nothing to mitigate the omission there.

13. One should not have to point out that at most one passage in the middle period dialogues clearly says any such thing (*Rep*. 596a 6-7), and in only one (or possibly two) other places are Forms for common nouns asserted at all (*Crat*. 389 and, some think, *Phaedo* 103c ff., cf. Vlastos, "Postscript to the Third Man", *SPM* p. 290n.). But old dogmas die hard.

14. The example is borrowed from Chomsky, *Syntactic Structures*, p. 15.

15. Moravcsik seems to be the only person who has seen the point at all clearly: cf. his "Being and Meaning" pp. 61-65. His whole account of meaning and falsehood in the *Sophist* (pp. 56-77) is the most interesting, and on the whole the best, analysis yet provided.

16. Commentators have however not given him credit for even this advance. Cornford, for example, thinks that it is only the fact that on his view *every* separate word is given a designation which marks his advance over the sophists. C. thinks that, as the sophists had thought that a false statement necessarily had to have some meaningless part, some part which named nothing, all Plato needs to do in order to refute them is to show how *all* significant sentences, even false ones, have meaningful parts. He thinks that the sophist is worried about the allegedly false statement "Theaetetus flies" because though he sees how "Theaetetus" has a meaning (it refers to Theaetetus), he does not see how "flies" does (since there is no flying going on for it to refer to). Hence he gives to Plato a theory (pp. 313-317) which, *without relying upon the discrimination of parts and functions in a logos* to which the Stranger devotes so much attention, provides a meaning (reference) for each word of any sentence, even a false one. This is achieved by introducing the theory of Forms as the meanings of the constituent words (or perhaps only the predicate-expressions) of a sentence. (Hence his oft-repeated claim that what is essential to Plato's solution of the problem of falsehood is his invocation of the theory of Forms.) "Theaetetus flies" thus has a meaning: "Theaetetus" names Theaetetus and "flies" refers to the Form of Flying, so the sentence as a whole has a meaning. This is supposed to satisfy the sophist. But it obviously doesn't. For even supposing that for the sophist "flies" seemed to have no meaning unless it referred to some concrete act of flying, the substitution of an abstract act of flying, in giving "flying" a meaning, also makes the sentence in question true. If each of the parts refers to some ὄν, then the whole sentence λέγει τὸ ὄν and is true. The sophist's problem is how they can be meaningful and yet λέγει τὰ μὴ ὄντα, and the introduction of Forms to be the meanings of some of the words of a sentence gets us nowhere. In fact, of course, the real work only now begins: we must show how the false statement *says* something meaningful but false. Cornford himself has belatedly (p. 315)

to bring in such an explanation (involving the idea of a relation between elements of reality referred to) but he does so without having provided a place for it in his formal account and without recognizing either its crucial importance for the problem under discussion or the obviously essential part in his own explanation which the Stranger gives it. As we should expect, the necessary part is the part the Stranger explicitly states and the unessential part is the part which Cornford has to invent for him. Taylor's account (*Plato: the Sophist and the Statesman*, pp. 66 ff.) like Cornford's dutifully records the analysis of the meaning of a sentence and then proceeds to ignore it. Moravcsik is the only writer known to me who has fully seen the point of the analysis (*op. cit.*, pp. 62-64, 73-77).

17. Usually translated "nouns" and "verbs", as Plato's examples (262b) encourage one to do. But the fact that Plato only mentions nouns and verbs should not be permitted to obscure the point he is evidently making: he certainly did not regard "Theaetetus is snub-nosed" as meaningless. Cf. n. 11 above.

18. So Cornford (*PTK*, p. 216), Taylor (*Plato: the Sophist and the Statesman*, p. 67), Ross (p. 116).

19. "Meaning and Being", pp. 66 ff.

20. *Op. cit.*, p. 74.

21. That the "any and all" must be strongly emphasized in the statement of the analysis is illustrated by the following version of the usual analysis (Taylor, *Plato: the Sophist and the Statesman*, p. 67): "Thus [the false proposition] affirms about him 'what is not' as though it were. But this only means that it affirms of him 'something that is, but is different' from what is. . . Flying is a genuine action; there *are* creatures which fly. . . but [flying] is *different* from the act which he is, *ex hypothesi*, in fact now performing. And this is enough to make the assertion false." But it isn't: twiddling one's thumbs is a different action from sitting. Does it follow that Theaetetus, who is sitting, is not twiddling his thumbs? (The importance of the addition "any and all", and the fact that nothing in Plato's account corresponds to it might in fact lead one to doubt whether we can be expected to provide it and interpret as the usual view does.)

22. E.g. the flux theory of reality, the idea that

investigation into the derivations of words can lead to understanding of what there is, conventionalism of various sorts, as well as the problems of meaning I shall be discussing.

23. Cf. Hermogenes' complaints on this score, 383a 4-384a 7, 427d 3-7.

24. E.g. by Shorey (Unity, pp. 54-55), Mrs. Sprague, p.17.

25. It probably only means "phrase": cf. n. 12 above.

26. I have interpreted 432d 11-433b 5 as saying something about the truth and falsehood of statements; in my view falsehood of a logos is here connected with the false attribution of names argued for above (430-431), and an analogy is drawn between a false logos, as a bad picture of a fact, and a bad name, as a faulty copy of a thing. This requires the assumption that once Socrates distinguishes between introducing a name and using it (430-431) he keeps the two things apart, at least through 433b: for as I construe 432e-433a, when Socrates speaks of a logos as saying something κακῶς he means that it says something false, and when he says that a logos may contain μὴ προσήκοντα ὀνόματα he means false names in the sense explained in 430-431, viz. wrongly applied names. But other interpretations of these admittedly obscure remarks are possible. Thus it might be that after 432c, where he turns to discuss not incorrect use but incorrect formation of names, Socrates does not return at all to the topic of falsehood. In that case 432e-433a will merely be extending the analysis of badly made names, remarking that if some letters of a name are wrong, and it nevertheless remains a copy of the thing, then *a fortiori* a logos that contains a name that contains some incorrect letters will fail to be as good a copy as it might have been of the things it names: but this will have no more to do with false statements than badly introduced names do with false names as explained in 430-431. A different interpretation would take Socrates to mean by sentences which say things κακῶς sentences which are false, but would take him to be making falsehood dependent not (as in 430-431) on the misapplication of a name with a previously fixed meaning but on the bare fact that it contains a badly made name. On this interpretation Socrates is saying in 432e that because names can have incorrect letters the logoi in which they occur can have incorrect names (viz. any name with any incorrect letters); but, forgetting his distinction

between incorrect use and incorrect formation, he now means to make logoi false by making them contain an incorrectly *formed* name. Thus if "horse" is a bad name for horses, any sentence in which "horse" is used in the ordinary way will contain a *false* name and so will itself be false. Now it seems to me that either of these views is possible (and the latter could be elaborated to make a rather full theory of falsehood). But they share one feature which inclines me to prefer the one I have adopted to either of them. In 432e 3-4 Socrates says that (as he has explained) a name may contain μὴ προσήκοντα γράμματα, and similarly a logos may contain a μὴ προσῆκον ὄνομα. Now on either of the two views mentioned a μὴ προσῆκον ὄνομα is one with some bad letters---one which κακῶς κεῖται. And it seems doubtful to me that it can mean this. It is certainly far more likely that μὴ προσήκοντα ὀνόματα here means what it does at 431b 2-5, viz., "names wrongly applied". And in that case one is justified in understanding by "names which do not fit", names which, as Socrates has explained, are applied (like pictures) to things they do not resemble.

27. It is important to observe that both here and throughout this part of the dialogue it is knowledge of *objects*, and never of *truths* which is meant. Cornford occasionally slips into talk of knowledge of truths (cf. *PTK*, pp. 137-8), and even comes close to translating the same concern into Plato's text (198b 1), but this is certainly a mistake.

28. Even this kind of mistake is in fact possible. Dr. Jekyll *was* Mr. Hyde, but he need not have been; if he were not, someone might still have thought to himself the very words"Dr. Jekyll is Mr. Hyde!" and been wrong but not unintelligible. This possibility is due, of course, to the fact that though a proper name designates an object it can be introduced on the basis of some description or set of descriptions. Thus before I discover (or think) that Dr. Jekyll and Mr. Hyde are the same person, Mr. Hyde is for me a man of a certain description, with certain characteristic occupations etc. Likewise, *mutatis mutandis*, for Dr. Jekyll. What I discover (or think I discover) is just that it is one and the same man who meets both descriptions and engages in both occupations. So even when I have two men in mind and give them their own proper names I need not render myself unintelligible by saying that the one is the other. But in general different proper names name different people, and if we assume that this is universally so, then Socrates' principle is unobjectionable.

29. But note 191d 5 ἐννοήσωμεν which does not appear to sort well with perceptual experience as the sole source of the imprints on the wax: though no doubt someone could over-interpret it so as to make it consistent with that supposition.

30. Hence not much weight should be attached to Socrates' excursus (194c 1-195b 1) on the ways in which differences in the quality of a person's wax block affect his intelligence and the likelihood that he will make mistakes and judge falsely. Similarly one need not be surprised that the remark at 197d 7-8 about the varieties of birds in one's aviary has not been satisfactorily construed as implying some classification on Plato's part of the objects of knowledge (cf. Campbell, p. 199, Cornford <u>PTK</u>, p. 132n.); nor can the remark (198a 4-b 6) about how <u>one</u> man teaches another his numbers, thereby stocking his aviary with the knowledge of the numbers, bear the weight which Cornford (p. 135-6), mistranslating ἐπιστήμας τῶν ἀριθμῶν (198b 1), attaches to it (cf. also Stoelzel, pp. 111-113, from whom Cornford seems to have gotten the idea). All these passages are elaborations of the models for their own sakes and do not form any part of the discussion of the problem about false belief which Plato introduces the similes to clarify and solve.

31. It is amusing to observe that Cornford first announces (p. 124) that Socrates in 193b 9 ff. is going to illustrate "the three cases in which mistake is possible", and then (p. 125), having translated the passage giving the illustrations, remarks that Socrates has not illustrated one of the three cases and that he will go on in 193d 10 ff. to repeat his explanation of "the two cases he has illustrated"

32. Cf. P.F. Strawson <u>Individuals</u> Ch. 1.

33. Cf. 198d 1-8.

34. Cf. 199b 1-5.

35. It is worth noting that here again, as at 196a-b, one is not supposed to <u>have</u> 12 in mind when he has 7+5 in mind; <u>he goes in hunt of 12</u> (199b 2-3) once he asks himself how much <u>7 and 5</u> make.

36. An ignorance of 11, as the development of the argument above shows, is something by having which in active use one is in fact thinking of 11 but not knowing it for 11: an

ignorance is just the same as a knowledge except that if one has the knowledge of something to hand he knows what thing he is thinking of. Cornford is therefore wrong to suggest that the "piece of ignorance" one is supposed to lay hold of is the "false belief...that 5+7=11" (p. 138). Cornford fails to observe that it is knowledge or ignorance of *objects* throughout here that is in question, not propositions. But he is at least consistent, since he thinks the ἐπιστῆμαι, no less than the ἀνεπιστημοσύναι, are propositional in form (p. 135). There is absolutely no warrant for this in the text, however, though Cornford translates some warrant into it at 198b 1. (Oddly enough he takes τοῦ αὐτοῦ πέρι 199e 5 with δοξάζειν, when he might have eked out his case by taking it, as Diès does, with ἀνεπιστημοσύνην, translating "now getting a knowledge and now an ignorance about the same thing".) It is easy to think that the ἐπιστῆμαι τῶν ἀριθμῶν must be knowledge of *truths* about the numbers; but once one sees (as Cornford of course does not: cf. his comments pp. 117-118 on the definition of falsehood as ἀλλοδοξία) that according to the atomistic theory of meaning being pursued here falsehood of whatever sort must reduce to mistaking one *object* for another, the emphasis on knowledge of an object which does not come down to a lot of knowledge of truths *about* it is seen to be both appropriate and necessary to the argument.

37. *PLE*, p. 37. Cf. also Robinson, "Forms and Error" p. 5, who sees the implication of the argument but is willing to believe it was a "slip" on Plato's part. The recognition that this argument sorts ill with the old knowledge-Forms/belief-empirical world dichotomy goes back to the nineteenth century at least: Stoelzel (p. 113n.) mentions, and attempts to rebut, interpretations to this effect by Schubart and von Stein.

38. It is worth pointing out that this fact wrecks Cherniss' interpretation of the second half of the dialogue. He thinks ("Economy", *SPM* pp. 5-6) to show the argument of the second half of the dialogue to be a coherent and well-argued defense of the old view, succinctly argued in *Tim.* 51d-e, that if knowledge and true opinion are different then there are Forms (the objects with which knowledge is concerned). The arguments of *Theaetetus* 201a-c and 208e-210a fit together to show that (a) knowledge and true belief are distinct and (b) since knowledge is not *identical* with true belief true belief cannot be an "essential element" of knowledge either, so that knowledge must have different objects from the objects of belief. By so interpreting the

second argument Cherniss makes its conclusion dependent upon that of the first; but as we have now seen the conclusion of the first (that knowledge is not identical with true belief) is dependent upon the assumption that not all objects of knowledge are Forms. Neither argument nor the sum of the two can, then, be interpreted as showing that true belief and knowledge must be distinguished in such a way that belief and knowledge have _different_ "objects". Of course this does not show that Plato did not _intend_ to be arguing as Cherniss represents him; but since one reason for accepting that he did so argue is (as Cherniss obviously believes) that the argument so construed is a good, clear and coherent one, it is worth pointing out that it is not. The argument of the _Theaetetus_ manifestly does not _prove_ the "epistemological necessity of the Ideas."

39. Pp. 113-114.

NOTES TO CHAPTER VI

1. Runciman, _PLE_ pp. 41-44, thinks that these closing lines of Socrates' exposition do not form part of the dream theory, and that therefore the dream nowhere contemplates giving an explanation of logos as a sufficient condition of knowledge. But there is no reason to take this radical line. The dream can be proposing a theory of logos as something to be added to true belief as well as enunciating a necessary condition of knowledge. (It should be observed that the necessary condition Runciman thinks the dream is producing [that "a combination of names is a necessary prerequisite of simples becoming either opinable or knowable", p. 44] is misguided. Simples are in the clearest possible way (202b 5-6) said to be _unknowable_; what is known when their names are put together is _not_ the simples themselves but the complexes they are parts of.)

2. One may grant, as I have done in what precedes, that the dream is partly (and perhaps by intention primarily) a theory of explanation and not one of language or semantics; nevertheless it contains the two root ideas of the atomistic theory, (a) designation as the fundamental linguistic act (201e 2-202a 2), and (b) the idea that to say something is to string names together (202b 2-5, 7, cf. 205d 8). On all this see below pp. 251 ff.

3. Endorsed by Cherniss, "Philosophical Economy", SPM p. 7 and argued by Cornford, PTK pp. 142 ff.

4. "Forms and Error", pp. 14-16. Robinson's own positive view (that Plato in the final section shows that his view that knowledge always involves logos, though he continues to accept it, is incoherent so far as he can tell) seems to me not very promising. The theory of simples and complexes expounded in the dream has to be attributed firmly to Plato in order for this interpretation to have any chance of being right (since it must have Plato arguing that there are some things of which there is knowledge but no logos); and I doubt that Plato can here be firmly adopting any theory of logos or any theory of complexes. Cf. Hackforth "Platonic Forms. . .", p. 57.

5. Diès offers an argument along traditional lines to show how this might be done ("L'Idée de la science dans Platon", Autour de Platon II. 465-469.)

6. Cf. Cornford PTK pp. 154, 162-3, as against p. 158; Cherniss "Philosophical Economy", SPM p. 7.

7. Hence Cornford's remarks at the end of his discussion are uninformative at best, and obfuscatory at worst. He writes: "The Platonist will draw the necessary inference. True knowledge has for its objects things of a different order---not sensible things, but intelligible Forms. . . . Such objects are necessarily unique; they do not become and perish or change in any respect." But as nothing in the preceding arguments, or Cornford's commentary on them, has suggested that the changingness and temporality of sensible things causes the failure of the attempt to define logos for them so as to permit knowledge of them, *these* features of Forms, though no doubt central to the conception of Forms in general, do not themselves have any relevance to the issues raised. Cornford should certainly have explained how the fact that the Form of Justice, say, is eternal and unchanging permits one to give a logos of it which is not open to the kinds of objections raised against the definitions of logos actually proposed.

8. I do not claim even to understand at all well the supposed fourth sense. At one point (p. 154) it appears to be definition through higher concepts, at another (pp. 141-2) it appears to be something not given of an individual (whether thing or concept) but, rather, of a belief or a judgement, though then it is not a sense which any one could suppose was appropriate either (e.g.) to the sun or to the Just Itself. Cf. Robinson, "Forms and Error", pp. 14-15.

9. "Plato's *Parmenides*", *SPM* pp. 136 ff., "Letters and Syllables", p. 443.

10. 207a 5-7 and 208d 1-3 seem quite ambiguous, and the examples of Theaetetus and his name, though they seem to lean towards logos as a *simple* list, are hardly decisive.

11. Cf. for example *Crat.* 425a 1-3, 431b 2-c 2 (where, as I have argued above, p. 187 and n. 25, the inclusion of ῥήματα as well as ὀνόματα is inconsequential) and *Soph.* 263d 1-4 (where virtually the same formula is understood differently, cf. pp. 167 ff.). In these, and other, places, it is always a statement which is said to be a combination, or an intermingling, etc., of names (or names and verbs).

12. It should be carefully noted that the second conception of a συλλαβή treats *it* as something over and above the elements and as *itself* a partless simple thing. The supposition is *not* (as Ryle, "Plato's 'Parmenides'", *SPM* pp. 137-138, thinks) that a complex may *consist of* letters *plus* an order of arrangement, which is then as much a simple (though a simple of a different kind) as the letters. The new simple thing being introduced on this second understanding of a συλλαβή is not something of which the syllable consists; it is the syllable itself (cf. 205c 1-2). There is nowhere in this discussion any allusion, so far as I can see, to any notion of an "order of arrangement" (Ryle) that has to be added in with the letters to make a syllable. (Aristotle's discussion in *Met.* Z.1041b 11-33 is to be *contrasted* with the *Tht.*'s discussion.)

13. Of course the *Parmenides* treats the one as simultaneously *both* of these, whereas in the *Tht.* the two conceptions are alternatives. But this does not matter for my purposes.

14. The use of examples in the learning of letters as an example of Example: the identity of letters in different syllables and ability to recognize the identity must be seen in the context of the definition of the statesman and the use of weaving as an example. What is it to recognize θεραπεία (if, cf. 278e 9, this is the στοιχεῖον which is being learned) or συγκριτική and διακριτική (if, cf. 282b, these are being learned), first in weaving and then in statesmanship? In what consists the identity of θεραπεία in the two? Letters are evidently not being thought of as *simple* elements in any sense.

15. In "Plato's 'Parmenides'" *SPM* pp. 137-138, the unpublished paper referred to by R.C. Cross ("Logos and Forms in Plato", pp. 434-435), and "Letters and Syllables", p. 443.

16. Hence I reject Runciman's idea (*PLE* pp. 47-48) that Plato is arguing against the dream theorist to the positive conclusion (which he thereafter regarded as an accomplished doctrine) that there must be knowledge of simples. For this to follow Plato would have himself to be firmly committed to the dream's (and Socrates') view of simples and complexes. And it is too much to say that he *accepted* this view. It is certainly too much to say, as Runciman does, that both *Theaetetus* and *Philebus* regard it as necessary that there should be knowledge of simples, on the ground that they both admit knowledge of letters (though differing as to what knowledge of such a simple comes to). For as soon as the *Philebus* sees that knowing a letter involves knowing how it can combine with others it no longer treats letters as simples in any sense in which the *Theaetetus* argues for knowledge of simples.

17. "TH" of course stands for the single Greek letter Theta.

18. Cf. 209c 7: τἆλλα ... ἐξ ὧν εἶ σύ, with 202e 1-2, στοιχεῖα ἐξ ὧν ἡμεῖς τε συγκείμεθα καὶ τἆλλα.

19. Ryle has made much of the distinction between letters as sounds and letters as characters, arguing that when Plato uses the letters-syllables analogy he must have primarily in mind letters as sounds (cf. "Letters and Syllables"). Ryle's reason for thinking so is just that the point he takes Plato to be making by the use of the analogy is only correct, or correct without qualification, of spoken letters and not of written. For the written "T" is a discrete and separable *part* of the words in which it appears, recognizable and teachable on its own; whereas the sound represented by "T" does not turn up on its own and is not a separate and discrete part of the spoken word. And according to Ryle, Plato's point in appealing to the letter and syllable analogy "in expounding his logical or semantic views"(p. 431), is to show the "independent-variability-without-separability of the meanings of parts of sentences" (p. 451): words, since they are parts of sentences, have meaning derivatively from the meanings of the sentences in which they occur, and therefore as meaningful elements are *aspects* and not parts: they are "distinguishables, not detachables; abstractables, not extractables" (p.436)

And just as the only independently existing linguistic units are complete statements, so the analogy Plato relies upon to make this point should take letters as sounds, where the elements have no independent existence, rather than as characters, where they obviously do exist separately. That Plato does not have letters as phonetic elements rather than written characters specially in mind is clear from many passages (e.g., *Tht.* 206a) and has been shown by Gallop (*Phil. Rev.* 1963 pp. 364-369). (Ryle also fails to notice that Plato's "logical and semantical views" were different in *Cratylus* and *Theaetetus* from *Sophist*, *Politicus* and *Philebus*, so that the use of the analogy should not in any case be uniform.) The absence of the distinction between phonetic elements and written characters suggests that Ryle's estimation of the point Plato uses the analogy to illustrate in his later dialogues is faulty. I think Plato never wishes to deny that letters---whether phonetic or written---can be met with on their own, nor that words and their meanings exist except as parts of sentences or propositions. His point is, rather, that to *know* one of these things is not to know merely what one might learn by looking very closely at it *as* it appears in isolation, but to know *about* it what kinds of functions it performs and how it differs from other similar things performing different functions. Whereas Ryle thinks---and wishes Plato to think---that syllables as independent existences are prior to letters, which never occur except in syllables, Plato in fact sees them as interconnected and neither in Ryle's way prior to the other.

20. Cf. Robinson, "Forms and Error", pp. 17-19 (replied to by Hackforth, "Platonic Forms", p. 58). But notice that I have not said that the Forms are not relevant to *any and all* questions about what knowledge is, but only that they are not necessary to an investigation of *the* question raised by the *Theaetetus*.

21. Cf. what the *Politicus* says (277a-287a) about τὰ τῶν πάντων στοιχεῖα (278d 1): this passage deserves much closer attention than it usually receives. One of these στοιχεῖα is (I think, cf. note 14 above) θεραπεία, which occurs both in weaving and in statesmanship. Knowing θεραπεία as it occurs in weaving is no simple operation: cf. 281b 7-d 3. Likewise having gotten to know θεραπεία in the case of weaving serves as a guide to getting to know θεραπεία in the case of statesmanship (cf. 287b ff.) in nothing like the way having practised picking out a man from a group of three others helps one to pick him out from a group of 20.

BIBLIOGRAPHY OF WORKS CITED

Certain periodicals and collections are referred to in the Bibliography by abbreviation, as follows:

AJP *American Journal of Philosophy*
CQ *Classical Quarterly*
PR *Philosophical Review*
SPM *Studies in Plato's Metaphysics*, ed. R.E. Allen, New York 1965.

Bischoff, H. "Die drei λόγοι des Theaitet", *Hermes* 74 (1939).

Brochard, V. *De l'erreur*, Paris 1897.

——— "Protagore et Démocrite", *Etudes de philosophie ancienne et de philosophie moderne*, Paris 1912.

Campbell, L. *The Theaetetus of Plato*, ed. 2, Oxford 1883.

Cherniss, H.F. *Aristotle's Criticism of Plato and the Academy*, Baltimore 1944.

——— "The Philosophical Economy of the Theory of Ideas", *AJP* 57 (1936); reprinted in *SPM*.

——— "The Relation of the *Timaeus* to Plato's Later Dialogues", *AJP* 78 (1957); reprinted in *SPM*.

——— Review of R. Robinson, *Plato's Earlier Dialectic*, *AJP* 68 (1947).

Chomsky, N. *Syntactic Structures*, 's-Gravenhage 1962.

Cornford, F.M. *Plato's Cosmology*, London 1937.

——— *Plato's Theory of Knowledge*, London 1935.

Cross, R.C. "Logos and Forms in Plato", *Mind* 63 (1954).

Diès, A. *Platon: Théétète* (vol. 8, pt. 2 of *Oeuvres Complètes*, Budé), ed. 3, Paris 1955.

——— "L'Idée de la science dans Platon", *Autour de Platon*, vol. II, Paris 1927.

Gallop, D. "Plato and the Alphabet", *PR* 72 (1963).

Grote, G. *Plato and the Other Companions of Socrates*, vol. II, London 1865.

Gulley, N. *Plato's Theory of Knowledge*, London 1962.

Hackforth, R. "Platonic Forms in the *Theaetetus*", *CQ* n. s. 7 (1957).

Horn, F. *Platonstudien*, 2te Reihe, Vienna 1904.

Jackson, H. "Plato's Later Theory of Ideas", *Journal of Philology* 1882-1882.

Lutoslawski, W. *The Origin and Growth of Plato's Logic*, London 1897.

Moravcsik, J.M.E. "Being and Meaning in the *Sophist*", *Acta Philosophica Fennica*, Fascicle 14 (1962).

Owen, G.E.L. "The Place of the *Timaeus* in Plato's Dialogues", *CQ* n.s. 3 (1953); reprinted in *SPM*.

——— "A Proof in the περὶ ἰδεῶν", *The Journal of Hellenic Studies* 77 part 1 (1957); reprinted in *SPM*.

Robinson, R. "Forms and Error in Plato's *Theaetetus*", *PR* 59 (1950).

Ross, W.D. *Plato's Theory of Ideas*, Oxford 1951.

Runciman, W.G. *Plato's Later Epistemology*, Cambridge 1962.

——— "Plato's *Parmenides*", *Harvard Studies in Classical Philology* 64 (1959); reprinted in *SPM*.

Ryle, G. "Letters and Syllables in Plato", *PR* 69 (1960).

——— "Plato's *Parmenides*", *Mind* 48 (1939); reprinted in *SPM*.

Shorey, P. *De Platonis Idearum Doctrina*, Munich 1884.

——— Introduction in *Plato: the Republic* (Loeb Classical Library), London 1930.

——— "Recent Platonism in England", *AJP* 9 (1888).

——— "The *Timaeus* of Plato", *AJP* 10 (1889).

——— *The Unity of Plato's Thought*, Chicago 1903.

Skemp, J.B. *Plato's Statesman*, London 1952.

Sprague, Mrs. R.K. *Plato's Use of Fallacy*, London 1962.

Stenzel, J. *Plato's Method of Dialectic*, tr. D.J. Allan, Oxford 1940.

Stoelzel, E. *Die Behandlung des Erkenntnisproblems bei Platon*, Halle 1908.

Strawson, P.F. *Individuals*, London 1959.

Susemihl, F. *Die Genetische Entwickelung der Platonischen Philosophie*, I, Leipzig 1855.

Taylor, A.E. *A Commentary on Plato's Timaeus*, Oxford 1928.

——— *Plato: the Man and his Work*, London 1926.

——— *Plato: the Sophist and the Statesman*, London 1961.

Vlastos, G. "Postscript to the Third Man", *PR* 65 (1956); reprinted in *SPM*.

Warburg, M. *Zwei Fragen zum Kratylos*, Berlin 1929.